Network Security with NetFlow and IPFIX

Big Data Analytics for Information Security

Omar Santos

Cisco Press

800 East 96th Street

Indianapolis, Indiana 46240 USA

Network Security with NetFlow and IPFIX

Omar Santos

Published by:
Cisco Press
800 East 96th Street
Indianapolis, IN 46240 USA

Printed in the United States of America

First Printing September 2015

Library of Congress Control Number: 2015945876

ISBN-13: 978-1-58714-438-7

ISBN-10: 1-58714-438-7

Warning and Disclaimer

This book is designed to provide information about network security using Cisco NetFlow. Every effort has been made to make this book as complete and as accurate as possible, but no warranty or fitness is implied.

The information is provided on an "as is" basis. The authors, Cisco Press, and Cisco Systems, Inc. shall have neither liability nor responsibility to any person or entity with respect to any loss or damages arising from the information contained in this book or from the use of the discs or programs that may accompany it.

The opinions expressed in this book belong to the author and are not necessarily those of Cisco Systems, Inc.

Trademark Acknowledgments

All terms mentioned in this book that are known to be trademarks or service marks have been appropriately capitalized. Cisco Press or Cisco Systems, Inc., cannot attest to the accuracy of this information. Use of a term in this book should not be regarded as affecting the validity of any trademark or service mark.

Special Sales

For information about buying this title in bulk quantities, or for special sales opportunities (which may include electronic versions; custom cover designs; and content particular to your business, training goals, marketing focus, or branding interests), please contact our corporate sales department at corpsales@pearsoned.com or (800) 382-3419.

For government sales inquiries, please contact governmentsales@pearsoned.com.

For questions about sales outside the U.S., please contact international@pearsoned.com.

Feedback Information

At Cisco Press, our goal is to create in-depth technical books of the highest quality and value. Each book is crafted with care and precision, undergoing rigorous development that involves the unique expertise of members from the professional technical community.

Readers' feedback is a natural continuation of this process. If you have any comments regarding how we could improve the quality of this book, or otherwise alter it to better suit your needs, you can contact us through email at feedback@ciscopress.com. Please make sure to include the book title and ISBN in your message.

We greatly appreciate your assistance.

Publisher: Paul Boger

Associate Publisher: Dave Dusthimer

Business Operation Manager, Cisco Press: Jan Cornelssen

Acquisitions Editor: Denise Lincoln

Managing Editor: Sandra Schroeder

Senior Development Editor: Christopher Cleveland

Project Editor: Mandie Frank

Copy Editor: Keith Cline

Technical Editors: Lou Ronnau, John Stuppi

Editorial Assistant: Vanessa Evans

Book Designer: Mark Shirar

Composition: CodeMantra

Senior Indexer: Cheryl Lenser

Proofreader: Sarah Kearns

Americas Headquarters
Cisco Systems, Inc.
San Jose, CA

Asia Pacific Headquarters
Cisco Systems (USA) Pte. Ltd.
Singapore

Europe Headquarters
Cisco Systems International BV
Amsterdam, The Netherlands

Cisco has more than 200 offices worldwide. Addresses, phone numbers, and fax numbers are listed on the Cisco Website at **www.cisco.com/go/offices**.

CCDE, CCENT, Cisco Eos, Cisco HealthPresence, the Cisco logo, Cisco Lumin, Cisco Nexus, Cisco StadiumVision, Cisco TelePresence, Cisco WebEx, DCE, and Welcome to the Human Network are trademarks; Changing the Way We Work, Live, Play, and Learn and Cisco Store are service marks; and Access Registrar, Aironet, AsyncOS, Bringing the Meeting To You, Catalyst, CCDA, CCDP, CCIE, CCIP, CCNA, CCNP, CCSP, CCVP, Cisco, the Cisco Certified Internetwork Expert logo, Cisco IOS, Cisco Press, Cisco Systems, Cisco Systems Capital, the Cisco Systems logo, Cisco Unity, Collaboration Without Limitation, EtherFast, EtherSwitch, Event Center, Fast Step, Follow Me Browsing, FormShare, GigaDrive, HomeLink, Internet Quotient, IOS, iPhone, iQuick Study, IronPort, the IronPort logo, LightStream, Linksys, MediaTone, MeetingPlace, MeetingPlace Chime Sound, MGX, Networkers, Networking Academy, Network Registrar, PCNow, PIX, PowerPanels, ProConnect, ScriptShare, SenderBase, SMARTnet, Spectrum Expert, StackWise, The Fastest Way to Increase Your Internet Quotient, TransPath, WebEx, and the WebEx logo are registered trademarks of Cisco Systems, Inc. and/or its affiliates in the United States and certain other countries.

All other trademarks mentioned in this document or website are the property of their respective owners. The use of the word partner does not imply a partnership relationship between Cisco and any other company. (0812R)

About the Author

Omar Santos is a Principal Engineer in the Cisco Product Security Incident Response Team (PSIRT) part of Cisco's Security Research and Operations. He mentors and leads engineers and incident managers during the investigation and resolution of security vulnerabilities in all Cisco products. Omar has been working with information technology and cyber security since the mid-1990s. Omar has designed, implemented, and supported numerous secure networks for Fortune 100 and 500 companies and for the U.S. government. Prior to his current role, he was a Technical Leader within the World Wide Security Practice and the Cisco Technical Assistance Center (TAC), where he taught, led, and mentored many engineers within both organizations.

Omar is an active member of the security community, where he leads several industry-wide initiatives and standard bodies. His active role helps businesses, academic institutions, state and local law enforcement agencies, and other participants that are dedicated to increasing the security of the critical infrastructure.

Omar is the author of several books and numerous whitepapers, articles, and security configuration guidelines and best practices. He has also delivered numerous technical presentations at many conferences and to Cisco customers and partners, in addition to many C-level executive presentations to many organizations. Omar is the author of the following Cisco Press books:

- *CCNA Security 210-260 Official Cert Guide*, ISBN-13: 9781587205668

- *Deploying Next-Generation Firewalls Live Lessons*, ISBN-13: 9781587205705

- *Cisco's Advanced Malware Protection (AMP)*, ISBN-13: 9781587144462

- *Cisco ASA Next-Generation Firewall, IPS, and VPN Services* (3rd Edition), ISBN-10: 1587143070

- *Cisco ASA: All-in-One Firewall, IPS, Anti-X, and VPN Adaptive Security Appliance* (2nd Edition), ISBN-10: 1587058197

- *Cisco ASA: All-in-One Firewall, IPS, and VPN Adaptive Security Appliance*, ISBN-10: 1587052091

- *Cisco Network Admission Control, Volume: Deployment and Management*, ISBN-10: 1587052253

- *End-to-End Network Security: Defense-in-Depth*, ISBN-10: 1587053322

About the Technical Reviewers

John Stuppi, CCIE No. 11154, is a Technical Leader in the Cisco Security Solutions (CSS) organization at Cisco, where he consults Cisco customers on protecting their network against existing and emerging cyber security threats. In this role, John is responsible for providing effective techniques using Cisco product capabilities to provide identification and mitigation solutions for Cisco customers who are concerned with current or expected security threats to their network environments. Current projects include helping customers leverage DNS and NetFlow data to identify and subsequently mitigate network-based threats. John has presented multiple times on various network security topics at Cisco Live, Black Hat, and other customer-facing cyber security conferences. In addition, John contributes to the Cisco Security Portal through the publication of whitepapers, Security Blog posts, and Cyber Risk Report articles. Prior to joining Cisco, John worked as a network engineer for JPMorgan, and then as a network security engineer at Time, Inc., with both positions based in New York City. John is also a CISSP (#25525) and holds an Information Systems Security (INFOSEC) professional certification. In addition, John has a Bachelor of Science in Electrical Engineering degree from Lehigh University and an MBA from Rutgers University. John lives in Ocean Township, New Jersey (a.k.a the Jersey Shore) with his wife, two kids, and his dog.

Lou Ronnau is a Consulting Engineer in the Cisco Security Solutions group at Cisco Systems, where he has worked for more than 20 years. In this position, he works with customers to identify and mitigate threats to the secure operation of their data networks. Lou has presented at Cisco Live and other industry security conferences and is a Cisco Press author. In his spare time, Lou enjoys flying as a private pilot and scuba diving.

Dedication

I want to dedicate this book to my lovely wife, Jeannette, and my two beautiful children, Hannah and Derek, who have inspired and supported me throughout the development of this book.

I also dedicate this book to my father, Jose, and write in memory of my mother, Generosa. Without their knowledge, wisdom, and guidance, I would not have the goals that I strive to achieve today.

Acknowledgments

I want to thank the technical editors, John Stuppi and Lou Ronnau, for their time and technical expertise. They verified my work and corrected me in all the major and minor mistakes that were hard to find.

I also want to thank the Cisco Press team, especially Denise Lincoln, Chris Cleveland, and Mandie Frank for their patience, guidance, and consideration. Their efforts are greatly appreciated.

Kudos to the Cisco product development teams for delivering such a great product portfolio.

Finally, I want to acknowledge the Cisco PSIRT and Security Research and Operations. Some of the best and brightest minds in the network security industry work there, supporting and protecting our Cisco customers, often under very stressful conditions and working miracles daily.

Contents at a Glance

Contents

Command Syntax Conventions

The conventions used to present command syntax in this book are the same conventions used in the IOS Command Reference. The Command Reference describes these conventions as follows:

- **Boldface** indicates commands and keywords that are entered literally as shown. In actual configuration examples and output (not general command syntax), boldface indicates commands that are manually input by the user (such as a **show** command).

- *Italic* indicates arguments for which you supply actual values.

- Vertical bars (|) separate alternative, mutually exclusive elements.

- Square brackets ([ ]) indicate an optional element.

- Braces ({ }) indicate a required choice.

- Braces within brackets ([{ }]) indicate a required choice within an optional element.

Introduction

Cisco NetFlow is now the primary network accounting technology in the industry. Visibility into the network is an indispensable tool for network and security professionals. In response to new requirements and cyber security headaches, network operators and security professionals are finding it critical to understand how the network is behaving. Cisco NetFlow creates an environment where network administrators and security professionals have the tools to understand who, what, when, where, and how network traffic is flowing.

Who Should Read This Book?

This book serves as comprehensive guide for any network and security professional who manages network security, installs and configures network security features to provide additional visibility. It encompasses topics from an introductory level to advanced topics on Cisco NetFlow, Cisco Cyber Threat Defense, and big data analytics tools such as Logstash, Kibana, Elasticsearch, and many others.

How This Book Is Organized

The following is an overview of how this book is organized:

- **Chapter 1, "Introduction to NetFlow and IPFIX":** This chapter provides an overview of Cisco NetFlow and IPFIX. Cisco NetFlow and IPFIX provide a key set of services for IP applications, including network traffic accounting, usage-based network billing, network planning, security, denial-of-service monitoring capabilities, and network monitoring. NetFlow provides valuable information about network users and applications, peak usage times, and traffic routing. Cisco invented NetFlow and is the leader in IP traffic flow technology.

- **Chapter 2, "Cisco NetFlow Versions and Features":** This chapter covers the different Cisco NetFlow versions and features available on each version. It also covers the NetFlow v9 export format and packet details, and includes a detailed comparison between NetFlow and IPFIX.

- **Chapter 3, "Cisco Flexible NetFlow":** Flexible NetFlow provides enhanced optimization of the network infrastructure, reduces costs, and improves capacity planning and security detection beyond other flow-based technologies available today. This chapter provides an introduction to Cisco's Flexible NetFlow, and it covers the Flexible NetFlow components and fields. It also provides step-by-step guidance on how to configure flexible NetFlow in Cisco IOS Software.

- **Chapter 4, "NetFlow Commercial and Open Source Monitoring and Analysis Software Packages":** This chapter provides details about the top commercial NetFlow analyzers. It also provides detailed information about the top open source NetFlow analyzers including SiLK, Flow-tools, FlowScan, NTop, EHNT, BPFT, Cflowd, Logstash, Kibana, Elasticsearch, and others.

- **Chapter 5, "Big Data Analytics and NetFlow"**: Big data analytics is a key and growing network security, monitoring, and troubleshooting trend. Cisco NetFlow provides a source of relevant big data that customers should be analyzing to improve the performance, stability, and security of their networks. This chapter describes how NetFlow is used for big data analytics for cyber security, along with other network telemetry capabilities such as firewall logs, syslog, SNMP, and authentication, authorization and accounting logs, in addition to logs from routers and switches, servers, and endpoint stations, among others.

- **Chapter 6, "Cisco Cyber Threat Defense and NetFlow"**: Cisco has partnered with Lancope to deliver a solution that provides visibility into security threats by identifying suspicious traffic patterns in the corporate network. These suspicious patterns are then augmented with circumstantial information necessary to determine the level of threat associated with a particular incident. This solution allows a network administrator or security professional to analyze this information in a timely, efficient, and cost-effective manner for advanced cyber threats. This chapter provides detailed coverage of Cisco Cyber Threat Defense Solution. Cisco Cyber Threat Defense Solution utilizes the Lancope StealthWatch System to analyze NetFlow information from Cisco switches, routers, and the Cisco ASA 5500 Next-Generation Firewalls to detect advanced and persistent security threats such as internally spreading malware, data leakage, botnet command-and-control traffic, and network reconnaissance. The Cisco ISE solution supplements StealthWatch NetFlow-based behavioral threat detection data with contextual information such as user identity, user authorization level, device type, and posture. This chapter provides design and configuration guidance when deploying the Cisco Cyber Threat Defense Solution.

- **Chapter 7, "Troubleshooting NetFlow"**: This chapter focuses on the different techniques and best practices available when troubleshooting NetFlow deployments and configurations. It assumes that you already have an understanding of the topics covered in previous chapters, such as configuration and deployment of NetFlow in all the supported devices.

- **Chapter 8, "Case Studies"**: This chapter covers several case studies and real-life scenarios on how NetFlow is deployed in large enterprises and in small and medium-sized businesses.

## Chapter 1

Introduction to NetFlow and IPFIX

This chapter covers the following topics:

- Introduction to NetFlow

- NetFlow versus IP accounting and billing

- NetFlow for network security

- Traffic engineering and network planning

- IP flow information export

- Supported platforms

- Introduction to Cisco's Cyber Threat Defense

- Cisco application visibility and control and NetFlow

- Deployment scenarios

This chapter provides an overview of Cisco NetFlow. Cisco NetFlow provides a key set of services for IP applications, including network traffic accounting, usage-based network billing, network planning, security, denial-of-service (DoS) monitoring capabilities, and network monitoring. NetFlow provides valuable information about network users and applications, peak usage times, and traffic routing.

Introduction to NetFlow

NetFlow is a Cisco application that provides comprehensive visibility into all network traffic that traverses a Cisco-supported device. Cisco invented NetFlow and is the leader in IP traffic flow technology. NetFlow was initially created for billing and accounting of network traffic and to measure other IP traffic characteristics such as bandwidth utilization and application performance. NetFlow has also been used as a network-capacity planning tool and to monitor network availability. Nowadays, NetFlow is used as a network security tool because its reporting capabilities provide nonrepudiation, anomaly detection, and investigative capabilities. As network traffic traverses a NetFlow-enabled device, the device collects traffic flow information and provides a network administrator or security professional with detailed information about such flows.

NetFlow provides detailed network telemetry that allows the administrator to

- See what is actually happening across the entire network.

- Identify DoS attacks.

- Quickly identify compromised endpoints and network infrastructure devices.

- Monitor network usage of employees, contractors, or partners.

- Obtain network telemetry during security incident response and forensics.

- Detect firewall misconfigurations and inappropriate access to corporate resources.

NetFlow supports both IP Version 4 (IPv4) and IP Version 6 (IPv6).

The Attack Continuum

Defending against cyber security attacks is becoming more challenging every day, and it is not going to get any easier. The threat landscape is evolving to a faster, more effective, and more efficient criminal economy profiting from attacks against users, enterprises, services providers, and governments. The organized cyber-crime and exchange of exploits is booming and fueling a very lucrative economy. Bad actors nowadays have a clear understanding of the underlying security technologies and their vulnerabilities. Hacker groups now follow software development lifecycles, just like enterprises follow their own. These bad actors perform quality-assurance testing against security products before releasing them into the underground economy. They continue to find ways to evade common security defenses. Attackers follow new techniques such as the following:

- Port and protocol hopping

- Encryption

- Droppers

- Social engineering

- Zero-day attacks

Security technologies and processes should not focus only on defending against Internet threats, but should also provide the ability to detect and mitigate the impact after a successful attack. Cisco has defined a framework around the attack continuum. Figure 1-1 illustrates the attack continuum.

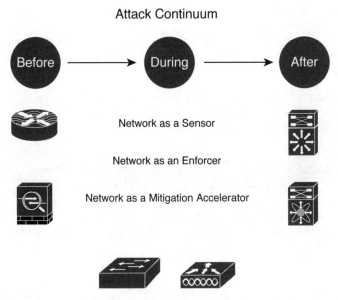

Figure 1-1 *The Attack Continuum*

Security professionals must maintain visibility and control across the extended network during the full attack continuum:

- Before the attack takes place

- During an active attack

- After an attacker starts to damage systems or steal information

Cisco next-generation security products provide protection throughout the attack continuum. Devices such as the ASA with FirePOWER Services available on the Cisco ASA 5500-X series and ASA 5585-X Adaptive Security Appliances and Cisco's Advanced Malware Protection (AMP) provide a security solution that help discover threats and enforce and harden policies before an attack takes place. In addition, you can detect attacks before, during, and after they have already taken place with NetFlow. These solutions provide the capabilities to contain and remediate an attack to minimize data loss and additional network degradation.

The Network as a Sensor and as an Enforcer

Many organizations fail use one of the strongest tools that can help protect against today's security threats: the network itself. For example, Cisco Catalyst switches, data center switches, Aggregation Services Routers (ASRs), Integrated Services Routers (ISRs), next-generation firewalls and intrusion prevention systems, NetFlow generation appliances, Advanced Malware Protection (AMP), and wireless products, in conjunction with the Cisco Application Centric Infrastructure, can protect you throughout the attack continuum: before, during, and after an attack.

The network can be used in security in three different fundamental ways:

■ **The network as a sensor:** NetFlow allows you to use the network as a sensor, giving you deep and broad visibility into unknown and unusual traffic patterns, in addition into compromised devices.

■ **The network as an enforcer:** You can use Cisco TrustSec to contain attacks by enforcing segmentation and user access control. Even when bad actors successfully breach your network defenses, you thus limit their access to only one segment of the network.

■ **The network as a mitigation accelerator:** The network can help you contain and mitigate breaches faster through automation with the Cisco Application Policy Infrastructure Controller Enterprise Module (APIC-EM). APIC-EM allows you to apply mitigations in an automated way in near real time to your whole enterprise. You can also combine these solutions with Cisco AMP and next-generation firewalls.

What Is a Flow?

A flow is a unidirectional series of packets between a given source and destination. In a *flow*, the same source and destination IP addresses, source and destination ports, and IP protocol are shared. This is often referred to as the *five-tuple*. Figure 1-2 shows an example of a flow between a client and a server.

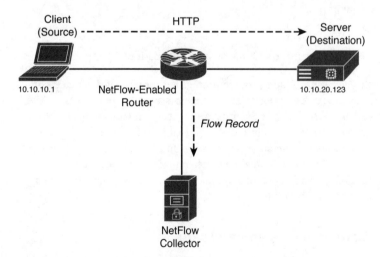

Figure 1-2   *Basic NetFlow Example*

In Figure 1-2, the client (source) establishes a connection to the server (destination). When the traffic traverses the router (configured for NetFlow), it generates a flow record. At the very minimum, the five-tuple is used to identify the flow in the NetFlow database of flows kept on the device. This database is often called the NetFlow cache.

Table 1-1 shows the five-tuple for the basic flow represented in Figure 1-2.

Table 1-1 *NetFlow Five-Tuple*

Field	Value
Source IP address	10.10.10.1
Destination IP address	10.10.20.123
Source port	13578
Destination port	80
Protocol	TCP

Depending on the version of NetFlow, the router can also gather additional information, such as type of service (ToS) byte, differentiated services code point (DSCP), the device's input interface, TCP flags, byte counters, and start and end times.

Flexible NetFlow, Cisco's next-generation NetFlow, can track a wide range of Layer 2, IPv4, and IPv6 flow information, such as the following:

- Source and destination MAC addresses
- Source and destination IPv4 or IPv6 addresses
- Source and destination ports
- ToS
- DSCP
- Packet and byte counts
- Flow time stamps
- Input and output interface numbers
- TCP flags and encapsulated protocol (TCP/UDP) and individual TCP flags
- Sections of packet for deep packet inspection
- All fields in IPv4 header, including IP-ID, TTL, and others
- All fields in IPv6 header, including Flow Label, Option Header, and others
- Routing information (next-hop address, source autonomous system number [ASN], destination ASN, source prefix mask, destination prefix mask, Border Gateway Protocol [BGP] next hop, BGP policy accounting traffic index)

Note   You can find detailed information about the versions of NetFlow in Chapter 2, "Cisco NetFlow Versions and Features."

NetFlow protocol data unit (PDU)s, also referred to as flow records, are generated and sent to a NetFlow collector after the flow concludes or expires (times out).

Note   Examples of open source and commercial NetFlow collectors are covered in detail in Chapter 4, "NetFlow Commercial and Open Source Monitoring and Analysis Software Packages."

There are three types of NetFlow cache:

- **Normal cache:** This is the default cache type in many infrastructure devices enabled with NetFlow and Flexible NetFlow. The entries in the flow cache are removed (aged out) based on the configured **timeout active** *seconds* and **timeout inactive** *seconds* settings.

- **Immediate cache:**

  - Flow accounts for a single packet

  - Desirable for real-time traffic monitoring and distributed DoS (DDoS) detection

  - Used when only very small flows are expected (for example, sampling)

Note   Immediate cache may result in a large amount of export data.

- **Permanent cache:**

  - Used to track a set of flows without expiring the flows from the cache.

  - The entire cache is periodically exported (update timer).

  - The cache is a configurable value.

  - After the cache is full, new flows will not be monitored.

  - Uses update counters rather than delta counters.

Many people often confuse a *flow* with a *session*. All traffic in a flow is going in the same direction; however, when the client establishes the HTTP connection (session) to the server and accesses a web page, it represents two separate flows. The first flow is the traffic from the client to the server, and the other flow is from the server to the client.

NetFlow Versus IP Accounting and Billing

NetFlow was originally created for IP accounting and billing purposes; however, it plays a crucial role for the following:

- Network security

- Traffic engineering

- Network planning

- Network troubleshooting

Do not confuse the feature in Cisco IOS Software called *IP Accounting* with NetFlow. IP Accounting is a great Cisco IOS tool, but it is not as robust or as well known as NetFlow.

Table 1-2 provides a comparison between some of the fundamental features provided by NetFlow and the IP Accounting feature in Cisco IOS.

Table 1-2 *NetFlow Versus IP Accounting*

Feature/Application	NetFlow	IP Accounting
Basic Layer 3 IP Accounting	Yes	Yes
IP Accounting for access control lists (ACLs)	No	Yes
IP Accounting MAC address	No	Yes
Easy results retrieval via Simple Management Network Protocol (SNMP) Management Information Base (MIB)	No	Yes
IP Accounting precedence	No	Yes
Network security	Yes	No
Traffic engineering	Yes	No
Network planning	Yes	No

NetFlow for Network Security

NetFlow is a tremendous security tool. It provides nonrepudiation, anomaly detection, and investigative capabilities. The Cisco Cyber Threat Defense (CTD) Solution uses NetFlow as the primary security visibility tool. Complete visibility is one of the key requirements when identifying and classifying security threats.

Note   An overview of Cisco CTD is covered later in this chapter and in detail in Chapter 6, "Cisco Cyber Threat Defense and NetFlow."

The first step in the process of preparing your network and staff to successfully identify security threats is achieving complete network visibility. You cannot protect against or mitigate what you cannot view/detect. You can achieve this level of network visibility through existing features on network devices you already have and on devices whose potential you do not even realize. In addition, you should create strategic network diagrams to clearly illustrate your packet flows and where, within the network, you may enable security mechanisms to identify, classify, and mitigate the threat. Remember that network security is a constant war. When defending against the enemy, you must know your own territory and implement defense mechanisms in place.

Anomaly Detection and DDoS Attacks

You can use NetFlow as an anomaly-detection tool. Anomaly-based analysis keeps track of network traffic that diverges from "normal" behavioral patterns. You must define what is considered to be normal behavior. You can use anomaly-based detection to mitigate DDoS attacks and zero-day outbreaks. DDoS attacks are often used maliciously to consume the resources of your hosts and network that would otherwise be used to serve legitimate users. The goal with these types of attacks is to overwhelm the victim network resources, or a system's resources such as CPU and memory. In most cases, this is done by sending numerous IP packets or forged requests.

A particularly dangerous attack is when an attacker builds up a more powerful attack with a more sophisticated and effective method of compromising multiple hosts and installing small attack daemons. This is what many call *zombies* or *bot hosts/nets*. Subsequently, an attacker can launch a coordinated attack from thousands of zombies onto a single victim. This daemon typically contains both the code for sourcing a variety of attacks and some basic communications infrastructure to allow for remote control.

Typically, an anomaly-detection system monitors network traffic and alerts and then reacts to any sudden increase in traffic and any other anomalies.

Note   NetFlow, along with other mechanisms such as syslog and SNMP, can be enabled within your infrastructure to provide the necessary data used for identifying and classifying threats and anomalies. Before implementing these anomaly-detection capabilities, you should perform traffic analysis to gain an understanding of general traffic rates and patterns. In anomaly detection, learning is generally performed over a significant interval, including both the peaks and valleys of network activity.

Figure 1-3 shows a graph of network traffic during a DDoS attack.

As you can see in the graph illustrated in Figure 1-3, the amount of traffic (in gigabits per second) increases around 2:00 p.m.. If the 2:00 p.m. spike is not a normal occurrence on other days, this may be an anomaly. In some cases, misconfigured hosts and servers can send traffic that consumes network resources unnecessarily. Having the necessary tools and mechanisms to identify and classify security threats and anomalies in the network is crucial.

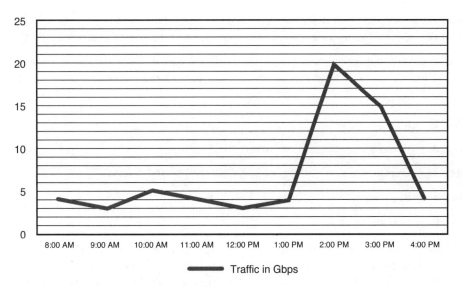

Figure 1-3 *Anomaly Detection and NetFlow Example*

Data Leak Detection and Prevention

Many network administrators, security professionals, and business leaders struggle in the effort to prevent data loss within their organization. The ability to identify anomalous behavior in data flows is crucial to detect and prevent data loss. The application of analytics to data collected via NetFlow can aid security professionals in detecting anomalous large amounts of data leaving the organization and abnormal traffic patterns inside of the organization.

Using NetFlow along with identity management systems, an administrator can detect who initiated the data transfer, the hosts (IP addresses) involved, the amount of data transferred, and the services used.

In addition, you can measure how long the communications lasted, and the frequency of the same connection attempts.

Tip Often, tuning is necessary, because certain traffic behavior could cause false positives. For instance, your organization may be legitimately sharing large amounts of data or streaming training to business partners and customers. In addition, analytics software that examines baseline behavior may be able to detect typical file transfers and incorporate them into existing baselines.

Incident Response and Network Security Forensics

NetFlow is often compared to a phone bill. When police want to investigate criminals, for instance, they often collect and investigate their phone records. NetFlow provides information about all network activity that can be very useful for incident response and network forensics. This information can help you discover indicators of compromise (IOC).

A six-step methodology on security incident handling has been adopted by many organizations, including service providers, enterprises, and government organizations, as follows:

Step 1.   Preparation

Step 2.   Identification

Step 3.   Containment

Step 4.   Eradication

Step 5.   Recovery

Step 6.   Lessons learned

NetFlow plays a crucial role in the preparation phase and identification phases. Information collected in NetFlow records can be used to identify, categorize, and scope suspected incidents as part of the identification. NetFlow data also provides great benefits for attack traceback and attribution. In addition, NetFlow provides visibility of what is getting into your network and what information is being exfiltrated out of your network.

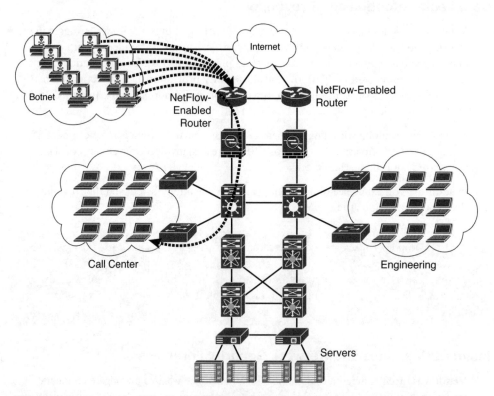

Figure 1-4   *Detecting What Is Getting into Your Network*

Figure 1-4 shows an example of how a botnet is performing a DDoS attack against the corporate network, while at the same time communicating with an internal host in the call center. NetFlow in this case can be used as an anomaly-detection tool for the DDoS attack and also as a forensics tool to potentially find others IOCs of more sophisticated attacks that may be carrying out incognito.

Figure 1-5 shows how a "stepping-stone" attack is carried out in the corporate network. A compromised host in the engineering department is extraditing large amounts of sensitive data to an attacker in the Internet from a server in the data center.

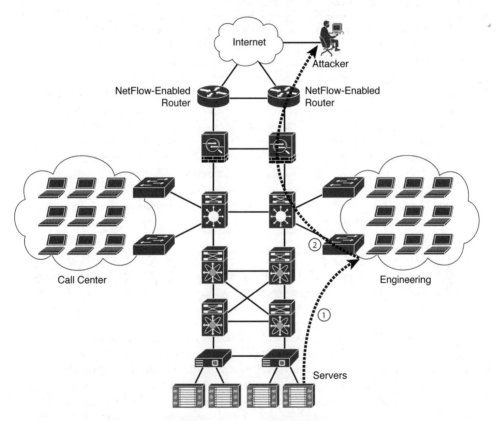

Figure 1-5 *Detecting What Is Getting Out of Your Network*

Note   More detailed real-life examples of IOCs are covered in Chapter 8, "Case Studies."

You can also use NetFlow in combination with DNS records to help you detect suspicious and malicious traffic, such as the following:

■ Suspicious requests to .gov, .mil, and .edu sites when you do not even do business with any of those entities

- Large amount of traffic leaving the organization late at night to suspicious sites

- Traffic to embargoed countries that should not have any business partners or transactions

- Suspicious virtual private network (VPN) requests and VPN traffic

- Requests and transactions to sites without any content

- Pornography sites or any other corporate policy violations

- Illegal file-sharing sites

Syslog and packet captures are also often used in network forensics; however, an area where these traditional network forensics tools fall short is in coverage. For instance, it is very difficult to deploy hundreds of sniffers (packet-capture devices) in the network of large organizations. In addition, the cost will be extremely high. When a security incident or breach is detected, the incident responders need answers fast! They do not have time to go over terabytes of packet captures, and they can definitely not analyze every computer on the network to find the root cause, miscreant, and source of the breach. You can use NetFlow to obtain a high-level view of what is happening in the network, and then the incident responder can perform a deep-dive investigation with packet captures and other tools later in the investigation. Sniffers can be then deployed as needed in key locations where suspicious activity is suspected. The beauty of NetFlow is that you can deploy it anywhere you have a supported router, switch, or Cisco ASA; alternatively, you can use Cisco NetFlow Generation Appliance (NGA).

Note   Step-by-step NetFlow configuration examples in Cisco routers, switches, Cisco ASA, and Cisco NGA are covered in Chapter 6, "Cisco Cyber Threat Defense and NetFlow," and Chapter 8, "Case Studies."

NetFlow can fill in some of the gaps and challenges regarding the collection of packet captures everywhere in the network. It is easier to store large amounts of NetFlow data because it is only a transactional record. Therefore, administrators can keep a longer history of events that occurred on their networks. Historical records can prove very valuable when investigating a breach. Network transactions can show you where an initial infection came from, what command-and-control channel was initiated by the malware, what other computers on the internal network were accessed by that infected host, and whether other hosts in the network reached out to the same attacker or command-and-control system, as demonstrated at a high-level in Figure 1-3 and Figure 1-4.

The logging facility on Cisco IOS routers, switches, Cisco ASA, and other infrastructure devices allows you to save syslog messages locally or to a remote host. By default, routers send logging messages to a logging process. The logging process controls the delivery of logging messages to various destinations, such as the logging buffer, terminal lines, a syslog server, or a monitoring event correlation system such as Cisco Prime Infrastructure, Splunk, and others. You can set the severity level of the messages to control the type of messages displayed, in addition to a time stamp to successfully track the reported information. Every security professional and incident responder knows how important it is to have good logs. There is no better way to find out what was happening in a router, switch, and firewall at the time that an attack occurred. However, like all things, syslog has limitations. You have to enable the collection of logs from each endpoint; so in many environments, syslog coverage is incomplete, and after a computer has been compromised, it is not possible to trust the logs coming from that device anymore. Syslog is extremely important, but it cannot tell you everything. Many network telemetry sources can also be correlated with NetFlow while responding to security incidents and performing network forensics, including the following:

- Dynamic Host Configuration Protocol (DHCP) logs

- VPN logs

- Network Address Translation (NAT) information

- 802.1x authentication logs

- Server logs (syslog)

- Web proxy logs

- Spam filters from e-mail security appliances such as the Cisco Email Security Appliance (ESA)

Table 1-3 lists different event types, their source, and respective events that can be combined with NetFlow while responding to security incidents and performing network forensics.

Table 1-3 *Network Telemetry Type, Sources, and Events*

Event Type	Source	Events
Attribution	DHCP server	IP assignments to machine
		MAC addresses
	VPN server	IP assignments to users
		VPN source addresses
	NAT gateway	NAT/PAT logs
	802.1x authentication logs	IP assignment to user
		MAC addresses
System activity	Syslog server	Authentication and authorization events
		Services starting and stopping
		Configuration changes
		Security events

Table 1-3 *continued*

Event Type	Source	Events
Web proxy logs	Web proxies (for example, Cisco Web Security [CWS], Web Security Appliance [WSA])	Web malware downloads Command and control check-ins
Spam filter logs	Spam filter (for example, Cisco Email Security Appliance [ESA])	Malicious URLs Malicious attachments
Firewall logs	Network firewalls (for example, Cisco ASA)	Accepted/denied connections
Web server logs	Web servers	Access logs Error logs

Tip It is extremely important that your syslog and other messages are time-stamped with the correct date and time. This is why the use of Network Time Protocol (NTP) is strongly recommended.

Network forensics can be an intimidating topic for many security professionals. Everyone knows that forensic investigation may entail many other sources of information from end hosts, servers, and any affected systems. Each forensics team needs to have awareness of many different areas, such as the following:

■ Have thorough knowledge of assets, risks, impact, and likelihood of events.

■ Practice incident response policies and procedures in mock events and collect things like NetFlow on a regular basis to analyze what is happening in the network.

■ Awareness of current vulnerabilities and threats.

■ Understand evidence handling and chain of custody. (Even NetFlow events can be used as evidence.)

■ Enact mitigation based on evidence collected.

■ Know the documentation requirements for evidence depending on your country and local laws.

■ Understand the analysis process during and after the incident.

■ Have a framework for communications, both within the team and external to the team.

Traffic Engineering and Network Planning

NetFlow can also be used for traffic engineering and network planning. For example, you can use NetFlow to understand many things that can be tuned and further engineered in the network, such as understanding what are non-mission-critical traffic taxing network resources like end users downloading audio or video files, or visiting Facebook, Twitter, and other social networking sites. Network configuration problems in infrastructure devices can be inferred by observing NetFlow. In the case of service providers, NetFlow correlation with BGP benefits peering and IP transit analysis (profitability, costs, violations, and so on). In enterprise networks, correlation with internal gateway protocols (Open Shortest Path First [OSPF], Enhanced Interior Gateway Routing Protocol [EIGRP], and Routing Information Protocol [RIP]) can provide similar benefits.

You can also use NetFlow as a troubleshooting tool. For instance, you might have users complaining that voice over IP (VoIP) calls or Cisco TelePresence video calls are failing or that the quality is very poor. Reviewing NetFlow data might indicate that many users are inappropriately streaming YouTube, Netflix, or Hulu videos. Using this data, the network administrator can create access lists to block traffic to some of these sites (or all) and/or create quality of service (QoS) policies to prioritize the VoIP and Cisco TelePresence traffic.

An example of capacity planning may be a planned merger with another company that will add hundreds or thousands of new users to internal corporate resources. Another example is a new application that may have numerous users where the network administrator might need to provision additional bandwidth or *capacity* to different areas of the network.

IP Flow Information Export

The Internet Protocol Flow Information Export (IPFIX) is a network flow standard led by the Internet Engineering Task Force (IETF). IPFIX was created to create a common, universal standard of export for flow information from routers, switches, firewalls, and other infrastructure devices. IPFIX defines how flow information should be formatted and transferred from an exporter to a collector. IPFIX is documented in RFC 7011 through RFC 7015 and RFC 5103. Cisco NetFlow Version 9 is the basis and main point of reference for IPFIX. IPFIX changes some of the terminologies of NetFlow, but in essence they are the same principles of NetFlow Version 9.

Note   The different NetFlow versions, as well as each of the components, packet types, and other detailed information, are covered in Chapter 2.

IPFIX defines different elements that are grouped into 12 groups according to their applicability:

1. Identifiers

2. Metering and exporting process configuration

3. Metering and exporting process statistics

4. IP header fields

5. Transport header fields

6. Sub-IP header fields

7. Derived-packet properties

8. Min/max flow properties

9. Flow time stamps

10. Per-flow counters

11. Miscellaneous flow properties

12. Padding

IPFIX is considered to be a *push protocol*. Each IPFIX-enabled device regularly sends IPFIX messages to configured collectors (receivers) without any interaction by the receiver. The sender controls most of the orchestration of the IPFIX data messages. IPFIX introduces the concept of *templates*, which make up these flow data messages to the receiver. IPFIX also allows the sender to use user-defined data types in its messages. IPFIX prefers the Stream Control Transmission Protocol (SCTP) as its transport layer protocol; however, it also supports the use of the Transmission Control Protocol (TCP) or User Datagram Protocol (UDP) messages.

Traditional Cisco NetFlow records are usually exported via UDP messages. The IP address of the NetFlow collector and the destination UDP port must be configured on the sending device. The NetFlow standard (RFC 3954) does not specify a specific NetFlow listening port. The standard or most common UDP port used by NetFlow is UDP port 2055, but other ports like 9555 or 9995, 9025, and 9026 can also be used. UDP port 4739 is the default port used by IPFIX.

IPFIX Architecture

IPFIX uses the following architecture terminology:

■ **Metering process (MP):** Generates flow records from packets at an observation point. It time stamps, samples, and classifies flows. The MP also maintains flows in an internal data structure and passes complete flow information to an exporting process (EP).

■ **EP:** Sends flow records via IPFIX from one or more MPs to one or more collecting processes (CPs).

■ **CP:** Receives records via IPFIX from one or more EPs.

Figure 1-6 illustrates these concepts and architecture.

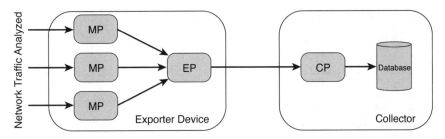

Figure 1-6 *IPFIX General Architecture*

IPFIX Mediators

IPFIX introduces the concept of mediators. Mediators collect, transform, and re-export IPFIX streams to one or more collectors. Their main purpose is to allow federation of IPFIX messages. Mediators include an intermediate process (ImP) that allows

- For NetFlow data to be kept anonymously.

- For NetFlow data to be aggregated.

- Filtering of NetFlow data.

- Proxying of web traffic.

- IP translation.

Figure 1-7 illustrates an example architecture that includes an IPFIX mediator.

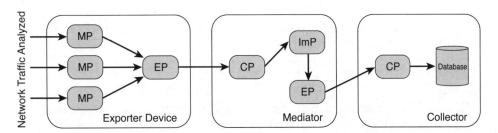

Figure 1-7 *IPFIX Mediator Example*

IPFIX Templates

An IPFIX template describes the structure of flow data records within a data set. Templates are identified by a template ID, which corresponds to set ID in the set header of the data set. Templates are composed of (information element [IE] and length) pairs. IEs provide field type information for each template. Figure 1-8 illustrates these concepts.

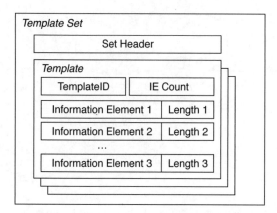

Figure 1-8 *IPFIX Template Structure*

A standard information models cover nearly all common flow collection use cases, such as the following:

- The traditional five-tuple (source IP address, destination IP address, source port, destination port, and IP protocol)

- Packet treatment such as IP next-hop IPv4 addresses, BGP destination ASN, and others

- Time stamps to nanosecond resolution

- IPv4, IPv6, ICMP, UDP, TCP header fields

- Sub-IP header fields such as source MAC address and wireless local area network (WLAN) service set identifier (SSID)

- Various counters (packet delta counts, total connection counts, top talkers, and so on)

- Flow metadata information such as ingress and egress interfaces, flow direction, virtual routing and forwarding (VRF) information

Note   There are numerous others defined at the Internet Assigned Numbers Authority (IANA) website: http://www.iana.org/assignments/ipfix/ipfix.xhtml.

Figure 1-9 includes an example of a template that includes different information element lengths and the association with the respective data set of flow records.

As illustrated in Figure 1-9, the template ID matches the set header of the related dataset (260) in this example. Then the data set includes a series of flow records. An example of the flow record is shown in the block diagram on the right.

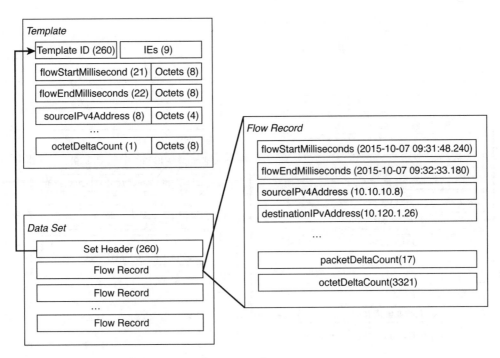

Figure 1-9 *Detailed IPFIX Template Example*

Option Templates

Option templates are a different type of IPFIX templates used to define records referred to as *options* that are associated with a specified scope. A scope may define an entity in the IPFIX architecture, including the exporting process, other templates, or a property of a collection of flows. Flow records describe flows, and option records define things other than flows, such as the following:

- Information about the collection infrastructure

- Metadata about flows or a set of flows

- Other properties of a set of flows

Figure 1-10 shows an example of an options template.

Introduction to the Stream Control Transmission Protocol (SCTP)

IPFIX uses SCTP, which provides a packet transport service designed to support several features beyond TCP or UDP capabilities. These features include the following:

- Packet streams

- Partial reliability (PR) extension

- Unordered delivery of packets or records
- Transport layer multihoming

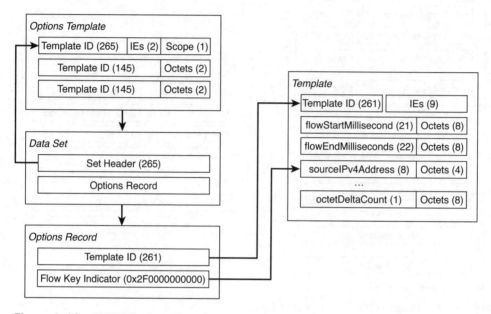

Figure 1-10 *IPFIX Options Template Example*

Many refer to SCTP as a simpler state machine than features provided by TCP with an "a la carte" selection of features. PR-SCTP provides a reliable transport with a mechanism to skip packet retransmissions. It allows for multiple applications with different reliability requirements to run on the same flow association. In other words, it combines the best effort reliability of UDP while still providing TCP-like congestion control.

SCTP ensures that IPFIX templates are sent reliably by improving end-to-end delay.

Note   RFC 6526 introduces additional features such as per-template drop counting with partial reliability and fast template reuse.

Supported Platforms

NetFlow is supported in many different platforms, including the following:

- Numerous Cisco IOS routers
- Cisco ISR Generation 2 routers

- Cisco Catalyst switches

- Cisco ASR 1000 series routers

- Cisco Carrier Routing System (CRS)

- Cisco Cloud Services Router (CSR)

- Cisco Network Convergence System (NCS)

- Cisco ASA 5500-X series next-generation firewalls

- Cisco NetFlow Generation Appliances (NGA)

- Cisco Wireless LAN Controllers

New platforms and additional support are being added on a regular basis by Cisco. The best way to obtain a full list of supported platforms is by visiting the Cisco Feature Navigator at http://tools.cisco.com/ITDIT/CFN/jsp/index.jsp.

Cisco Feature Navigator enables you to quickly find the right Cisco IOS, IOS XE, and IOS XR software release and platform for any feature that you want to enable in your network, including NetFlow.

Introduction to Cisco Cyber Threat Defense

The Cisco Cyber Threat Defense Solution provides visibility into security threats by identifying suspicious traffic patterns in the corporate network. These suspicious patterns are then augmented with circumstantial information necessary to determine the level of threat associated with a particular incident.

The Cisco CTD Solution uses NetFlow telemetry and contextual information from the Cisco network infrastructure. This solution allows a network administrator or security professional to analyze this information in a timely, efficient, and cost-effective manner for advanced cyber threats, such as the following:

- Network reconnaissance

- Malware proliferation across the network for the purpose of stealing sensitive data or creating back doors to the network

- Communications between the attacker (or command and control servers) and the compromised internal hosts

- Data exfiltration

Cisco has partnered with Lancope to deliver this solution. The Lancope StealthWatch System, available from Cisco, aggregates and normalizes considerable amounts of NetFlow data to apply security analytics to detect malicious and suspicious activity. The StealthWatch Management Console provides a rich graphical unit interface (GUI) with many visualizations and telemetry information.

The following are the primary components of the Lancope StealthWatch System:

- FlowCollector, which is a physical or virtual appliance that collects NetFlow data from infrastructure devices.

- StealthWatch Management Console.

- Flow licenses, which are required to aggregate flows at the StealthWatch Management Console. (Flow licenses define the volume of flows that may be collected.)

The following are optional components of the Lancope StealthWatch System:

- **FlowSensor:** A physical or virtual appliance that can generate NetFlow data when legacy Cisco network infrastructure components are not capable of producing line-rate, unsampled NetFlow data. Alternatively, you can use the Cisco NGA.

- **FlowReplicator:** A physical appliance used to forward NetFlow data as a single data stream to other devices.

Chapter 6 provides detailed information about the Cisco CTD Solution, along with sample configurations and best practices

Cisco Application Visibility and Control and NetFlow

The Cisco Application Visibility and Control (AVC) solution is a collection of services available in several Cisco network infrastructure devices to provide application-level classification, monitoring, and traffic control. The Cisco AVC solution is supported by the Cisco Integrated Services Routers Generation 2 (ISR G2), Cisco ASR 1000 Series Aggregation Service Routers (ASR 1000s), and Cisco Wireless LAN Controllers (WLCs). The following are the capabilities Cisco AVC combines:

- Application recognition

- Metrics collection and exporting

- Management and reporting systems

- Network traffic control

Application Recognition

Cisco AVC uses existing Cisco Network Based Application Recognition Version 2 (NBAR2) to provide deep packet inspection (DPI) technology to identify a wide variety of applications within the network traffic flow, using Layer 3 to Layer 7 data.

NBAR works with QoS features to help ensure that the network bandwidth is best used to fulfill its main primary objectives. The benefits of combining these features include the ability to guarantee bandwidth to critical applications, limit bandwidth to other applications, drop selective packets to avoid congestion, and mark packets appropriately so that the network and the service provider's network can provide QoS from end to end.

Metrics Collection and Exporting

Cisco AVC includes an embedded monitoring agent that is combined with NetFlow to provide a wide variety of network metrics data. Examples of the type of metrics the monitoring agent collects include the following:

- TCP performance metrics such as bandwidth usage, response time, and latency
- VoIP performance metrics such as packet loss and jitter

These metrics are collected and exported in NetFlow v9 or IPFIX format to a management and reporting system.

Note   In Cisco IOS routers, metrics records are sent out directly from the data plane when possible, to maximize system performance. However, if more complex processing is required on the Cisco AVC-enabled device, such as if the user requests that a router keep a history of exported records, the records may be exported from the route processor at a lower speed.

Management and Reporting Systems

Management and reporting systems, such as Cisco Prime Infrastructure or third-party tools such as Lancope and many others, receive the network metrics data in NetFlow v9 or IPFIX format.

Note   NetFlow commercial and open source software management and reporting systems are covered in detail in Chapter 4, "NetFlow Commercial and Open Source Monitoring and Analysis Software Packages."

Control

As previously mentioned, administrators can use QoS capabilities to control application prioritization. Protocol discovery features in Cisco AVC shows you the mix of applications currently running on the network. This helps you define QoS classes and polices, such as how much bandwidth to provide to mission-critical applications and how to determine which protocols should be policed. Per-protocol bidirectional statistics are available such as packet and byte counts, as well as bit rates.

After administrators classify the network traffic, they can apply the following QoS features:

- Class-based weighted fair queuing (CBWFQ) for guarantee bandwidth
- Enforcing bandwidth limits using policing

■ Marking for differentiated service downstream or from the service provider using type of service (ToS) bits or DSCPs in the IP header

■ Drop policy to avoid congestion using weighted random early detection (WRED)

Deployment Scenarios

You can enable NetFlow on network devices at all layers of the network to record and analyze all network traffic and identify threats such as malware that could be spreading laterally through the internal network; in other words, malware that spreads between adjacent hosts in the network. The following sections describe different types of NetFlow deployment scenarios within an enterprise network. These deployment scenarios include the following:

■ User access layer

■ Wireless LANs

■ Internet edge

■ Data center

■ NetFlow in site-to-site and remote-access VPNs

Tip   As a best practice, NetFlow should be enabled as close to the access layer as possible (user access layer, data center access layer, in VPN termination points, and so on). Another best practice is that all NetFlow records belonging to a flow should be sent to the same collector.

Deployment Scenario: User Access Layer

Figure 1-11 shows an enterprise corporate network where NetFlow is enabled at the access layer in a call center. NetFlow is enabled at the access layer switches. In this example, a host in the call center is compromised and is attempting to infect another machine in the engineering department.

If the access switches do not support NetFlow, you can deploy a Cisco NGA or Lancope StealthWatch FlowSensor to generate the NetFlow data. Cisco NGA or the Lancope StealthWatch FlowSensor must be placed in a Layer 1 or Layer 2 adjacent manner to the monitoring area of the network.

Note   To gain network visibility, Test Access Ports (TAPs) or Switched Port Analyzer (SPAN) ports must be configured when the Cisco NGA or the Lancope StealthWatch FlowSensor are deployed.

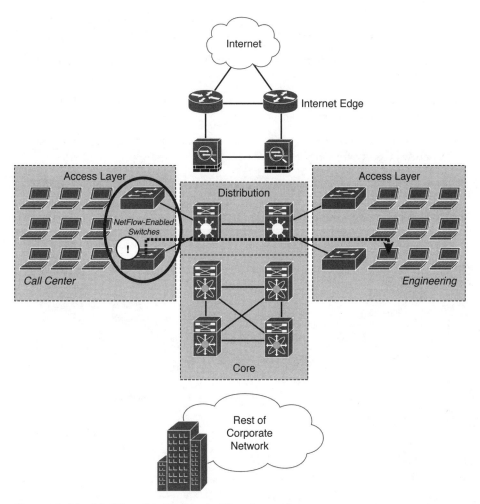

Figure 1-11 *NetFlow Enabled at the User Access Layer*

Deployment Scenario: Wireless LAN

NetFlow can be enabled in wireless LAN (WLAN) deployments. An administrator can configure NetFlow in combination with Cisco AVC in Cisco WLCs. The following are a few facts about the hardware and software requirements for AVC and NetFlow support in Cisco WLCs:

■ Cisco AVC works on traffic from Cisco wireless access points (APs) configured in local mode or enhanced local mode. APs configured in local mode provide wireless service to clients in addition to limited time-sliced attacker scanning. There is an enhanced local mode feature (just called *enhanced local mode*) that, like local mode, provides wireless service to clients, but when scanning off-channel, the radio dwells on the channel for an extended period of time, allowing enhanced attack detection.

- Cisco AVC also works with FlexConnect central switching and OfficeExtend Access Point (OEAP) traffic.

- Cisco AVC is based on port, destination, and heuristics, which allows reliable packet classification with deep visibility.

- Cisco AVC looks into the initial setup of the client flow (first 10 to 20 packets), so loading on the controller system is minimal.

- Cisco AVC and NetFlow support is available for all Cisco controllers supporting Cisco WLC Software Version 7.4 or later.

Figure 1-12 shows a simple topology where an AP is providing wireless connectivity to clients in the corporate network while managed by a Cisco WLC. NetFlow is enabled in the Cisco WLC, as well as other Cisco AVC features.

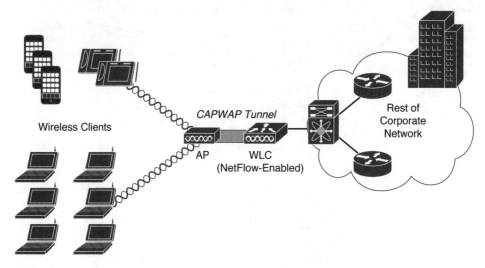

Figure 1-12 *NetFlow Enabled in WLANs*

Cisco WLC and APs establish a Control And Provisioning of Wireless Access Points (CAPWAP) tunnel between them for communication.

> **Note** CAPWAP is an IETF standard that is based on its predecessor, the Lightweight Access Point Protocol (LWAPP). CAPWAP provides an upgrade path from Cisco products that use LWAPP to next-generation Cisco wireless products to interoperate with third-party APs and to manage radio frequency identification (RFID) readers and similar devices.

Deployment Scenario: Internet Edge

You can also deploy NetFlow in the Internet edge to see what traffic is knocking on your door and what is leaving your network. The Cisco ASR 1000 series routers provide multigigabit performance to meet the requirements for Internet gateway functions for medium and large organizations. The architecture of the Cisco ASRs include the Cisco QuantumFlow Processor that provides a lot of high-performance features such as application layer gateways (ALGs), all Layer 4 to Layer 7 zone-based firewall session processing, high-speed NAT and firewall translation logging, as well as NetFlow Event Logging (NEL). NEL uses NetFlow v9 templates to log binary syslog to NEL collectors, allowing not only the use of NAT at multigigabit rates but also the ability to record NAT and firewall session creation and teardown records at very high speeds.

Note   You can use Cisco Feature Navigator to get details of all NAT- and firewall-related features for the Cisco ASR 1000 series routers at http://tools.cisco.com/ITDIT/CFN/jsp/index.jsp.

Figure 1-13 shows how two ASR Cisco ASR 1000 series routers connected to two different Internet service providers (ISPs) and enabled for NetFlow. The ISP edge is a critical part of the Internet edge because it provides the interface to the public Internet infrastructure.

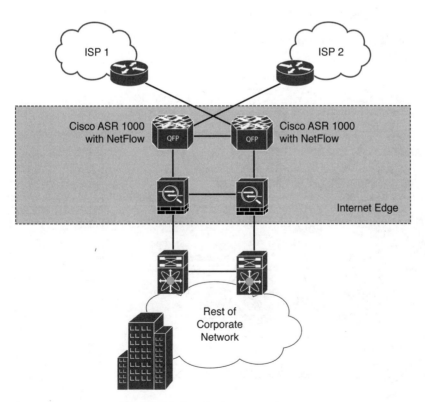

Figure 1-13   *NetFlow Enabled at the Internet Edge*

The Internet edge can be built out of many platforms and components that may fail or that may be subject to attack. Designing a redundant architecture helps eliminate single points of failure, thereby improving the availability and resiliency of the network.

> **Tip**   The Internet edge should be designed with several layers of redundancy including redundant interfaces and standby devices. Redundant interfaces at various points of the architecture provide alternative paths. Dynamic routing protocols should be used for path selection. The design allows for the use of multiple ISP connections, each served by different interfaces.

Deployment Scenario: Data Center

The data center can be a very complex world. It not only provides a rich set of services and architectures, but it also hosts the crown jewels of your organization. It is extremely important to maintain visibility of everything that is happening in the data center. The concept of "north-to-south" and "east-to-west" is often used when trying to describe the types of communication (or flow) within and to the outside of the data center:

- North-to-south is the communication needs with end-users and external entities.

- East-to-west is the communication between entities in the data center.

Figure 1-14 illustrates the concepts of north-to-south and east-to-west communication.

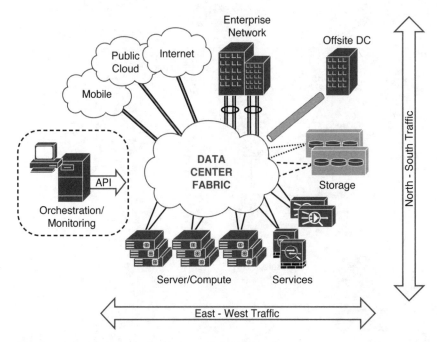

Figure 1-14   *Data Center Concepts of North-to-South and East-to-West Communication*

The data center has many different high-throughput and low-latency requirements, in addition to increasing high-availability requirements. In addition, automated provisioning and control with orchestration, monitoring, and management tools are crucial.

The data center architecture consists of three primary modular layers with hierarchical interdependencies:

- **Data center foundation:** Primary building block of the data center on which all other services rely. Despite of the size of the data center, the foundation must be resilient, scalable, and flexible to support data center services that add value, performance, and reliability. The data center foundation provides the computing necessary to support the applications that process information and the seamless transport between servers, storage, and the end users who access the applications.

- **Data center services:** Include infrastructure components to enhance the security of the applications and access to critical data. It also includes virtual switching services to extend the network control in a seamless manner from the foundation network into the hypervisor systems on servers to increase control and lower operational costs (as well as other application resilience services).

- **User services:** Include e-mail, order processing, and file sharing or any other applications in the data center that rely on the data center foundation and services like database applications, modeling, and transaction processing.

Figure 1-15 illustrates some of the components of the data center services architecture.

Examples of the data center service insertion components include the following:

- Firewalls

- Intrusion prevention systems (IPS)

- Application delivery features

- Server load balancing

- Network analysis tools (such as NetFlow)

- Virtualized services deployed in a distributed manner along with virtual machines

- Traffic direction with vPath and Nexus 1000v

- Application Centric Infrastructure (ACI) automated framework components for service insertion

Note   ACI in the data center is a holistic architecture with centralized automation and policy-driven application profiles. Its main goal is to provide software flexibility with the scalability of hardware performance and simplified automation by an application-driven policy model with real-time application health monitoring. ACI is covered in more detail in Chapter 8.

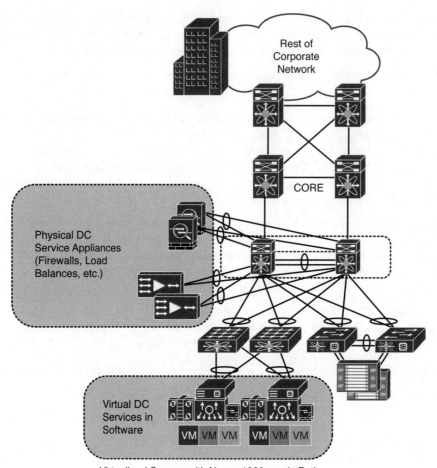

Figure 1-15   *Data Center Services Architecture*

NetFlow collection in large data centers can be very challenging because of the large amount of data being generated at very high rates. In this case, the Cisco NGA provides a high-performance solution for flow visibility in multigigabit data centers. The Cisco NGA has four 10G monitoring interfaces and up to four independent flow caches and flow monitors. In other words, the Cisco NGA can receive up to 40 gigabits of data and support various combinations of data ports, record templates, and export parameters.

Note   The Cisco NGA supports up to 64 million active flows.

Figure 1-16 shows how two Cisco NGAs are deployed in the data center services architecture.

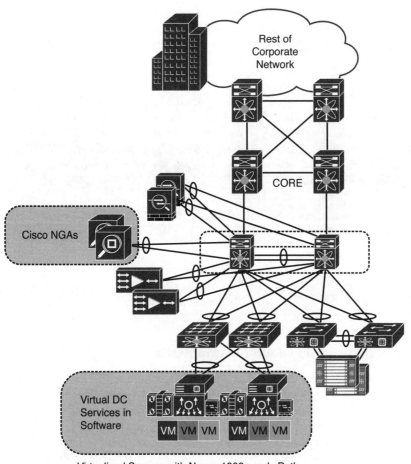

Virtualized Servers with Nexus 1000v and vPath

Figure 1-16 *Cisco NGA in the Data Center*

The Cisco NGA can be placed to receive data from the physical access, aggregation, and core layers is to maintain complete visibility of all traffic within the data center, in addition to traffic that is leaving the data center (north-to-south and east-to-west traffic). Traffic within the virtual environment (VM-to-VM traffic) can be monitored using the Nexus 1000V, and traffic entering and leaving the data center can be monitored using edge devices such as the Cisco ASA and Nexus 7000. Strategically placing the NGA in the aggregation and core layers ensures effective monitoring of traffic within the data center, and provides additional statistics for traffic leaving the data center.

If the deployment of the Cisco NGA is not possible, you can enable NetFlow in the Cisco ASA or enabled in any other strategic areas of the data center such as data center distribution switches and access switches.

The Cisco Nexus 7000 series switches support NetFlow in hardware with the F2, Enhanced F2, and F3 series modules. Without these modules, NetFlow is supported in software. If NetFlow generation is performed in software, it consumes more CPU resources.

Tip   The Cisco Nexus 7000 supports SPAN ports that can be used to send the raw traffic to a Cisco NGA for NetFlow generation in hardware. The SPAN method using NGA is the best recommendation for NetFlow in a data center environment because it minimizes design considerations around NetFlow cache size. This maintains the performance of the Nexus 7000 without losing NetFlow information. When SPAN is configured locally, the SPAN source is one or both of the following:

- One or more physical interfaces

- One or more VLANs

Note   SPAN of primary and or secondary private VLANs (PVLANs) is also supported.

Public, Private, and Hybrid Cloud Environments

In the case of cloud implementations, Cisco Cloud Services Router (CSR) 1000V series also support NetFlow. The Cisco CSR provides direct connectivity of cloud-hosted applications, private WAN integration, and other data center network capabilities to simplify application onboarding. Cisco customers can buy the Cisco CSR directly from Cisco or from their public cloud provider on a per-usage basis. The Cisco CSR is deployed in the cloud provider data center and works with Cisco routers in the enterprise to deliver end-to-end cloud optimization.

Furthermore, the Cisco CSR can also be deployed in multitenant environments. Figure 1-17 shows how Cisco CSRs are deployed in virtual environments for two cloud tenants. NetFlow can be enabled on those virtual routers to maintain visibility of tenant communication with the rest of the world.

The Cisco Nexus 1000V VSM supports NetFlow. However, it performs NetFlow generation in software. It cannot be configured as an aggregation device as the Nexus 7000 does. In busy data centers, there could be a performance impact in the Nexus 1000V when NetFlow is configured.

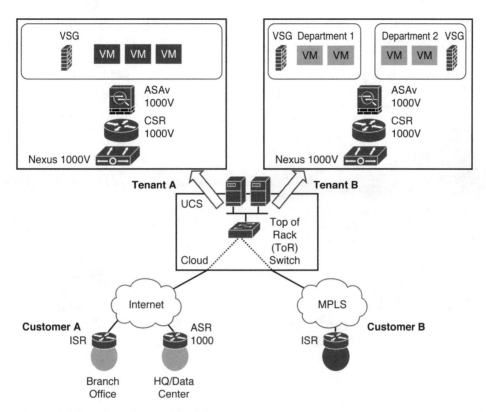

Figure 1-17   *Cisco CSR and NetFlow*

Deployment Scenario: NetFlow in Site-to-Site and Remote VPNs

Many organizations deploy VPNs to provide data integrity, authentication, and data encryption to ensure confidentiality of the packets sent over an unprotected network or the Internet. VPNs are designed to avoid the cost of unnecessary leased lines. You can also strategically enable NetFlow in VPN termination points for both site-to-site and remote-access VPN scenarios.

NetFlow Remote-Access VPNs

Remote-access VPNs enable users to work from remote locations such as their homes, hotels, and other premises as if they were directly connected to their corporate network.

Figure 1-18 shows how two remote-access VPN clients connect to a Cisco ASA in the corporate network.

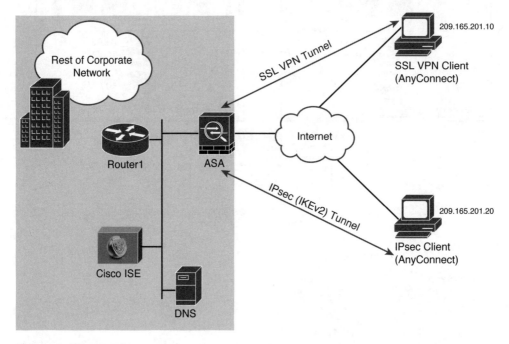

Figure 1-18 *NetFlow in Remote-Access VPNs*

The remote-access clients use the Cisco AnyConnect Secure Mobility Client. One is creating a Secure Sockets Layer (SSL) VPN tunnel, and the other is creating an IPsec tunnel.

Note Detailed configurations of the Cisco ASA and the Cisco AnyConnect Secure Mobility Solution can be learned in the Cisco Press book *Cisco ASA: All-in-One Next-Generation Firewall, IPS, and VPN Services*, 3rd Edition.

NetFlow Secure Event Logging (NSEL) can be enabled at the Cisco ASA to monitor traffic from any type of remote-access client VPN termination.

NetFlow Site-to-Site VPNs

Site-to-site (otherwise known as LAN-to-LAN) VPNs enable organizations to establish VPN tunnels between two or more network infrastructure devices in different sites so that they can communicate over a shared medium such as the Internet. Many organizations use IPsec, generic routing encryption (GRE), and Multiprotocol Label Switching (MPLS) VPN as site-to-site VPN protocols. Typically, site-to-site VPN tunnels are terminated between two or more network infrastructure devices, whereas remote-access VPN tunnels are formed between a VPN headend device and an end-user workstation or hardware VPN client. Figure 1-19 shows a site-to-site VPN example.

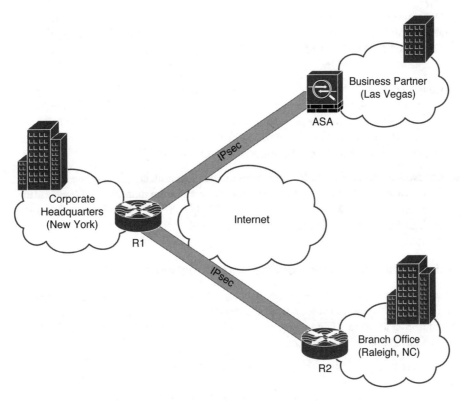

Figure 1-19 *NetFlow in Site-to-Site VPNs*

In Figure 1-19, two site-to-site VPNs are terminated in the router (R1) at the corporate headquarters. One of the tunnels connects to a Cisco ASA at a business partner, and the second tunnel connects the corporate headquarters to a remote branch office in Raleigh, North Carolina. In the example, NetFlow can be enabled in R1 to monitor traffic coming from both of the remote locations. In addition, the business partner can enable NSEL in the Cisco ASA to also maintain visibility of the VPN traffic. To make things more complicated, an administrator could also enable NetFlow in the router at the remote branch office in Raleigh (R2).

NetFlow Collection Considerations and Best Practices

The following are several best practices and general recommendations when preparing and designing where to enable NetFlow in your organization:

- **Minimizing NetFlow overhead:** NetFlow collection should be done as close to the NetFlow generator as possible. For instance, in the data center, NetFlow can be enabled as close to the servers or assets you want to monitor. Another example is in access switches of a network segment where the users you want to monitor reside.

- **Asymmetric routing considerations:** All devices in the asymmetric route should send NetFlow records to the same collector, not to different collectors.

- **Distributed deployment:** In a distributed deployment, FlowCollectors are deployed at multiple sites and are usually placed close to the source producing the highest number of NetFlow records. This deployment has the advantage of limiting the overhead introduced by NetFlow.

- **Centralized deployment:** In a centralized deployment, all NetFlow collectors are placed in a single location. In some cases, the collector can be configured behind a load balancer. This provides the benefit of a single collection location and possibly a single IP address globally for NetFlow collection. This deployment offers advantages in environments where NetFlow generators are far apart.

- **Bandwidth consideration:** It is not recommended to collect NetFlow over wide-area network (WAN) connections because there might be limitations in bandwidth between sites to consider, as well. You should plan ahead and identify the monitoring locations that make more sense for your environment.

Determining the Flows per Second and Scalability

One of the most important steps in the planning and design of NetFlow deployments is to determine and measure the flows per second (fps) volume that will be generated by the monitoring locations. The volume or fps indicates how many records the collectors must be able to receive and analyze.

Many different factors affect the volume of NetFlow records generated by network infrastructure devices. Forecasting an exact number can be difficult. As a general rule, a NetFlow-enabled device can generate between 1000 and 5000 fps per 1 gigabit per second (Gbps) of traffic passing through such device. The number of fps fundamentally depends on the following:

- Number of unique flows passing through the NetFlow-enabled device.

- Number of new connections per second.

- The lifetime of each of the flows. Some flows can be short-lived and others may be long-lived.

The network overhead introduced by NetFlow is also influenced by the number of fps and the NetFlow record size.

Tip Cisco recommends NetFlow v9, which results in an average of 34 NetFlow records per 1500-byte packet. Cisco also recommends an active timer of 60 seconds and an inactive timer of 15 seconds.

Careful planning is required when enabling NetFlow in high-impact areas of your network. You can start by enabling NetFlow in certain areas of your network and become familiar with the impact it may have in the rest of your deployment. A few tools are available that you can use to forecast the impact of enabling NetFlow in your network.

An example is the Lancope NetFlow Bandwidth Calculator available at http://www.
lancope.com/resource-center/netflow-bandwidth-calculator-stealthwatch-calculator/.

Note   Using random-sampled NetFlow provides NetFlow data for a subset of traffic
in a Cisco router by processing only one randomly selected packet out of a series of
sequential packets. The number of packets or "randomness" is a user-configurable
parameter. This type of statistical traffic sampling substantially reduces the overheard
in CPU and other resources while providing NetFlow data. However, the main use of
random-sampled NetFlow is for traffic engineering, capacity planning, and applications
where full NetFlow is not needed for an accurate view of network traffic.

Summary

NetFlow and IPFIX provide comprehensive visibility into network traffic across an organization. This visibility has many benefits for network security, IP accounting, billing,
traffic engineering, and network capacity planning. NetFlow technology is supported
across Cisco routers, switches, Cisco ASA, Cisco WLC, virtual routers, and the Cisco
NGA. This chapter provided an overview of NetFlow and IPFIX. It provided information about the supported platforms, in addition to several tips when enabling NetFlow
telemetry implemented at all layers of the network. This chapter provided an overview
of how NetFlow enables you to use the network as a sensor, as well as how other
advanced security technologies can enable you to use the network as an enforcer and as
an attack-mitigation accelerator. Several deployment scenarios were covered at the end
of the chapter, providing a conceptual overview of where NetFlow can be enabled in
your organization to maintain visibility of the access layer, wireless network, the Internet
edge, the data center, and site-to-site and remote-access VPN termination points. Several
best practices and general recommendations were covered that can help you when preparing and designing where to enable NetFlow in your organization.

## Chapter 2

Cisco NetFlow Versions and Features

This chapter covers the following topics:

- NetFlow versions and respective features

- NetFlow v9 export format and packet details

- NetFlow and IPFIX comparison

NetFlow Versions and Respective Features

NetFlow was invented by Cisco to provide full network visibility, as mentioned in Chapter 1, "Introduction to NetFlow and IPFIX." This section provides an overview of all NetFlow versions and the respective features that are supported.

Table 2-1 lists of all versions of NetFlow and a brief description of the features supported.

Table 2-1 *NetFlow Versions*

NetFlow Version	Description
Version 1 (v1)	(Obsolete) The first implementation of NetFlow. NetFlow v1 was limited to IPv4 without IP network masks and autonomous system numbers (ASNs).
Version 2 (v2)	Never released.
Version 3 (v3)	Never released.
Version 4 (v4)	Never released.
Version 5 (v5)	Popular NetFlow version on many routers from different vendors. Limited to IPv4 flows.

Table 2-1   *continued*

NetFlow Version	Description
Version 6 (v6)	(Obsolete) No longer supported by Cisco.
Version 7 (v7)	(Obsolete) Like version 5 with a source router field.
Version 8 (v8)	(Obsolete) Several aggregation form, but only for information that is already present in Version 5 records
Version 9 (v9)	Template-based, available (as of 2009) on some recent routers. Mostly used to report flows like IPv6, Multiprotocol Label Switching (MPLS), or even plain IPv4 with Border Gateway Protocol (BGP) next hop.
IPFIX	IPFIX is an IETF standard based on NetFlow v9 with several extensions. IPFIX was covered in detail in Chapter 1.

NetFlow v1 Flow Header Format and Flow Record Format

Table 2-2 lists the NetFlow v1 flow header format, and Table 2-3 lists the attributes of the NetFlow v1 flow record format.

Table 2-2   *NetFlow v1 Flow Header Format*

Bytes	Contents	Description
0–1	version	NetFlow export format version number
2–3	count	Number of flows exported in this packet (1–24)
4–7	sys_uptime	Current time in milliseconds since the export device booted
8–11	unix_secs	Current count of seconds since 0000 UTC 1970
12–16	unix_nsecs	Residual nanoseconds since 0000 UTC 1970

Table 2-3   *NetFlow v1 Flow Record Format*

Bytes	Contents	Description
0–3	srcaddr	Source IP address
4–7	dstaddr	Destination IP address
8–11	nexthop	IP address of next-hop router
12–13	input	SNMP index of input interface
14–15	output	SNMP index of output interface
16–19	dPkts	Packets in the flow
20–23	dOctets	Total number of Layer 3 bytes in the packets of the flow
24–27	first	SysUptime at start of flow

Table 2-3 *continued*

Bytes	Contents	Description
28–31	last	SysUptime at the time the last packet of the flow was received
32–33	srcport	TCP/UDP source port number or equivalent
34–35	dstport	TCP/UDP destination port number or equivalent
36–37	pad1	Unused (0) bytes
38	prot	IP protocol type (for example, TCP = 6; UDP = 17)
39	tos	IP type of service (ToS)
40	flags	Cumulative OR of TCP flags
41–48	pad2	Unused (0) bytes

NetFlow v5 Flow Header Format and Flow Record Format

Table 2-4 lists the NetFlow v5 flow header format, and Table 2-5 lists the attributes of the NetFlow v5 flow record format.

Table 2-4 *NetFlow v5 Flow Header Format*

Bytes	Contents	Description
0–1	version	NetFlow export format version number
2–3	count	Number of flows exported in this packet (1–30)
4–7	sys_uptime	Current time in milliseconds since the export device booted
8–11	unix_secs	Current count of seconds since 0000 UTC 1970
12–15	unix_nsecs	Residual nanoseconds since 0000 UTC 1970
16–19	flow_sequence	Sequence counter of total flows seen
20	engine_type	Type of flow-switching engine
21	engine_id	Slot number of the flow-switching engine
22–23	sampling_interval	First two bits hold the sampling mode; remaining 14 bits hold value of sampling interval

Table 2-5 *NetFlow v5 Flow Record Format*

Bytes	Contents	Description
0–3	srcaddr	Source IP address
4–7	dstaddr	Destination IP address
8–11	nexthop	IP address of next-hop router
12–13	input	Simple Network Management Protocol (SNMP) index of input interface

Table 2-5 *continued*

Bytes	Contents	Description
14–15	output	SNMP index of output interface
16–19	dPkts	Packets in the flow
20–23	dOctets	Total number of Layer 3 bytes in the packets of the flow
24–27	first	SysUptime at start of flow
28–31	last	SysUptime at the time the last packet of the flow was received
32–33	srcport	TCP/UDP source port number or equivalent
34–35	dstport	TCP/UDP destination port number or equivalent
36	pad1	Unused (0) bytes
37	tcp_flags	Cumulative OR of TCP flags
38	prot	IP protocol type (for example, TCP = 6; UDP = 17)
39	tos	IP type of service (ToS)
40–41	src_as	Autonomous system number (ASN) of the source, either origin or peer
42–43	dst_as	ASN of the destination, either origin or peer
44	src_mask	Source address prefix mask bits
45	dst_mask	Destination address prefix mask bits
46–47	pad2	Unused (0) bytes

NetFlow v7 Flow Header Format and Flow Record Format

Table 2-6 lists the NetFlow v7 flow header format, and Table 2-7 lists the attributes of the NetFlow v7 flow record format.

Table 2-6 *NetFlow v7 Flow Header Format*

Bytes	Contents	Description
0–1	version	NetFlow export format version number
2–3	count	Number of flows exported in this packet (1–30)
4–7	sys_uptime	Current time in milliseconds since the export device booted
8–11	unix_secs	Current count of seconds since 0000 UTC 1970
12–15	unix_nsecs	Residual nanoseconds since 0000 UTC 1970
16–19	flow_sequence	Sequence counter of total flows seen
20–23	reserved	Unused (0) bytes

Table 2-7 *NetFlow v7 Flow Record Format*

Bytes	Contents	Description
0–3	srcaddr	Source IP address
4–7	dstaddr	Destination IP address
8–11	nexthop	IP address of next-hop router
12–13	input	SNMP index of input interface
14–15	output	SNMP index of output interface
16–19	dPkts	Packets in the flow
20–23	dOctets	Total number of Layer 3 bytes in the packets of the flow
24–27	first	SysUptime at start of flow
28–31	last	SysUptime at the time the last packet of the flow was received
32–33	srcport	TCP/UDP source port number or equivalent
34–35	dstport	TCP/UDP destination port number or equivalent
36	pad1	Unused (0) bytes
37	tcp_flags	Cumulative OR of TCP flags
38	prot	IP protocol type (for example, TCP = 6; UDP = 17)
39	tos	IP type of service (ToS)
40–41	src_as	ASN of the source, either origin or peer
42–43	dst_as	ASN of the destination, either origin or peer
44	src_mask	Source address prefix mask bits
45	dst_mask	Destination address prefix mask bits
46–47	flags	Flags indicating, among other things, what flows are invalid
48–51	router_sc	IP address of the router that is bypassed by the Catalyst 5000 series switch. (This is the same address the router uses when it sends NetFlow export packets. This IP address is propagated to all switches bypassing the router through the Fibre Channel Protocol [FCP].)

NetFlow Version 9

The most popular version of NetFlow is Version 9. The NetFlow v9 format is template based. Templates provide a flexible design to the record format. This feature allows for future enhancements to NetFlow services without requiring fundamental changes to the underlying flow record format.

The following are the benefits of using NetFlow templates:

■ Provides a vendor-neutral support for companies that create applications that provide collector or analysis capabilities for NetFlow are not required to reinvent their product each time a new NetFlow feature is added.

■ New features can be added to NetFlow more quickly, without breaking current implementations and with backward compatibility.

The NetFlow Version 9 record format consists of a packet header followed by at least one or more template or data FlowSets. A template FlowSet provides a description of the fields that will be present in future data FlowSets. These data FlowSets may occur later within the same export packet or in subsequent export packets. Figure 2-1 shows a basic illustration of the NetFlow v9 export packet.

| Packet Header | Template FlowSet | Data FlowSet | Data FlowSet | ·········· | Template FlowSet | Data FlowSet |

Figure 2-1 *NetFlow v9 Export Packet*

Figure 2-2 shows a more detailed illustration of the NetFlow v9 export packet and the relationship between each field and attributes.

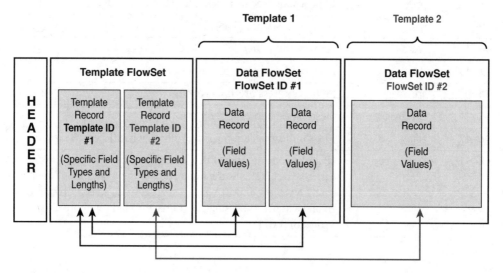

Figure 2-2 *NetFlow v9 Export Packet Details*

The format of the NetFlow v9 packet header is very similar to its predecessors, and it is illustrated in Figure 2-3.

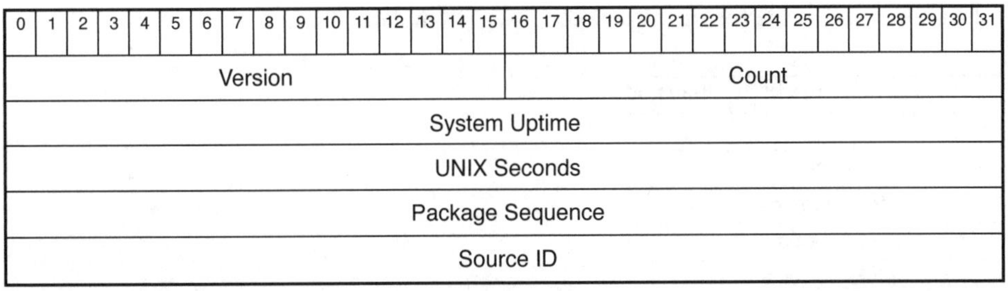

0	1	2	3	4	5	6	7	8	9	10	11	12	13	14	15	16	17	18	19	20	21	22	23	24	25	26	27	28	29	30	31
Version																Count															
System Uptime																															
UNIX Seconds																															
Package Sequence																															
Source ID																															

Figure 2-3 *NetFlow v9 Packet Header Format*

Table 2-8 lists the NetFlow v9 packet header field descriptions.

Table 2-8 *NetFlow v9 Packet Header Field Descriptions*

Field Name	Value
Version	The version of NetFlow records exported in this packet. The hexadecimal value 0x0009 represents NetFlow v9.
Count	Number of FlowSet records (both template and data) contained within the export packet.
System Uptime	Time in milliseconds since the device started.
UNIX Seconds	Seconds since 0000 coordinated universal time (UTC) 1970.
Sequence Number	Incremental sequence counter of all export packets sent by this export device; this value is cumulative, and it can be used to identify whether any export packets have been missed. **Note:** This is a change from the NetFlow Version 5 and Version 8 headers, where this number represented "total flows."
Source ID	A 32-bit value that is used to ensure uniqueness for all flows exported from a particular NetFlow-enabled device. The Source ID field is the equivalent of the Engine Type and Engine ID fields found in the NetFlow v5 and v8 headers. The format of this field is vendor specific. In Cisco's implementation, the first 2 bytes are reserved for future expansion, and will always be 0. Byte 3 provides uniqueness with respect to the routing engine on the exporting device. Byte 4 provides uniqueness with respect to the particular line card or Versatile Interface Processor on the exporting device. NetFlow collectors should use the combination of the source IP address plus the Source ID field to associate an incoming NetFlow export packet with a unique instance of NetFlow on a particular device.

As previously mentioned, templates are one of the main benefits of NetFlow v9 because they provide flexibility to allow a NetFlow collector or display application to process NetFlow data without necessarily knowing the format of the data in advance.

Figure 2-4 shows the format of the NetFlow v9 template FlowSet.

0 1 2 3 4 5 6 7 8 9 10 11 12 13 14 15
Flowset_Id=0
Length
Template_Id
Field_Count
Field_1_Type
Field_1_Length
Field_2_Type
Field_2_Length
Field_3_Type
Field_3_Length
...
Field_N_Type
Field_N_Length
Template_Id
Field_Count
Field_1_Type
Field_1_Length
...
Field_N_Type
Field_N_Length

Figure 2-4   *NetFlow v9 Template FlowSet Format*

Table 2-9 lists the NetFlow v9 template FlowSet field descriptions.

Table 2-9   *NetFlow v9 Template FlowSet Field Descriptions*

Field	Description
flowset_id	The flowset_id is used to distinguish template records from data records. A template record always has a flowset_id in the range of 0 to 255. Currently, the template record that describes flow fields has a flowset_id of 0, and the template record that describes option fields (described later) has a flowset_id of 1. A data record always has a non-0 flowset_id greater than 255.
length	Length refers to the total length of this FlowSet. Because an individual template FlowSet may contain multiple template IDs (as illustrated earlier), the length value should be used to determine the position of the next FlowSet record, which could be either a template or a data FlowSet.
	Length is expressed in type/length/value (TLV) format, meaning that the value includes the bytes used for the flowset_id and the length bytes themselves, in addition to the combined lengths of all template records included in this FlowSet.

Table 2-9 *continued*

Field	Description
template_id	As a router generates different template FlowSets to match the type of NetFlow data it will be exporting, each template is given a unique ID. This uniqueness is local to the router that generated the template_id.
	Templates that define data record formats begin numbering at 256 because 0 through 255 are reserved for FlowSet IDs.
field_count	This field gives the number of fields in this template record. Because a template FlowSet may contain multiple template records, this field allows the parser to determine the end of the current template record and the start of the next.
field_type	This numeric value represents the type of the field. The possible values of the field type are vendor specific. Cisco-supplied values are consistent across all platforms that support NetFlow Version 9.
	At the time of the initial release of the NetFlow Version 9 code (and after any subsequent changes that could add new field-type definitions), Cisco provides a file that defines the known field types and their lengths.
	Table 2-10 details the currently defined field types.
field_length	This number gives the length of the field_type field, in bytes.

Table 2-10 lists the NetFlow v9 field type definitions.

Table 2-10 *NetFlow v9 Field Type Definitions*

Field Type	Value	Length (Bytes)	Description
IN_BYTES	1	N (default is 4)	Incoming counter with length N × 8 bits for number of bytes associated with an IP flow.
IN_PKTS	2	N (default is 4)	Incoming counter with length N × 8 bits for the number of packets associated with an IP flow.
FLOWS	3	N	Number of flows that were aggregated; default for N is 4.
PROTOCOL	4	1	IP protocol byte.
SRC_TOS	5	1	Type of service byte setting when entering incoming interface.
TCP_FLAGS	6	1	Cumulative of all the TCP flags seen for this flow.
L4_SRC_PORT	7	2	TCP/UDP source port number (for example, FTP, Telnet, or equivalent).

Table 2-10   *continued*

Field Type	Value	Length (Bytes)	Description
IPV4_SRC_ADDR	8	4	IPv4 source address.
SRC_MASK	9	1	The number of contiguous bits in the source address subnet mask (that is, the submask in slash notation).
INPUT_SNMP	10	N	Input interface index; default for N is 2, but higher values could be used.
L4_DST_PORT	11	2	TCP/UDP destination port number (for example, FTP, Telnet, or equivalent).
IPV4_DST_ADDR	12	4	IPv4 destination address.
DST_MASK	13	1	The number of contiguous bits in the destination address subnet mask (that is, the submask in slash notation).
OUTPUT_SNMP	14	N	Output interface index; default for N is 2, but higher values could be used.
IPV4_NEXT_HOP	15	4	IPv4 address of next-hop router.
SRC_AS	16	N (default is 2)	Source BGP ASN, where N could be 2 or 4.
DST_AS	17	N (default is 2)	Destination BGP ASN, where N could be 2 or 4.
BGP_IPV4_NEXT_HOP	18	4	Next-hop router's IP in the BGP domain.
MUL_DST_PKTS	19	N (default is 4)	IP multicast outgoing packet counter with length N × 8 bits for packets associated with the IP flow.
MUL_DST_BYTES	20	N (default is 4)	IP multicast outgoing byte counter with length N × 8 bits for bytes associated with the IP flow.
LAST_SWITCHED	21	4	System uptime at which the last packet of this flow was switched.
FIRST_SWITCHED	22	4	System uptime at which the first packet of this flow was switched.

Table 2-10 *continued*

Field Type	Value	Length (Bytes)	Description
OUT_BYTES	23	N (default is 4)	Outgoing counter with length N × 8 bits for the number of bytes associated with an IP flow.
OUT_PKTS	24	N (default is 4)	Outgoing counter with length N × 8 bits for the number of packets associated with an IP flow.
MIN_PKT_LNGTH	25	2	Minimum IP packet length on incoming packets of the flow.
MAX_PKT_LNGTH	26	2	Maximum IP packet length on incoming packets of the flow.
IPV6_SRC_ADDR	27	16	IPv6 source address.
IPV6_DST_ADDR	28	16	IPv6 destination address.
IPV6_SRC_MASK	29	1	Length of the IPv6 source mask in contiguous bits.
IPV6_DST_MASK	30	1	Length of the IPv6 destination mask in contiguous bits.
IPV6_FLOW_LABEL	31	3	IPv6 flow label as per RFC 2460 definition.
ICMP_TYPE	32	2	Internet Control Message Protocol (ICMP) packet type; reported as ((ICMP Type * 256) + ICMP code).
MUL_IGMP_TYPE	33	1	Internet Group Management Protocol (IGMP) packet type.
SAMPLING_INTERVAL	34	4	When using sampled NetFlow, the rate at which packets are sampled. For example, a value of 100 indicates that 1 of every 100 packets is sampled.
SAMPLING_ALGORITHM	35	1	The type of algorithm used for sampled NetFlow: 0x01 deterministic sampling, 0x02 random sampling.
FLOW_ACTIVE_TIMEOUT	36	2	Timeout value (in seconds) for active flow entries in the NetFlow cache.
FLOW_INACTIVE_TIMEOUT	37	2	Timeout value (in seconds) for inactive flow entries in the NetFlow cache.

Table 2-10 *continued*

Field Type	Value	Length (Bytes)	Description
ENGINE_TYPE	38	1	Type of flow switching engine: RP = 0, VIP/Linecard = 1.
ENGINE_ID	39	1	ID number of the flow switching engine.
TOTAL_BYTES_EXP	40	N (default is 4)	Counter with length N × 8 bits for bytes for the number of bytes exported by the observation domain.
TOTAL_PKTS_EXP	41	N (default is 4)	Counter with length N × 8 bits for bytes for the number of packets exported by the observation domain.
TOTAL_FLOWS_EXP	42	N (default is 4)	Counter with length N × 8 bits for bytes for the number of flows exported by the observation domain.
* Vendor Proprietary*	43	N/A	N/A
IPV4_SRC_PREFIX	44	4	IPv4 source address prefix (specific for Catalyst architecture).
IPV4_DST_PREFIX	45	4	IPv4 destination address prefix (specific for Catalyst architecture).
MPLS_TOP_LABEL_TYPE	46	1	MPLS top label type: 0x00 UNKNOWN 0x01 TE-MIDPT 0x02 ATOM 0x03 VPN 0x04 BGP 0x05 LDP.
MPLS_TOP_LABEL_IP_ADDR	47	4	Forwarding Equivalent Class corresponding to the MPLS top label.
FLOW_SAMPLER_ID	48	1	Identifier shown in show flow-sampler.
FLOW_SAMPLER_MODE	49	1	The type of algorithm used for sampling data: 0x02 random sampling. Use in connection with FLOW_SAMPLER_MODE.
FLOW_SAMPLER_RANDOM_INTERVAL	50	4	Packet interval at which to sample. Use in connection with FLOW_SAMPLER_MODE.
* Vendor Proprietary*	51	N/A	N/A

Table 2-10 *continued*

Field Type	Value	Length (Bytes)	Description
MIN_TTL	52	1	Minimum Time to Live (TTL) on incoming packets of the flow.
MAX_TTL	53	1	Maximum TTL on incoming packets of the flow.
IPV4_IDENT	54	2	The IP v4 identification field.
DST_TOS	55	1	Type of service byte setting when exiting outgoing interface.
IN_SRC_MAC	56	6	Incoming source MAC address.
OUT_DST_MAC	57	6	Outgoing destination MAC address.
SRC_VLAN	58	2	Virtual LAN identifier associated with ingress interface.
DST_VLAN	59	2	Virtual LAN identifier associated with egress interface.
IP_PROTOCOL_VERSION	60	1	Internet Protocol version set to 4 for IPv4, set to 6 for IPv6. If not present in the template, Version 4 is assumed.
DIRECTION	61	1	Flow direction: 0 = ingress flow, 1 = egress flow.
IPV6_NEXT_HOP	62	16	IPv6 address of the next-hop router.
BPG_IPV6_NEXT_HOP	63	16	Next-hop router in the BGP domain.
IPV6_OPTION_HEADERS	64	4	Bit-encoded field identifying IPv6 option headers found in the flow.
* Vendor Proprietary*	65	N/A	N/A
* Vendor Proprietary*	66	N/A	N/A
* Vendor Proprietary*	67	N/A	N/A
* Vendor Proprietary*	68	N/A	N/A
* Vendor Proprietary*	69	N/A	N/A
MPLS_LABEL_1	70	3	MPLS label at position 1 in the stack.
MPLS_LABEL_2	71	3	MPLS label at position 2 in the stack.

Table 2-10   *continued*

Field Type	Value	Length (Bytes)	Description
MPLS_LABEL_3	72	3	MPLS label at position 3 in the stack.
MPLS_LABEL_4	73	3	MPLS label at position 4 in the stack.
MPLS_LABEL_5	74	3	MPLS label at position 5 in the stack.
MPLS_LABEL_6	75	3	MPLS label at position 6 in the stack.
MPLS_LABEL_7	76	3	MPLS label at position 7 in the stack.
MPLS_LABEL_8	77	3	MPLS label at position 8 in the stack.
MPLS_LABEL_9	78	3	MPLS label at position 9 in the stack.
MPLS_LABEL_10	79	3	MPLS label at position 10 in the stack.
IN_DST_MAC	80	6	Incoming destination MAC address.
OUT_SRC_MAC	81	6	Outgoing source MAC address.
IF_NAME	82	N (default specified in template)	Shortened interface name (for example, FE1/0).
IF_DESC	83	N (default specified in template)	Full interface name (for example, FastEthernet 1/0).
SAMPLER_NAME	84	N (default specified in template)	Name of the flow sampler.
IN_PERMANENT_ BYTES	85	N (default is 4)	Running byte counter for a permanent flow.
IN_PERMANENT_ PKTS	86	N (default is 4)	Running packet counter for a permanent flow.
* Vendor Proprietary*	87	N/A	N/A
FRAGMENT_OFFSET	88	2	The fragment-offset value from fragmented IP packets.

Table 2-10 *continued*

Field Type	Value	Length (Bytes)	Description
FORWARDING STATUS	89	1	Forwarding status is encoded on 1 byte, with the 2 left bits giving the status and the 6 remaining bits giving the reason code.
MPLS PAL RD	90	8 (array)	MPLS PAL route distinguisher.
MPLS PREFIX LEN	91	1	Number of consecutive bits in the MPLS prefix length.
SRC TRAFFIC INDEX	92	4	BGP policy accounting source traffic index.
DST TRAFFIC INDEX	93	4	BGP policy accounting destination traffic index.
APPLICATION DESCRIPTION	94	N	Description of the application.
APPLICATION TAG	95	1+n	8 bits of engine ID, followed by *n* bits of classification.
APPLICATION NAME	96	N	Application name associated with a classification.
*** Not used ***	97	N/A	N/A
postipDiffServCode-Point	98	1	The value of a differentiated services code point (DSCP) encoded in the Differentiated Services field, after modification.
replication factor	99	4	Multicast replication factor.
Deprecated	100	N	Deprecated.
*** Not used ***	101	N/A	N/A
layer2packetSection-Offset	102		Layer 2 packet section offset.
layer2packetSection-Size	103		Layer 2 packet section size.
layer2packetSection-Data	104		Layer 2 packet section data.
*** Reserved for future use ***	105 thru 127	N/A	N/A

Figure 2-5 shows the NetFlow v9 template FlowSet format.

0	1	2	3	4	5	6	7	8	9	10	11	12	13	14	15
Flowset Id=Template ID
Length
Record 1 - Field 1 Value
Record 1 - Field 2 Value
Record 1 - Field 3 Value
Record 1 - Field 4 Value
•
•
•
Record 1 - Field N Value
Record 2 - Field 1 Value
Record 2 - Field 2 Value
Record 2 - Field 3 Value
•
•
•
Record 2 - Field N Value
•
•
•
Padding

Figure 2-5   *NetFlow v9 Template FlowSet Format*

Table 2-11 lists the NetFlow v9 data FlowSet definitions.

Table 2-11   *NetFlow v9 Data FlowSet Definitions*

Field	Description
flowset_id	A FlowSet ID precedes each group of records within a NetFlow Version 9 data FlowSet. The FlowSet ID maps to a (previously received) template_id. The collector and display applications should use the flowset_id to map the appropriate type and length to any field values that follow.
length	This field gives the length of the data FlowSet. Length is expressed in TLV format, meaning that the value includes the bytes used for the flowset_id and the length bytes themselves, as well as the combined lengths of any included data records.

Table 2-11 *continued*

Field	Description
record_N through field_M	The remainder of the Version 9 data FlowSet is a collection of field values. The type and length of the fields have been previously defined in the template record referenced by the flowset_id/template_id.
padding	Padding should be inserted to align the end of the FlowSet on a 32-bit boundary. Pay attention that the length field will include those padding bits.

As you learned in Chapter 1, IPFIX is modeled after NetFlow v9. This is why many of these NetFlow v9 concepts and fields are very similar to IPFIX. Just like IPFIX, NetFlow v9 has the concept of options templates used to supply metadata about the NetFlow process itself. Figure 2-6 illustrates the format of the options template.

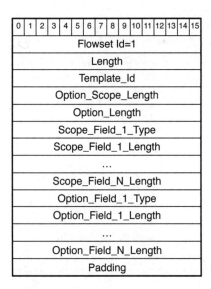

Figure 2-6 *NetFlow v9 Options Template Format*

Table 2-12 lists the NetFlow v9 data options template definitions.

Table 2-12 *NetFlow v9 Data Options Template Definitions*

Field	Description
flowset_id = 1	The flowset_id is used to distinguish template records from data records. A template record always has a flowset_id of 1. A data record always has a non-0 flowset_id that is greater than 255.

Table 2-12 *continued*

Field	Description
length	This field gives the total length of this FlowSet. Because an individual template FlowSet may contain multiple template IDs, the length value should be used to determine the position of the next FlowSet record, which could be either a template or a data FlowSet.
	Length is expressed in TLV format, meaning that the value includes the bytes used for the flowset_id and the length bytes themselves, as well as the combined lengths of all template records included in this FlowSet.
template_id	As a router generates different template FlowSets to match the type of NetFlow data it will be exporting, each template is given a unique ID. This uniqueness is local to the router that generated the template_id. The template_id is greater than 255. Template IDs less than 255 are reserved.
option_scope_length	This field gives the length in bytes of any scope fields contained in this options template. (The use of scope is described later.)
options_length	This field gives the length (in bytes) of any Options field definitions contained in this options template.
scope_field_N_type	This field gives the relevant portion of the NetFlow process to which the options record refers. Currently defined values follow:
	0x0001 System
	0x0002 Interface
	0x0003 Line Card
	0x0004 NetFlow Cache
	0x0005 Template
	For instance, Random Sampled NetFlow can be implemented on a per-interface basis. So, if the options record were reporting on how sampling is configured, the scope for the report would be 0x0002 (interface).
scope_field_N_length	This field gives the length (in bytes) of the Scope field, as it would appear in an options record.
option_field_N_type	This numeric value represents the type of the field that appears in the options record. Possible values are detailed in template FlowSet format (shown earlier).
option_field_N_length	This number is the length (in bytes) of the field, as it would appear in an options record.
padding	Padding is inserted to align the end of the FlowSet on a 32-bit boundary.

NetFlow and IPFIX Comparison

In Chapter 1, you learned that IPFIX was derived from NetFlow v9. The IPFIX standard specifications (RFC 5101 and RFC 5102) were co-authored by Benoit Clais, who also co-authored the NetFlow Version 9 RFC (RFC 3954).

IPFIX introduces several extensions, the most popular of which is the *Information Element identifiers*. These identifiers are compatible with the *field types* used by NetFlow v9 that you learned about in the previous sections of this chapter.

There are several similar concepts between NetFlow v9 and IPFIX. The first identifier in NetFlow v9 is called *IN_BYTES* and in IPFIX is called *octetDeltaCount*.

As you learned earlier in this chapter, NetFlow v9 has 127 *field types*. IPFIX defines 238, many of which are the same that are defined in NetFlow v9. IPFIX allows a vendor ID to be specified, whereby the vendor can stick proprietary information into NetFlow.

The Cisco Flexible NetFlow IPFIX Export Format feature allows a NetFlow-enabled device to export packets using the IPFIX export protocol.

Note   This feature was introduced in Cisco IOS Software Version 15.2(4)M and Cisco IOS XE Release 3.7S. Cisco Flexible NetFlow is covered in Chapter 3, "Cisco Flexible NetFlow."

Summary

This chapter covered all the historical versions of NetFlow, but concentrated on providing in-depth technical information about NetFlow v9, its packet format, templates, and numerous fields. It also provided a high-level comparison with IPFIX.

Cisco Flexible NetFlow

This chapter covers the following topics:

- Introduction to Cisco's Flexible NetFlow

- Flexible NetFlow components and fields

- Flexible NetFlow configuration

Introduction to Cisco's Flexible NetFlow

Flexible NetFlow provides enhanced optimization of the network infrastructure, reduces costs, and improves capacity planning and security detection beyond other flow-based technologies available today. Flexible NetFlow supports IPv6 and Network-Based Application Recognition (NBAR) 2 for IPv6 starting in Cisco IOS Software Version 15.2(1)T. It also supports IPv6 transition techniques (IPv6 inside IPv4). Flexible NetFlow can detect the following tunneling technologies that give full IPv6 connectivity for IPv6-capable hosts that are on the IPv4 Internet but that have no direct native connection to an IPv6 network:

- Teredo

- Intra-Site Automatic Tunnel Addressing Protocol (ISATAP)

- 6to4

- 6rd

Note Flexible NetFlow classification inside Teredo, ISATAP, 6to4, and 6rd was introduced in Cisco IOS Software Version 15.2(2)T. Export over IPv6 was introduced in Cisco IOS Software Version 15.2(2)T, Cisco IOS XE 3.7.0S, and Cisco Nexus Software Version 4.2.1.

Simultaneous Application Tracking

Flexible NetFlow tracks different applications simultaneously. For instance, security monitoring, traffic analysis, and billing can be tracked separately, and the information customized per application.

Flexible NetFlow allows the network administrator or security professional to create multiple flow caches or information databases to track. Conventionally, NetFlow has a single cache, and all applications use the same cache information. Flexible NetFlow supports the collection of specific security information in one flow cache and traffic analysis in another. Subsequently, each NetFlow cache serves a different purpose. For instance, multicast and security information can be tracked separately and the results sent to two different collectors. Figure 3-1 shows the Flexible NetFlow model and how three different monitors are used. Monitor 1 exports Flexible NetFlow data to Exporter 1, Monitor 2 exports Flexible NetFlow data to Exporter 2, and Monitor 3 exports Flexible NetFlow data to Exporter 1 and Exporter 3.

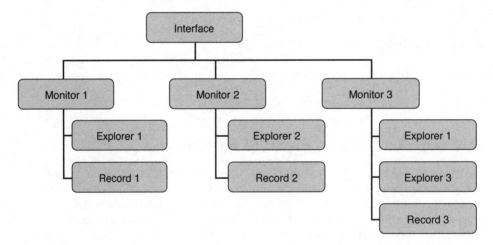

Figure 3-1   *The Flexible NetFlow Model*

The following are the Flexible NetFlow components:

- Records
- Flow monitors
- Flow exporters
- Flow samplers

In Flexible NetFlow, the administrator can specify what to track, resulting in fewer flows. This helps to scale in busy networks and use fewer resources that are already taxed by other features and services.

Flexible NetFlow Records

Records are a combination of key and non-key fields. In Flexible NetFlow, records are appointed to flow monitors to define the cache that is used for storing flow data. There are seven default attributes in the IP packet identity or "key fields" for a flow and for a device to determine whether the packet information is unique or similar to other packets sent over the network. Fields such as TCP flags, subnet masks, packets, and number of bytes are *non-key fields*. However, they are often collected and exported in NetFlow or in IPFIX.

Flexible NetFlow Key Fields

There are several Flexible NetFlow key fields in each packet that is forwarded within a NetFlow-enabled device. The device looks for a set of IP packet attributes for the flow and determines whether the packet information is unique or similar to other packets. In Flexible NetFlow, key fields are configurable, which enables the administrator to conduct a more granular traffic analysis.

Table 3-1 lists the key fields related to the actual flow, device interface, and Layer 2 services.

Table 3-1 *Flexible NetFlow Key Fields Related to Flow, Interface, and Layer 2*

	Flow	**Interface**	**Layer 2**
Fields	Sampler ID	Input	Source VLAN
	Direction	Output	Destination VLAN
	Class ID		Dot1q Priority
			Source MAC Address
			Destination MAC Address

Table 3-2 lists the IPv4- and IPv6-related key fields.

Table 3-2 *Flexible NetFlow IPv4 and IPv6 Key Fields*

	IPv4	**IPv6**
Fields	IP (Source or Destination)	IP (Source or Destination)
	Prefix (Source or Destination)	Prefix (Source or Destination)
	Mask (Source or Destination)	Mask (Source or Destination)
	Minimum-Mask (Source or Destination)	Minimum-Mask (Source or Destination)
	Protocol	Protocol
	Fragmentation Flags	Traffic Class

Table 3-2 *continued*

	IPv4	IPv6
Fields	Fragmentation Offset	Flow Label
	Identification	Option Header
	Header Length	Header Length
	Total Length	Payload Length
	Payload Size	Payload Size
	Packet Section (Header)	Packet Section (Header)
	Packet Section (Payload)	Packet Section (Payload)
	Time to Live (TTL)	DSCP
	Options bitmap	Extension Headers
	Version	Hop-Limit
	Precedence	Length
	DSCP	Next-Header
	TOS	Version

Table 3-3 lists the Layer 3 routing protocol-related key fields.

Table 3-3 *Flexible NetFlow Layer 3 Routing Protocol Key Fields*

	Routing
Fields	Source or Destination AS (autonomous system)
	Peer AS
	Traffic Index
	Forwarding Status
	Input VRF Name
	IGP Next Hop
	BGP Next Hop

Table 3-4 lists the transport related key fields.

Table 3-4 *Flexible NetFlow Transport Key Fields*

	Transport
Fields	Destination Port
	Source Port
	ICMP Code
	ICMP Type

Table 3-4   *continued*

	Transport
Fields	IGMP Type (IPv4 only)
	TCP ACK Number
	TCP Header Length
	TCP Sequence Number
	TCP Window-Size
	TCP Source Port
	TCP Destination Port
	TCP Urgent Pointer

Table 3-5 lists the Layer 3 routing protocol-related key fields.

Table 3-5   *Flexible NetFlow Layer 3 Routing Protocol Key Fields*

	Application
Fields	Application ID

Table 3-6 lists the multicast-related key fields.

Table 3-6   *Flexible NetFlow Multicast Key Fields*

	Multicast
Fields	Replication Factor (IPv4 only)
	RPF Check Drop (IPv4 only)
	Is-Multicast

Flexible NetFlow Non-Key Fields

There are several non-key Flexible NetFlow fields. Table 3-7 lists the non-key fields that are related to counters such as byte counts, number of packets, and more. Network administrators can use non-key fields for different purposes. For instance, the number of packets and amount of data (bytes) can be used for capacity planning and also to identify denial-of-service (DoS) attacks, in addition to other anomalies in the network. You will learn how these are used throughout the book and in Chapter 8, "Case Studies."

Table 3-7   *Flexible NetFlow Counters Non-Key Fields*

	Counters
Fields	Bytes
	Bytes Long
	Bytes Square Sum
	Bytes Square Sum Long
	Packets
	Packets Long
	Bytes Replicated
	Bytes Replicated Long
	Packets Replicated
	Packets Replicated Long

Table 3-8 lists the time stamp-related non-key fields.

Table 3-8   *Flexible NetFlow Multicast Non-Key Fields*

	Time Stamp
Fields	sysUpTime First Packet
	sysUpTime First Packet
	Absolute First Packet
	Absolute Last Packet

Table 3-9 lists the IPv4-only non-key fields.

Table 3-9   *Flexible NetFlow Multicast Non-Key Fields*

	IPv4 Only
Fields	Total Length Minimum
	Total Length Maximum
	TTL Minimum
	TTL Maximum

Table 3-10 lists the IPv4 and IPv6 non-key fields.

Table 3-10   *Flexible NetFlow Multicast Non-Key Fields*

	IPv4 and IPv6
Fields	Total Length Minimum
	Total Length Maximum

NetFlow Predefined Records

Flexible NetFlow includes several predefined records that can help an administrator or security professional start deploying NetFlow within their organization. Alternatively, they can create their own customized records for more granular analysis. As Cisco evolves Flexible NetFlow, many popular user-defined flow records could be made available as predefined records to make them easier to implement.

The predefined records guarantee backward compatibility with legacy NetFlow collectors. Predefined records have a unique blend of key and non-key fields that allows network administrators and security professionals to monitor different types of traffic in their environment without any customization.

Note   Flexible NetFlow predefined records that are based on the aggregation cache schemes in legacy NetFlow do not perform aggregation. Alternatively, the predefined records track each flow separately.

User-Defined Records

As the name indicates, Flexible NetFlow gives network administrators and security professionals the flexibility to create their own records (user-defined records) by specifying key and non-key fields to customize the data collection. The values in non-key fields are added to flows to provide additional information about the traffic in the flows. A change in the value of a non-key field does not create a new flow. In most cases, the values for non-key fields are taken from only the first packet in the flow. Flexible NetFlow enables you to capture counter values such as the number of bytes and packets in a flow as non-key fields.

Flexible NetFlow adds a new NetFlow v9 export format field type for the header and packet section types. A device configured for Flexible NetFlow communicates with the collector the configured section sizes in the corresponding NetFlow v9 export template fields.

Flow Monitors

In Flexible NetFlow, *flow monitors* are applied to the network device interfaces to perform network traffic monitoring. Flow data is collected from the network traffic and added to the flow monitor cache during the monitoring process based on the key and non-key fields in the flow record.

Flow Exporters

The entities that export the data in the flow monitor cache to a remote system are called *flow exporters*. Flow exporters are configured as separate entities. Flow exporters are assigned to flow monitors. An administrator can create several flow exporters and assign them to one or more flow monitors. A flow exporter includes the destination address of the reporting server, the type of transport (User Datagram Protocol [UDP] or Stream Control Transmission Protocol [SCTP]), and the export format corresponding of the NetFlow version or IPFIX.

Note You can configure up to eight flow exporters per flow monitor.

Flow Samplers

Flow samplers are created as separate components in a router's configuration. Flow samplers are used to reduce the load on the device that is running Flexible NetFlow by limiting the number of packets that are selected for analysis.

Flow sampling exchanges monitoring accuracy for router performance. When you apply a sampler to a flow monitor, the overhead load on the router of running the flow monitor is reduced because the number of packets that the flow monitor must analyze is reduced. The reduction in the number of packets that are analyzed by the flow monitor causes a corresponding reduction in the accuracy of the information stored in the flow monitor's cache.

Flexible NetFlow Configuration

The following sections provide step-by-step configuration guidance on how to enable and configure Flexible NetFlow in a Cisco IOS device. Figure 3-2 show the configuration steps in a sequential graphical representation.

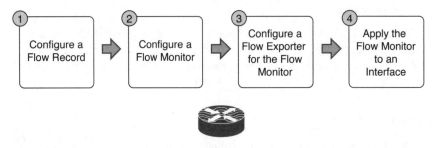

Figure 3-2 *Flexible NetFlow Configuration Steps*

The configuration steps, which are described in detailed in the corresponding sections, are as follows:

Step 1.   Configure a flow record.

Step 2.   Configure a flow monitor.

Step 3.   Configure a flow exporter for the flow monitor.

Step 4.   Apply the flow monitor to an interface.

The topology shown in Figure 3-3 is used in the following examples.

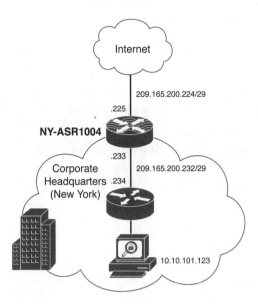

Figure 3-3 *Flexible NetFlow Configuration Example Topology*

A Cisco ASR 1004 at the New York headquarters is configured for Flexible NetFlow. The outside network is 209.165.200.224/29, and the inside network is 209.165.200.232/29.

Configure a Flow Record

The following are the steps required to configure a customized flow record.

Note There are hundreds of possible ways to configure customized flow records. The following steps can be followed to create one of the possible variations. You can create a customized flow record depending on your organization's requirements.

Step 1. Log in to your router and enter into enable mode with the **enable** command:

```
NY-ASR1004>enable
```

Step 2. Enter into configuration mode with the **configure terminal** command:

```
NY-ASR1004#configure terminal
Enter configuration commands, one per line.  End with CNTL/Z.
```

Step 3. Create a flow record with the **flow record** command. In this example, the record name is NY-ASR-FLOW-RECORD-1. After entering the **flow record**

command, the router enters flow record configuration mode. You can also use the **flow record** command to edit an existing flow record:

```
NY-ASR1004(config)# flow record NY-ASR-FLOW-RECORD-1
```

Step 4.   (Optional) Enter a description for the new flow record:

```
NY-ASR1004(config-flow-record)# description FLOW RECORD 1 for basic
  traffic analysis
```

Step 5.   Configure a key field for the flow record using the **match** command. In this example, the IPv4 destination address is configured as a key field for the record:

```
NY-ASR1004(config-flow-record)# match ipv4 destination address
```

The output of the **match ?** command shows all the primary options for the key field categories that you learned earlier in this chapter.

```
NY-ASR1004(config-flow-record)# match ?
  application  Application fields
  flow         Flow identifying fields
  interface    Interface fields
  ipv4         IPv4 fields
  ipv6         IPv6 fields
  routing      Routing attributes
  transport    Transport layer fields
```

Step 6.   Configure a non-key field with the **collect** command. In this example, the input interface is configured as a non-key field for the record:

```
NY-ASR1004(config-flow-record)#collect interface input
```

The output of the **collect ?** command shows all the options for the non-key field categories that you learned earlier in this chapter:

```
NY-ASR1004(config-flow-record)# collect ?
  application  Application fields
  counter      Counter fields
  flow         Flow identifying fields
  interface    Interface fields
  ipv4         IPv4 fields
  ipv6         IPv6 fields
  routing      Routing attributes
  timestamp    Timestamp fields
  transport    Transport layer fields
```

Step 7.   Exit configuration mode with the **end** command and return to privileged EXEC mode:

```
NY-ASR1004(config-flow-record)# end
```

Note   You can configure Flexible NetFlow to support NBAR with the **match application name** command under Flexible NetFlow flow record configuration mode.

You can use the **show flow record** to show the status and fields for the flow record. If multiple flow records are configured in the router, you can use the **show flow record** *name* command to show the output of a specific flow record, as shown in Example 3-1.

Example 3-1 *Output of the show flow record Command*

```
NY-ASR1004# show flow record NY-ASR-FLOW-RECORD-1
flow record NY-ASR-FLOW-RECORD-1:
 Description:        Used for basic traffic analysis
 No. of users:      0
 Total field space: 8 bytes
 Fields:
   match ipv4 destination address
   collect interface input
```

Use the **show running-config flow record** command to show the flow record configuration in the running configuration, as shown in Example 3-2.

Example 3-2 *Output of the show Running-config flow record Command*

```
NY-ASR1004# show running-config flow record
Current configuration:
!
flow record NY-ASR-FLOW-RECORD-1
 description Used for basic traffic analysis
 match ipv4 destination address
 collect interface input
!
```

Configuring a Flow Monitor for IPv4 or IPv6

The following are the steps required to configure a flow monitor for IPv4 or IPv6 implementations. In the following examples, a flow monitor is configured for the previously configured flow record.

Step 1. Log in to your router and enter into enable mode with the **enable** command:

```
NY-ASR1004>enable
```

Step 2. Enter into configuration mode with the **configure terminal** command:

```
NY-ASR1004# configure terminal
Enter configuration commands, one per line.  End with CNTL/Z.
```

Step 3. Create a flow monitor with the **flow monitor** command. In this example, the flow monitor is called **NY-ASR-FLOW-MON-1**:

```
NY-ASR1004(config)# flow monitor NY-ASR-FLOW-MON-1
```

Step 4.   (Optional) Enter a description for the new flow monitor:

```
NY-ASR1004(config-flow-monitor)# description monitor for IPv4 traffic
   in NY
```

Step 5.   Identify the record for the flow monitor:

```
NY-ASR1004(config-flow-monitor)# record netflow NY-ASR-FLOW-RECORD-1
```

In the following example, the **record ?** command is used to see all the flow monitor record options:

```
NY-ASR1004(config-flow-monitor)# record ?
  NY-ASR-FLOW-RECORD-1  Used for basic traffic analysis
  netflow               Traditional NetFlow collection schemes
  netflow-original      Traditional IPv4 input NetFlow with origin ASs
```

Step 6.   Exit configuration mode with the **end** command and return to privileged EXEC mode:

```
NY-ASR1004(config-flow-record)# end
```

You can use the **show flow monitor** to show the status and configured parameters for the flow monitor, as shown in Example 3-3.

Example 3-3   *Output of the show flow monitor Command*

```
NY-ASR1004# show flow monitor
Flow Monitor NY-ASR-FLOW-MON-1:
  Description:        monitor for IPv4 traffic in NY
  Flow Record:        NY-ASR-FLOW-RECORD-1
  Cache:
    Type:             normal (Platform cache)
    Status:           not allocated
    Size:             200000 entries
    Inactive Timeout: 15 secs
    Active Timeout:   1800 secs
    Update Timeout:   1800 secs
```

Use the **show running-config flow monitor** command to display the flow monitor configuration in the running configuration, as shown in Example 3-4.

Example 3-4   *Output of the show Running-config flow monitor Command*

```
NY-ASR1004# show running-config flow monitor
Current configuration:
!
flow monitor NY-ASR-FLOW-MON-1
 description monitor for IPv4 traffic in NY
 record NY-ASR-FLOW-RECORD-1
 cache entries 200000
```

Configuring a Flow Exporter for the Flow Monitor

Complete the following steps to configure a flow exporter for the flow monitor to export the data that is collected by NetFlow to a remote system for further analysis and storage. This is an optional step. IPv4 and IPv6 are supported for flow exporters.

> **Note** Flow exporters use UDP as the transport protocol and use the NetFlow v9 export format. Each flow exporter supports only one destination. If you want to export the data to multiple destinations, you must configure multiple flow exporters and assign them to the flow monitor.

Step 1. Log in to the router and enter into enable and configuration mode, as you learned in previous steps.

Step 2. Create a flow exporter with the **flow exporter** command. In this example, the exporter name is NY-EXPORTER-1:

```
NY-ASR1004(config)# flow exporter NY-EXPORTER-1
```

Step 3. (Optional) Enter a description for the exporter:

```
NY-ASR1004(config-flow-exporter)# description exports to New York
    Collector
```

Step 4. Configure the export protocol using the **export-protocol** command. In this example, NetFlow v9 is used. You can also configure legacy NetFlow v5 with the **netflow-v5** keyword or IPFIX with the **ipfix** keyword. IPFIX support was added in Cisco IOS Software Release 15.2(4)M and Cisco IOS XE Release 3.7S:

```
NY-ASR1004(config-flow-exporter)# export-protocol netflow-v9
```

Step 5. Enter the IP address of the destination host with the **destination** command. In this example, the destination host is 10.10.10.123:

```
NY-ASR1004(config-flow-exporter)# destination 10.10.10.123
```

Step 6. You can configure the UDP port used by the flow exporter with the **transport udp** command. The default is UDP port 9995.

Step 7. Exit the Flexible NetFlow flow monitor configuration mode with the **exit** command and specify the name of the exporter in the flow monitor:

```
NY-ASR1004(config)# flow monitor NY-ASR-FLOW-MON-1
NY-ASR1004(config-flow-monitor)# exporter NY-EXPORTER-1
```

You can use the **show flow exporter** command to view the configured options for the Flexible NetFlow exporter, as demonstrated in Example 3-5.

Example 3-5   *Output of the show flow exporter Command*

```
NY-ASR1004# show flow exporter
Flow Exporter NY-EXPORTER-1:
  Description:              exports to New York Collector
  Export protocol:         NetFlow Version 9
  Transport Configuration:
    Destination IP address: 10.10.10.123
    Source IP address:     209.165.200.225
    Transport Protocol:    UDP
    Destination Port:      9995
    Source Port:           55939
    DSCP:                  0x0
    TTL:                   255
    Output Features:       Used
```

You can use the **show running-config flow exporter** command to view the flow exporter configuration in the command-line interface (CLI), as demonstrated in Example 3-6.

Example 3-6   *Output of the show Running-config flow exporter Command*

```
NY-ASR1004# show running-config flow exporter
Current configuration:
!
flow exporter NY-EXPORTER-1
 description exports to New York Collector
 destination 10.10.10.123
```

You can use the **show flow monitor name NY-ASR-FLOW-MON-1 cache format
record** command to display the status and flow data in the NetFlow cache for the flow
monitor, as demonstrated in Example 3-7.

Example 3-7   *Output of the show flow monitor Name NY-ASR-FLOW-MON-1 Cache
Format Record Command*

```
NY-ASR1004# show flow monitor name NY-ASR-FLOW-MON-1 cache format record
  Cache type:                   Normal (Platform cache)
  Cache size:                   200000
  Current entries:                   4
  High Watermark:                    4
  Flows added:                     132
  Flows aged:                       42
    - Active timeout   ( 3600 secs)    3
    - Inactive timeout (   15 secs)   94
    - Event aged                       0
    - Watermark aged                   0
    - Emergency aged                   0
```

```
IPV4 DESTINATION ADDRESS:   10.10.20.5
ipv4 source address:        10.10.10.42
trns source port:           25
trns destination port:      25
counter bytes:              34320
counter packets:            1112
IPV4 DESTINATION ADDRESS:   10.10.1.2
ipv4 source address:        10.10.10.2
trns source port:           20
trns destination port:      20
counter bytes:              3914221
counter packets:            5124
IPV4 DESTINATION ADDRESS:   10.10.10.200
ipv4 source address:        10.20.10.6
trns source port:           32
trns destination port:      3073
counter bytes:              82723
counter packets:            8232
```

Applying a Flow Monitor to an Interface

A flow monitor must be applied to at least one interface. To apply the flow monitor to an interface, use the **ip flow monitor** *name* **input** command in interface configuration mode, as demonstrated in Example 3-8.

Example 3-8   *Applying the flow monitor to an Interface*

```
NY-ASR1004(config)# interface FastEthernet0/1/1
NY-ASR1004(config-if)# ip flow monitor NY-ASR-FLOW-MON-1 input
```

In Example 3-8, the flow monitor NY-ASR-FLOW-MON-1 is applied to interface FastEthernet0/1/1.

Example 3-9 shows the complete configuration.

Example 3-9   *Flexible NetFlow Configuration*

```
flow record NY-ASR-FLOW-RECORD-1
 description Used for basic traffic analysis
 match ipv4 destination address
 collect interface input
!
!
flow exporter NY-EXPORTER-1
```

```
 description exports to New York Collector
 destination 10.10.10.123
!
!
flow monitor NY-ASR-FLOW-MON-1
 description monitor for IPv4 traffic in NY
 record NY-ASR-FLOW-RECORD-1
 exporter NY-EXPORTER-1
 cache entries 200000
!
interface FastEthernet0/1/1
 ip address 209.165.200.233 255.255.255.248
 ip flow monitor NY-ASR-FLOW-MON-1 input
```

Flexible NetFlow IPFIX Export Format

Starting with Cisco IOS Software Version 15.2(4)M and Cisco IOS XE Software Version 3.7S, a feature was added to enable you to send export Flexible NetFlow packets using the IPFIX export protocol. This feature is enabled with the **export-protocol ipfix** sub-command under the flow exporter. Example 3-10 shows how the Flexible NetFlow IPFIX Export Format feature is enabled in the flow exporter configured in the previous example (Example 3-9).

Example 3-10 *Flexible NetFlow Configuration*

```
flow exporter NY-EXPORTER-1
 description exports to New York Collector
 destination 10.10.10.123
  export-protocol ipfix
```

Summary

Flexible NetFlow is the Cisco next generation of NetFlow. It allows network administrators and security professionals to create their own customized records for more granular network analysis. This chapter provided an in-depth description Cisco's Flexible NetFlow, its components, and fields. It then showed you how to create Flexible NetFlow flow records, configure a flow monitor, configure a flow exporter for the flow monitor, and apply the flow monitor to an interface.

## Chapter 4

NetFlow Commercial and Open Source Monitoring and Analysis Software Packages

This chapter covers the following topics:

- Commercial NetFlow monitoring and analysis software packages

- Open source NetFlow monitoring and analysis software packages

Commercial NetFlow Monitoring and Analysis Software Packages

There are several commercial NetFlow monitoring and analysis software packages in the industry. Table 4-1 lists the most popular.

Table 4-1 *Examples of Commercial NetFlow Monitoring and Analysis Software*

Commercial Software	Description	Website
ManageEngine NetFlow Analyzer	A web-based bandwidth monitoring tool.	http://manageengine.adventnet.com/products/netflow
NetUsage	Tool for network traffic monitoring, capacity planning, business justification, and cost control.	http://www.netusage.net
Caligare	Traffic monitoring and network anomalies detection.	http://www.caligare.com/
Evident Software Evident Analyze	Tool for billing and traffic analysis.	http://www.evidentsoftware.com/products/anlz_functions.aspx
Fluke Networks	Traffic analysis, NetFlow collection, and low-cost Windows-based NetFlow product.	http://www.flukenetworks.com/

Table 4-1 *continued*

Commercial Software	Description	Website
NetFlow Insight	Traffic analysis, NetFlow collection using HP Insight Network Performance Monitoring.	http://www.openview.hp.com/products/ovpi_net/
IBM NetFlow Aurora	NetFlow traffic profiling tool commercially available as Tivoli Netcool Performance Flow Analyzer (TNPFA).	http://www.zurich.ibm.com/aurora
IdeaData NetFlow Auditor	Tool used for network troubleshooting, security monitoring, and baseline trending.	http://www.netflowauditor.com
InfoVista 5View NetFlow	NetFlow monitoring tool.	http://www.infovista.com/products/NetFlow-Monitoring-Network-Traffic-Analysis
Lancope StealthWatch	Traffic analysis, NetFlow collection, and security monitoring tool suite part of Cisco's Cyber Threat Defense Solution.	http://lancope.com
Paessler PRTG	Network monitoring tool suite.	http://www.paessler.com
Plixer International Scrutinizer	Plixer offers free and commercial NetFlow reporting software. Scrutinizer is an incident response and network monitoring suite of tools.	http://www.plixer.com
SolarWinds NetFlow Traffic Analyzer	NetFlow traffic analyzer and performance management tool.	http://www.solarwinds.com/netflow-traffic-analyzer.aspx

Two of the most popular commercial products are Lancope's StealthWatch solution and Plixer Scrutinizer, as described in greater detail in the sections that follow.

Lancope's StealthWatch Solution

Lancope's StealthWatch solution is a key component of the Cisco Cyber Threat Defense (CTD) Solution. One of the key benefits of Lancope's StealthWatch is its capability to scale in large enterprises. It also provides integration with the Cisco Identity Services Engine (ISE) for user identity information. Cisco ISE is a security policy management and control system that you can use for access control and security compliance for wired, wireless, and virtual private network (VPN) connections.

Note   The Cisco CTD Solution is covered in detail in Chapter 6, "Cisco Cyber Threat Defense and NetFlow."

One other major benefit of Lancope's StealthWatch is its graphical interface, which includes great visualizations of network traffic, customized summary reports, and integrated security and network intelligence for drill-down analysis.

Figure 4-1 shows a screenshot of Lancope's StealthWatch Management Console (SMC).

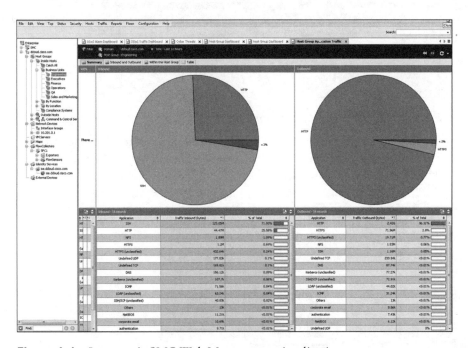

Figure 4-1   *Lanscope's SMC Web Management Application*

In Figure 4-1, a summary report of inbound and outbound traffic for a predefined host group in the inside network (Engineering) is displayed.

Figure 4-2 shows a report of the top applications observed in the network for the client and server host group called Inside Hosts. In this report, you can see that the top application observed was Skype. You can drill down each application and host to get more detailed information about what is happening in the network.

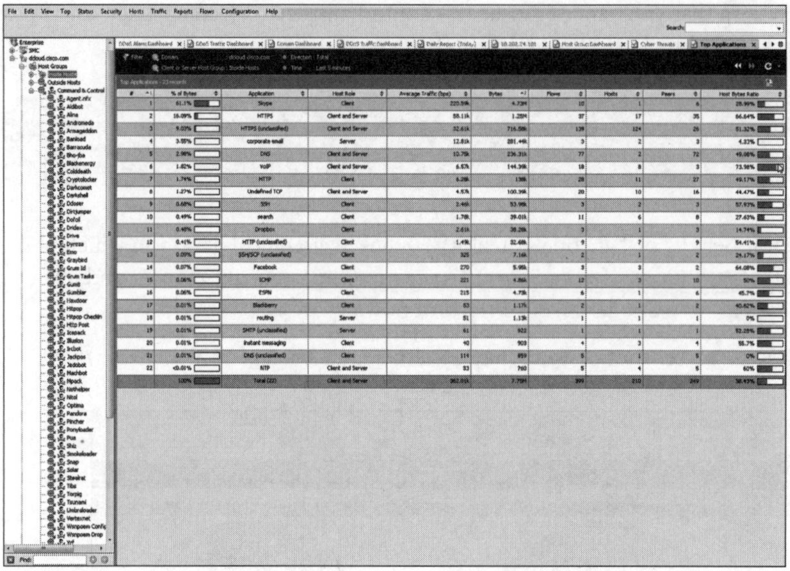

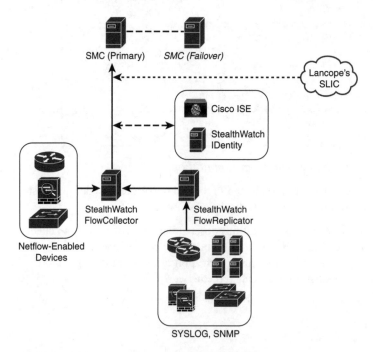

Figure 4-2   *Lancope's SMC Top Applications Report*

Lancope has a security research initiative that tracks emerging threat information from around the world called the StealthWatch Labs Intelligence Center (SLIC). Figure 4-3 illustrates the major components of Lancope's StealthWatch solution.

Figure 4-3   *The Lancope's StealthWatch Solution*

The following are the primary components of the Lancope StealthWatch solution shown in Figure 4-1:

- **StealthWatch Management Console:** Provides centralized management, configuration, and reporting of the other StealthWatch components. It can be deployed in a physical server or a virtual machine (VM). The StealthWatch Management Console provides high-availability features (failover), as shown in Figure 4-1.

- **FlowCollector:** A physical or virtual appliance that collects NetFlow data from infrastructure devices.

- **FlowSensor:** A physical or virtual appliance that can generate NetFlow data when legacy Cisco network infrastructure components are not capable of producing line-rate, unsampled NetFlow data. Alternatively, the Cisco NetFlow Generator Appliance (NGA) can be used.

- **FlowReplicator:** A physical appliance used to forward NetFlow data as a single data stream to other devices.

- **StealthWatch IDentity:** Provides user identity monitoring capabilities. Administrators can search on user names to obtain a specific user network activity. Identity data can be obtained from the StealthWatch IDentity appliance or through integration with the Cisco ISE.

Note Lancope StealthWatch also support usernames within NetFlow records from Cisco ASA appliances.

Lancope's StealthWatch solution supports a feature called *Network Address Translation (NAT) stitching*. NAT stitching uses data from network devices to combine NAT information from inside a firewall (or a NAT device) with information from outside the firewall (or a NAT device) to identify which IP addresses and users are part of a specific flow.

Note More information about Lancope's StealthWatch solution is covered in Chapter 6, "Cisco Cyber Threat Defense and NetFlow," and Chapter 8, "Case Studies."

Plixer's Scrutinizer

Plixer's Scrutinizer is another commercial NetFlow monitoring and analysis software package that has gone through interoperability tests by Cisco. Scrutinizer is used for incident response and network monitoring. Just like several components of Lancope's StealthWatch solution, Scrutinizer is available as a physical or virtual appliance.

Plixer also sells two other products that provide additional network visibility: FlowPro and Flow Replicator.

FlowPro is an appliance that can be deployed in a specific area of the corporate network to perform deep packet inspection (DPI) combining NetFlow/IPFIX data. Plixer's Flow Replicator allows several sources of network device and server log data to be replicated to different destinations. Flow Replicator can also be configured as a syslog to IPFIX gateway. It converts syslog messages and forwards them on inside IPFIX datagrams.

Open Source NetFlow Monitoring and Analysis Software Packages

The number of open source NetFlow monitoring and analysis software packages is on the rise. You can use these open source tools to successfully identify security threats within your network.

Table 4-2 lists the most popular open source NetFlow monitoring and analysis software packages.

Table 4-2   *Examples of Open Source NetFlow Monitoring and Analysis Software*

Open Source Software	Description	Website
cflowd	Traffic flow analysis tool provided by the Center for Applied Internet Data Analysis.	http://www.caida.org/tools/measurement/cflowd
flowtools	Tool set for collecting and working with NetFlow data created by Mark Fullmer.	http://www.splintered.net/sw/flow-tools
flowviewer	FlowViewer is a web-based interface to flow tools and SiLK.	http://sourceforge.net/projects/flowviewer
flowd	Small-packaged NetFlow collector.	http://www.mindrot.org/projects/flowd
IPFlow	NetFlow collector developed by Christophe Fillot of the University of Technology of Compiegne, France.	http://www.ipflow.utc.fr
NFdump	NetFlow analysis toolkit under the BSD license.	http://nfdump.sourceforge.net
NfSen	Web interface for NFdump.	http://sourceforge.net/projects/nfsen
Stager	Provides visualizations for NFdump.	https://trac.uninett.no/stager

Table 4-2 *Continued*

Open Source Software	Description	Website
Panoptis	NetFlow tool for detecting denial-of-service attacks. Development is fairly limited.	http://panoptis.sourceforge.net
Plixer's Scrutinizer NetFlow Analyzer	Scrutinizer NetFlow Analyzer a free version of Plixer's Scrutinizer.	http://www.plixer.com/Support/free-tools.html
SiLK	System for Internet-Level Knowledge (SiLK) is a NetFlow collector and analysis tool developed by the Carnegie Mellon University's CERT Network Situational Awareness Team (CERT NetSA).	https://tools.netsa.cert.org/silk
iSiLK	iSiLK is a graphical front end for the SiLK toolkit.	http://tools.netsa.cert.org/isilk
Elasticsearch, Logstash, and Kibana (ELK)	A distributed, scalable, open source big data analytics platform.	https://www.elastic.co/

Two of the most popular open source NetFlow collection and analysis toolkits are NFdump (sometimes used with NfSen or Stager) and SiLK, as described in greater detail in the sections that follow.

NFdump

NFdump is a set of Linux-based tools that support NetFlow Versions 5, 7, and 9. You can download NFdump from http://nfdump.sourceforge.net and install it from source. Alternatively, you can easily install NFdump in multiple Linux distributions such as Ubuntu using **sudo apt-get install nfdump**, as shown in Example 4-1.

Example 4-1 *Installing NFdump in Ubuntu*

```
omar@server1:~$ sudo apt-get install nfdump
[sudo] password for omar:
Reading package lists... Done
Building dependency tree
Reading state information... Done
The following packages were automatically installed and are no longer required:
  linux-headers-3.13.0-53 linux-headers-3.13.0-53-generic
  linux-headers-3.13.0-54 linux-headers-3.13.0-54-generic
  linux-image-3.13.0-53-generic linux-image-3.13.0-54-generic
  linux-image-extra-3.13.0-53-generic linux-image-extra-3.13.0-54-generic
Use 'apt-get autoremove' to remove them.
```

```
The following extra packages will be installed:
  fontconfig fonts-dejavu fonts-dejavu-core fonts-dejavu-extra libcairo2
  libdatrie1 libdbi1 libgraphite2-3 libharfbuzz0b libpango-1.0-0
  libpangocairo-1.0-0 libpangoft2-1.0-0 libpixman-1-0 librrd4 libthai-data
  libthai0 libxcb-render0 libxcb-shm0 libxrender1 ttf-dejavu ttf-dejavu-core
  ttf-dejavu-extra
Suggested packages:
  ttf-baekmuk ttf-arphic-gbsn00lp ttf-arphic-bsmi00lp ttf-arphic-gkai00mp
  ttf-arphic-bkai00mp
The following NEW packages will be installed:
  fontconfig fonts-dejavu fonts-dejavu-core fonts-dejavu-extra libcairo2
  libdatrie1 libdbi1 libgraphite2-3 libharfbuzz0b libpango-1.0-0
  libpangocairo-1.0-0 libpangoft2-1.0-0 libpixman-1-0 librrd4 libthai-data
  libthai0 libxcb-render0 libxcb-shm0 libxrender1 nfdump ttf-dejavu
  ttf-dejavu-core ttf-dejavu-extra
0 upgraded, 23 newly installed, 0 to remove and 9 not upgraded.
Need to get 4,903 kB of archives.
After this operation, 17.1 MB of additional disk space will be used.
Do you want to continue? [Y/n] Y
...<output omitted>
```

Table 4-3 lists all the components of the NFdump toolkit.

Table 4-3 *NFdump Components*

Component	Description
nfcapd	The NetFlow capture daemon. A separate nfcapd process needs to be launched for each NetFlow stream.
nfdump	Reads the NetFlow data from the files stored by nfcapd. The output and syntax is very similar to the Linux-based packet-capture tool tcpdump.
nfprofile	Filters the NetFlow data recorded by nfcapd and stores the filtered data into files for later use. The filters are referred to as *profiles*.
nfreplay	Replays NetFlow data.
nfclean.pl	Pearl sample script to cleanup historical NetFlow data.
ft2nfdump	Converts flow tools data from files or from standard input into nfdump format.

Figure 4-4 illustrates the NFdump architecture and main components.

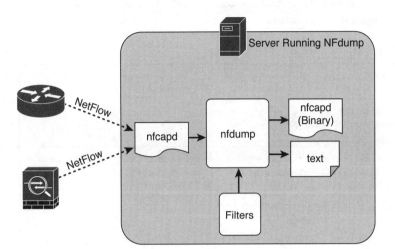

Figure 4-4 *NFdump Architecture*

Routers, firewalls, and any other NetFlow-enabled infrastructure devices can send NetFlow records to NFdump, as shown in Figure 4-4. The command to capture the NetFlow data is **nfcapd**. All processed NetFlow records are stored in one or more binary files. These binary files are read by **nfdump** and can be displayed in plain text to standard output (stdout) or written to another file. Example 4-2 demonstrates how the **nfcapd** command is used to capture and store NetFlow data in a directory called net-flow. The server is configured to listen to port 9996 for NetFlow communication.

Example 4-2 *Using the nfcapd Command*

```
omar@server1:~$ nfcapd -w -D -l netflow -p 9996
omar@server1:~$ cd netflow
omar@server1:~/netflow$ ls -l
total 544
-rw-r--r-- 1 omar omar  20772 Jun 18 00:45 nfcapd.201506180040
-rw-r--r-- 1 omar omar  94916 Jun 18 00:50 nfcapd.201506180045
-rw-r--r-- 1 omar omar  84108 Jun 18 00:55 nfcapd.201506180050
-rw-r--r-- 1 omar omar  78564 Jun 18 01:00 nfcapd.201506180055
-rw-r--r-- 1 omar omar 106732 Jun 18 01:05 nfcapd.201506180100
-rw-r--r-- 1 omar omar  73692 Jun 18 01:10 nfcapd.201506180105
-rw-r--r-- 1 omar omar  76996 Jun 18 01:15 nfcapd.201506180110
-rw-r--r-- 1 omar omar    276 Jun 18 01:15 nfcapd.current
```

Flows are read either from a single file or from a sequence of files. In Example 4-2, a series of files were created by the **nfcapd** daemon. Example 4-3 shows the command options of the **nfcapd** daemon command.

Example 4-3   *nfcapd Daemon Command Options*

```
omar@ server1:~$ nfcapd  -h
usage nfcapd [options]
-h              this text you see right here
-u userid       Change user to username
-g groupid      Change group to groupname
-w              Sync file rotation with next 5min (default) interval
-t interval     set the interval to rotate nfcapd files
-b host         bind socket to host/IP addr
-j mcastgroup   Join multicast group <mcastgroup>
-p portnum      listen on port portnum
-l basdir       set the output directory. (no default)
-S subdir       Sub directory format. see nfcapd(1) for format
-I Ident        set the ident string for stat file. (default 'none')
-H              Add port histogram data to flow file.(default 'no')
-n Ident,IP,logdir  Add this flow source - multiple streams
-P pidfile      set the PID file
-R IP[/port]    Repeat incoming packets to IP address/port
-s rate         set default sampling rate (default 1)
-x process      launch process after a new file becomes available
-z              Compress flows in output file.
-B bufflen      Set socket buffer to bufflen bytes
-e              Expire data at each cycle.
-D              Fork to background
-E              Print extended format of netflow data. for debugging purpose only.
-T              Include extension tags in records.
-4              Listen on IPv4 (default).
-6              Listen on IPv6.
-V              Print version and exit.
```

Example 4-4 demonstrates how to use the **nfdump** command to process and analyze all files that were created by **nfcapd** in the netflow directory.

Example 4-4   *Processing and Displaying the nfcapd Files with nfdump*

```
omar@server1::~$ nfdump -R netflow -o extended -s srcip -s ip/flows
Top 10 Src IP Addr ordered by flows:
Date first seen        Duration Proto    Src IP Addr    Flows(%)
  Packets(%)      Bytes(%)      pps     bps   bpp
2015-06-13 22:35:10.805    2.353 any      192.168.1.140  1582(19.5)
  0(-nan)       0(-nan)       0        0     0
```

```
2015-06-13 22:35:10.829      2.380 any       192.168.1.130    875(10.8)
   0(-nan)          0(-nan)        0         0       0
2015-06-13 22:35:10.805      2.404 any       192.168.1.168    807( 9.9)
   0(-nan)          0(-nan)        0         0       0
2015-06-13 22:35:11.219      1.839 any       192.168.1.142    679( 8.4)
   0(-nan)          0(-nan)        0         0       0
2015-06-13 22:35:10.805      2.258 any       192.168.1.156    665( 8.2)
   0(-nan)          0(-nan)        0         0       0
2015-06-13 22:35:10.805      2.297 any       192.168.1.205    562( 6.9)
   0(-nan)          0(-nan)        0         0       0
2015-06-13 22:35:10.805      2.404 any       192.168.1.89     450( 5.5)
   0(-nan)          0(-nan)        0         0       0
2015-06-13 22:35:11.050      1.989 any       10.248.91.231    248( 3.1)
   0(-nan)          0(-nan)        0         0       0
2015-06-13 22:35:11.633      1.342 any       192.168.1.149    234( 2.9)
   0(-nan)          0(-nan)        0         0       0
2015-06-13 22:35:11.040      2.118 any       192.168.1.157    213( 2.6)
   0(-nan)          0(-nan)        0         0       0


Top 10 IP Addr ordered by flows:
Date first seen          Duration Proto     IP Addr        Flows(%)
   Packets(%)       Bytes(%)       pps      bps   bpp
2015-06-13 22:35:10.805      2.353 any       192.168.1.140   1582(19.5)
   0(-nan)          0(-nan)        0         0       0
2015-06-13 22:35:10.805      2.353 any       10.8.8.8        1188(14.6)
   0(-nan)          0(-nan)        0         0       0
2015-06-13 22:35:10.805      2.297 any       192.168.1.1     1041(12.8)
   0(-nan)          0(-nan)        0         0       0
2015-06-13 22:35:10.829      2.380 any       192.168.1.130    875(10.8)
   0(-nan)          0(-nan)        0         0       0
2015-06-13 22:35:10.805      2.404 any       192.168.1.168    807( 9.9)
   0(-nan)          0(-nan)        0         0       0
2015-06-13 22:35:11.219      1.839 any       192.168.1.142    679( 8.4)
   0(-nan)          0(-nan)        0         0       0
2015-06-13 22:35:10.805      2.258 any       192.168.1.156    665( 8.2)
   0(-nan)          0(-nan)        0         0       0
2015-06-13 22:35:10.805      2.297 any       192.168.1.205    562( 6.9)
   0(-nan)          0(-nan)        0         0       0
2015-06-13 22:35:10.825      2.277 any       10.190.38.99     467( 5.8)
   0(-nan)          0(-nan)        0         0       0
2015-06-13 22:35:10.805      2.404 any       192.168.1.89     450( 5.5)
   0(-nan)          0(-nan)        0         0       0


Summary: total flows: 8115, total bytes: 0, total packets: 0, avg bps: 0, avg
   pps: 0, avg bpp: 0
Time window: 2015-06-13 22:35:10 - 2015-06-13 22:35:13
Total flows processed: 8115, Blocks skipped: 0, Bytes read: 457128
Sys: 0.009s flows/second: 829924.3   Wall: 0.008s flows/second: 967222.9
```

In Example 4-4, you can see the top talkers (top hosts that are sending the most traffic in the network). You can refer to the **nfdump** man pages for details about usage of the **nfdump** command (using the **man nfdump** command). Example 4-5 shows an excerpt of the output of the **nfdump** man pages showing several examples of the **nfdump** command usage.

Example 4-5   *nfdump Man Pages Excerpt*

```
EXAMPLES

       nfdump -r /and/dir/nfcapd.201107110845 -c 100 'proto tcp and ( src ip
172.16.17.18 or dst ip 172.16.17.19 )' Dumps the first 100 netflow records which
match the given filter:


       nfdump -r /and/dir/nfcapd.201107110845 -B Map matching flows as bin-
directional single flow.


       nfdump -R /and/dir/nfcapd.201107110845:nfcapd.200407110945 'host 192.168.1.2'
Dumps all netflow records of host 192.168.1.2 from July 11 08:45 - 09:45


       nfdump -M /to/and/dir1:dir2 -R nfcapd.200407110845:nfcapd.200407110945 -s
record -n 20 Generates the Top 20 statistics from 08:45 to 09:45 from 3 sources


       nfdump -r /and/dir/nfcapd.201107110845 -s record -n 20 -o extended Generates
the Top 20 statistics, extended output format


       nfdump -r /and/dir/nfcapd.201107110845 -s record -n 20 'in if 5 and bps >
10k' Generates the Top 20 statistics from flows comming from interface 5


       nfdump -r /and/dir/nfcapd.201107110845 'inet6 and proto tcp and ( src port >
1024 and dst port 80 ) Dumps all port 80 IPv6 connections to any web server.

NOTES
       Generating the statistics for data files of a few hundred MB is no problem.
However be careful if you want to create statistics of several GB of data. This
may consume a lot of memory and can take a while. Flow anonymization has moved
into nfanon.

SEE ALSO
       nfcapd(1), nfanon(1), nfprofile(1), nfreplay(1)
```

NfSen

NfSen is the graphical web-based front end for NFdump. You can download and obtain more information about NFSen at http://nfsen.sourceforge.net.

SiLK

The SiLK analysis suite is a very popular open source command-line Swiss army knife developed by CERT. Administrators and security professionals combine these tools in various ways to perform detailed NetFlow analysis. SiLK includes numerous tools and plug-ins.

The SiLK Packing System includes several applications (daemons) that collect NetFlow data and translate them into a more space efficient format. SiLK stores these records into service-specific binary flat files for use by the analysis suite. Files are organized in a time-based directory hierarchy. The following are the SiLK daemons:

- **flowcap:** Listens to flow generators and stores the data in temporary files.

- **rwflowpack:** Processes flow data either directly from a flow generator or from files generated by flowcap. Then it converts the data to the SiLK flow record format.

- **rwflowappend:** Appends flow records to hourly files organized in a time-based directory tree.

- **rwsender:** Watches an incoming directory for files, moves the files into a processing directory, and transfers the files to one or more rwreceiver processes.

- **rwreceiver:** Receives and processes files transferred from one or more rwsender processes and stores them in a destination directory.

- **rwpollexec:** Monitors a directory for incoming files and runs a user-specified command on each file.

- **rwpackchecker:** Reads SiLK flow records and checks for unusual patterns that may indicate data file corruption.

- **packlogic-twoway and packlogic-generic:** Plug-ins that rwflowpack may use when categorizing flow records.

SiLK Configuration Files

The following are the SiLK configuration files:

- **silk.conf:** Defines the classes, types, and sensors

- **sensor.conf:** Defines sensors and probes used by rwflowpack and flowcap

Filtering, Displaying, and Sorting NetFlow Records with SiLK

The following are the tools included in SiLK used for filtering, displaying, and sorting NetFlow records:

- **rwfilter:** The most important analysis tool in SiLK. It is an application for querying NetFlow records stored in SiLK's database.

- **rwcut:** Prints the attributes of NetFlow records in a delimited/columnar format. It can be integrated with plug-ins written in C or PySiLK.

- **rwsort:** Sorting utility for SiLK's NetFlow records.

SiLK's Python Extension

SiLK's Python Extension (PySiLK) can be used to read, manipulate, and write SiLK NetFlow records in Python. PySiLK can be deployed as a standalone Python program or to write plug-ins for several SiLK applications. SiLK Python plug-in (silkpython.so) can be used by PySiLK to define new partitioning rules for rwfilter; new key fields for rwcut, rwgroup, and rwsort; and fields in rwstats and rwuniq.

Counting, Grouping, and Mating NetFlow Records with Silk

The following are the tools included in SiLK used for counting, grouping, and mating NetFlow records:

- **rwcount:** Used to count and summarize NetFlow records across time (referred to as *time bins*). Its output includes counts of bytes, packets, and flow records for each time bin.

- **rwuniq:** User-specified key unique record attributes. It can print columns for the total byte, packet, and/or flow counts for each bin. rwuniq can also count the number of individual values for a field.

- **rwstats:** Summarizes NetFlow records just like rwuniq, but sorts the results by a value field to generate a Top-N or Bottom-N list and prints the results.

- **rwtotal:** Summarizes NetFlow records by a specified key and print the sum of the byte, packet, and flow counts for flows matching such key. rwtotal is faster than rwuniq because it uses a fixed amount of memory; however, it has a limited set of keys.

- **rwaddrcount:** Organizes NetFlow records by the source or destination IPv4 address and prints the byte, packet, and flow counts for each IP.

- **rwgroup:** Groups NetFlow records by a user-specified key that include record attributes, labels the records with a group ID that is stored in the Next-Hop IP field, and writes the resulting binary flows to a file or to standard output.

- **rwmatch:** Matches records as queries and responses, marks mated records with an identifier that is stored in the Next-Hop IP field, and writes the binary flow records to the output.

SiLK IPset, Bag, and Prefix Map Manipulation Tools

The following are the tools included in SiLK for IPset, bag, and prefix map manipulation:

- **rwset:** Generates binary IPset files containing the source IP addresses or destination IP addresses in NetFlow records.

- **rwsetbuild:** Reads IP addresses in canonical form or in classless interdomain routing (CIDR) notation from an input file or from the standard input and write a binary IPset file.

- **rwsetcat:** Prints the contents of a binary IPset file as text along with additional information from the NetFlow record.

- **rwsetmember:** Determines whether the specified IP address or CIDR block is included in an IPset.

- **rwsettool:** Unifies and determines the intersection, difference, and sampling functions on the input IPset files, generating a new IPset file.

- **rwbag:** Reads NetFlow records and builds binary bags containing key-count pairs.

- **rwbagbuild:** Creates a binary bag file.

- **rwbagcat:** Prints binary bag files as text.

- **rwbagtool:** Adds or subtracts attributes within binary bag files and produces a new binary bag file.

- **rwpmapbuild:** Generates a binary prefix map file for use with the Address Type (addrtype) and Prefix Map (pmapfilter) utilities.

- **rwpmapcat:** Prints a prefix map file as text.

- **rwpmaplookup:** Finds information about specific IP addresses, ports, or protocol information in a binary prefix map file and prints the result as text.

- **rwipaimport:** Used to import a SiLK IPset, bag, or prefix map files into the IP Address Association (IPA) data store.

- **rwipaexport:** Used to export a set of IP addresses from the IPA data store to a SiLK IPset, bag, or prefix map.

IP and Port Labeling Files

The addrtype file in SiLK allows an administrator to map an IPv4 address to an integer denoting the IP as internal, external, or nonroutable. The country code file (**ccfilter**) maps an IPv4 address to a two-letter, lowercase abbreviation of the country where the IP address is located. The prefix map file (pmapfilter) associates IP addresses or protocol/port pairs to string labels based on a user-defined map file. The map file is created by **rwpmapbuild.**

SiLK Runtime Plug-Ins

The following are SiLK's runtime plug-ins:

- **flowrate:** Adds switches and fields to compute packets/second, bytes/second, bytes/packet, payload-bytes, and payload-bytes/second. This plug-in must be loaded explicitly in SiLK after initial installation.

- **int-ext-fields:** Prints fields containing internal and external IPs and ports (int-ip, ext-ip, int-port, and ext-port).

- **ipafilter:** Known as the IP Association (IPA) plug-in. It works with rwfilter to partition flows based on data in an IPA data store. rwfilter will automatically load this plug-in if it is available. This plug-in requires that SiLK be compiled with IPA support.

- **silk-plugin:** Enables an administrator to create SiLK plug-ins using C.

SiLK Utilities for Packet Capture and IPFIX Processing

The following are the utilities included in SiLK for packet capture and IPFIX processing:

- **rwp2yaf2silk:** Converts a packet-capture (pcap) file to a single file of SiLK flow records. It requires the yaf and rwipfix2silk commands.

- **rwipfix2silk:** Converts IPFIX records to the SiLK flow record format.

- **rwsilk2ipfix:** Converts SiLK flow records to IPFIX format.

- **rwpcut:** Reads a packet-capture file and prints its contents in a textual form similar to that produced by rwcut.

- **rwpdedupe:** Detects and removes duplicate records from multiple packet capture input files.

- **rwpmatch:** Filters a packet-capture file by writing only packets whose five-tuple and time stamp match corresponding records in a SiLK flow file.

- **rwptoflow:** Generates a SiLK flow record for every packet.

- **rwpdu2silk:** Creates a stream of SiLK flow records from a file containing NetFlow v5 PDU records.

Utilities to Detect Network Scans

The following are the utilities included in SiLK for network scan detection:

- **rwscan:** Used to detect scanning activity from SiLK flow records.

- **rwscanquery:** Used to query the scan database generated by rwscan.

SiLK Flow File Utilities

The following are the flow file utilities included in SiLK:

- **rwappend:** Appends the SiLK flow records contained SiLK files.

- **rwcat:** Reads SiLK flow records from the files named on the command line. Similar to the Linux **cat** command.

- **rwcompare:** Compares two SiLK flow files to determine whether they contain the same flow records.

- **rwdedupe:** Removes any duplicate flow records. rwdedupe will reorder the records as part of its processing.

- **rwnetmask:** "Zeroizes" the least significant bits of the source, destination, or next-hop IP addresses, and writes the resulting records to a file or standard output.

- **rwrandomizeip:** Substitutes records using a pseudo-random IP address for the source and destination IP addresses in a stipulated input file.

- **rwsplit:** Splits SiLK files in a set of subfiles from the input.

- **rwswapbytes:** Changes the byte order of the records in a given input SiLK flow file.

Additional SiLK Utilities

The following are several additional SiLK utilities:

- **rwfileinfo:** Prints file information, including file type, version, and other attributes.

- **rwsiteinfo:** Prints information about the sensors, classes, and types specified in the silk.conf file.

- **rwtuc:** Creates SiLK flow records from textual input.

- **rwfglob:** Prints the list of files that rwfilter would normally process for a given set of file selection switches.

- **num2dot:** Processes delimited text from the standard input, converts integer values in the specified columns to dotted-decimal IP address, and prints the result to standard output.

- **rwresolve:** Processes delimited text from the standard input, attempts to resolve the IP addresses in the specified columns to hostnames, and prints the result to the standard output.

- **rwrecgenerator:** Creates SiLK flow records using a pseudo-random number generator.

- **rwgeoip2ccmap:** Generates the country code mapping file required by the ccfilter utility from the MaxMind GeoIP database. For more information about the MaxMind GeoIP database, go to https://www.maxmind.com/en/geolocation_landing.

- **rwidsquery:** Invokes rwfilter to find flow records matching Cisco Sourcefire Snort signatures.

- **silk_config:** Prints information about how SiLK was compiled. This information can be used for troubleshooting purposes.

Note   Chapter 8, "Case Studies" provides several examples of how SiLK is used in a small and medium-sized enterprise.

Elasticsearch, Logstash, and Kibana Stack

Elasticsearch ELK stack is a very powerful open source analytics platform. ELK stands for Elasticsearch, Logstash, and Kibana. Figure 4-5 illustrates the main components of ELK.

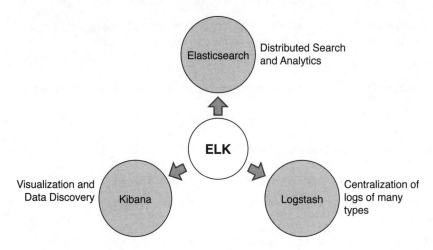

Figure 4-5   *ELK Components*

The following sections provide details about the components illustrated in Figure 4-5.

Elasticsearch

Elasticsearch is the name of a distributed search and analytics engine, but it is also the name of the company founded by the folks behind Elasticsearch and Apache Lucene. Elasticsearch is built on top of Apache Lucene, which is a high-performance search and information retrieval library that is written in Java. Elasticsearch is a schema-free, full text search engine with multilanguage support. It provides support for geolocation, suggestive search, autocompletion, and search snippets.

Logstash

Logstash offers centralized log aggregation of many types, such as network infrastructure device logs, server logs, and also Netflow. Logstash is written in JRuby and runs in a Java Virtual Machine (JVM). It has a very simple message-based architecture. Logstash has a single agent that is configured to perform different functions in combination with the other ELK components. Figure 4-6 illustrates Logstash's architecture.

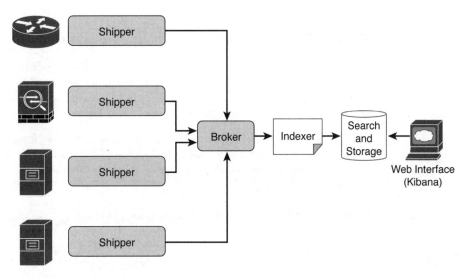

Figure 4-6 *Logstash's Architecture*

In Figure 4-6, you can see the four major components in the Logstash ecosystem. The following are the details of each component:

■ **The shipper:** Sends events to Logstash. Typically, remote agents will only run this component.

■ **The broker and indexer:** Receive and index the events.

■ **The search and storage:** Allows you to search and store events.

■ **The web interface:** A web-based interface. This web-based interface is called Kibana, and we cover it in the following sessions.

Logstash is very scalable because servers running Logstash can run one or more of these aforementioned components independently.

Kibana

Kibana is an analytics and visualization platform architected for Elasticsearch. It provides real-time summary and charting of streaming data, with the ability to share and embed dashboards.

Elasticsearch Marvel and Shield

Marvel and Shield are two additional components that can be integrated with ELK:

- **Marvel:** Provides monitoring of an Elasticsearch deployment. It uses Kibana to visualize the data. It provides a detailed explanation of things that are happening within the ELK deployment that are very useful for troubleshooting and additional analysis. You can obtain information about Marvel at http://www.elasticsearch.org/overview/marvel.

- **Shield:** Provides security features to ELK such as role-based access control, authentication, IP filtering, encryption of ELK data, and audit logging. Shield is not free, and it requires a license. You can obtain more information about Shield at http://www.elasticsearch.org/overview/shield.

Elasticsearch also provides integration with big data platforms such as Hadoop.

Note   Hadoop is covered in Chapter 5, "Big Data Analytics and NetFlow."

The following sections provide several tips and guidance on how to deploy ELK for NetFlow analysis.

ELK Deployment Topology

The topology illustrated in Figure 4-7 is used in the following examples.

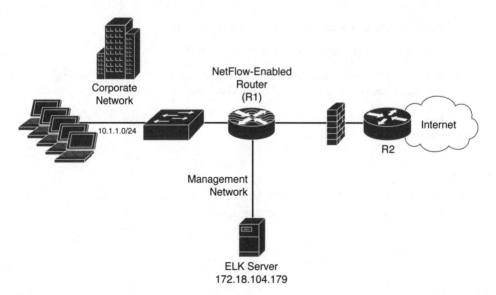

Figure 4-7   *ELK Deployment Topology*

In Figure 4-7, a NetFlow-enabled router (R1) is deployed in the network to monitor traffic between the corporate network and the Internet. ELK is installed on a server running Ubuntu Server to collect and analyze NetFlow records generated by R1.

Installing ELK

Java is required for Elasticsearch and Logstash to work. You can install OpenJDK or Oracle Java. In the following example, Oracle Java is installed. You can use the **sudo add-apt-repository -y ppa:webupd8team/java** command to add the Oracle Java Personal Package Archive (PPA) to the Ubuntu Server, as shown in Example 4-6.

Example 4-6 *Adding the Oracle Java PPA*

```
omar@elk-srv1:~$ sudo add-apt-repository -y ppa:webupd8team/java
gpg: keyring `/tmp/tmpe2orytku/secring.gpg' created
gpg: keyring `/tmp/tmpe2orytku/pubring.gpg' created
gpg: requesting key EEA14886 from hkp server keyserver.ubuntu.com
gpg: /tmp/tmpe2orytku/trustdb.gpg: trustdb created
gpg: key EEA14886: public key "Launchpad VLC" imported
gpg: Total number processed: 1
gpg:               imported: 1  (RSA: 1)
OK
omar@omar-srv1:~$
```

After you add the PPA, update the apt package database with the **sudo apt-get update** command, as shown in Example 4-7.

Example 4-7 *Updating the apt Package Database*

```
omar@elk-srv1:~$ sudo apt-get update
sudo: unable to resolve host omar-srv1
Ign http://us.archive.ubuntu.com trusty InRelease
Ign http://us.archive.ubuntu.com trusty-updates InRelease
Ign http://us.archive.ubuntu.com trusty-backports InRelease
Hit http://us.archive.ubuntu.com trusty Release.gpg
Ign http://security.ubuntu.com trusty-security InRelease
Get:1 http://us.archive.ubuntu.com trusty-updates Release.gpg [933 B]
Get:2 http://us.archive.ubuntu.com trusty-backports Release.gpg [933 B]
Ign http://ppa.launchpad.net trusty InRelease
Hit http://us.archive.ubuntu.com trusty Release
Get:3 http://security.ubuntu.com trusty-security Release.gpg [933 B]
<...output omited>
Ign http://us.archive.ubuntu.com trusty/multiverse Translation-en_US
Ign http://us.archive.ubuntu.com trusty/restricted Translation-en_US
Ign http://us.archive.ubuntu.com trusty/universe Translation-en_US
Fetched 4,014 kB in 6s (590 kB/s)
Reading package lists... Done
omar@omar-srv1:~$
```

Install the latest stable version of Oracle Java with the **sudo apt-get -y install oracle-javaXX-installer** command (XX is the version of Java). Oracle Java 8 is installed as follows:

```
omar@elk-srv1:~$ sudo apt-get -y install oracle-java8-installer
```

Installing Elasticsearch

The following are the steps necessary in order to install Elasticsearch in Ubuntu Server:

Step 1.   Add the Elasticsearch public GPG key into apt with the following command:

```
wget -O - http://packages.elasticsearch.org/GPG-KEY-elasticsearch |
    sudo apt-key add -
```

Step 2.   Create the Elasticsearch source list with the following command:

```
echo 'deb http://packages.elasticsearch.org/elasticsearch/1.4/debian
    stable main' |
sudo tee /etc/apt/sources.list.d/elasticsearch.list
```

Step 3.   Use the **sudo apt-get update** command to update your apt package database.

Step 4.   Install Elasticsearch with the **sudo apt-get -y install elasticsearch=1.4.4** command. In this example, Elasticsearch Version 1.4.4 is installed. For the latest version of Elasticsearch, visit https://www.elastic.co.

Step 5.   The Elasticsearch configuration resides in the /etc/elasticsearch/elasticsearch.yml file. To edit the configuration file, use your favorite editor. (Vi is used in this example: **sudo vi /etc/elasticsearch/elasticsearch.yml.**) It is a best practice to restrict access to the Elasticsearch installation on port 9200 to only local host traffic. Uncomment the line that specifies network.host in the elasticsearch.yml file and replace its value with **localhost**. Example 4-8 includes the complete elasticsearch.yml file for your reference.

Example 4-8   *The elasticsearch.yml Configuration File*

```
# This file contains an overview of various configuration settings,
# targeted at operations staff. Application developers should
# consult the guide at <http://elasticsearch.org/guide>.
#
# The installation procedure is covered at
# <http://elasticsearch.org/guide/en/elasticsearch/reference/current/setup.html>.
#
# Elasticsearch comes with reasonable defaults for most settings,
# so you can try it out without bothering with configuration.
#
# Most of the time, these defaults are just fine for running a production
# cluster. If you're fine-tuning your cluster, or wondering about the
# effect of certain configuration option, please _do ask_ on the
# mailing list or IRC channel [http://elasticsearch.org/community].
```

```
# Any element in the configuration can be replaced with environment variables
# by placing them in ${...} notation. For example:
#
#node.rack: ${RACK_ENV_VAR}

# For information on supported formats and syntax for the config file, see
# <http://elasticsearch.org/guide/en/elasticsearch/reference/current/setup-configu-
  ration.html>


#################################### Cluster ###################################

# Cluster name identifies your cluster for auto-discovery. If you're running
# multiple clusters on the same network, make sure you're using unique names.
#
#cluster.name: elasticsearch



#################################### Node ######################################

# Node names are generated dynamically on startup, so you're relieved
# from configuring them manually. You can tie this node to a specific name:
#
#node.name: "Franz Kafka"

# Every node can be configured to allow or deny being eligible as the master,
# and to allow or deny to store the data.
#
# Allow this node to be eligible as a master node (enabled by default):
#
#node.master: true
#
# Allow this node to store data (enabled by default):
#
#node.data: true

# You can exploit these settings to design advanced cluster topologies.
#
# 1. You want this node to never become a master node, only to hold data.
#    This will be the "workhorse" of your cluster.
#
#node.master: false
#node.data: true
#
```

```
# 2. You want this node to only serve as a master: to not store any data and
#    to have free resources. This will be the "coordinator" of your cluster.
#
#node.master: true
#node.data: false
#
# 3. You want this node to be neither master nor data node, but
#    to act as a "search load balancer" (fetching data from nodes,
#    aggregating results, etc.)
#
#node.master: false
#node.data: false


# Use the Cluster Health API [http://localhost:9200/_cluster/health], the
# Node Info API [http://localhost:9200/_nodes] or GUI tools
# such as <http://www.elasticsearch.org/overview/marvel/>,
# <http://github.com/karmi/elasticsearch-paramedic>,
# <http://github.com/lukas-vlcek/bigdesk> and
# <http://mobz.github.com/elasticsearch-head> to inspect the cluster state.


# A node can have generic attributes associated with it, which can later be used
# for customized shard allocation filtering, or allocation awareness. An attribute
# is a simple key value pair, similar to node.key: value, here is an example:
#
#node.rack: rack314


# By default, multiple nodes are allowed to start from the same installation loca-
  tion
# to disable it, set the following:
#node.max_local_storage_nodes: 1



################################### Index ###################################

# You can set a number of options (such as shard/replica options, mapping
# or analyzer definitions, translog settings, ...) for indices globally,
# in this file.
#
# Note, that it makes more sense to configure index settings specifically for
# a certain index, either when creating it or by using the index templates API.
#
# See <http://elasticsearch.org/guide/en/elasticsearch/reference/current/index-mod-
  ules.html> and
# <http://elasticsearch.org/guide/en/elasticsearch/reference/current/indices-create-
  index.html>
# for more information.
```

```
# Set the number of shards (splits) of an index (5 by default):
#
#index.number_of_shards: 5

# Set the number of replicas (additional copies) of an index (1 by default):
#
#index.number_of_replicas: 1

# Note, that for development on a local machine, with small indices, it usually
# makes sense to "disable" the distributed features:
#
#index.number_of_shards: 1
#index.number_of_replicas: 0

# These settings directly affect the performance of index and search operations
# in your cluster. Assuming you have enough machines to hold shards and
# replicas, the rule of thumb is:
#
# 1. Having more *shards* enhances the _indexing_ performance and allows to
#    _distribute_ a big index across machines.
# 2. Having more *replicas* enhances the _search_ performance and improves the
#    cluster _availability_.
#
# The "number_of_shards" is a one-time setting for an index.
#
# The "number_of_replicas" can be increased or decreased anytime,
# by using the Index Update Settings API.
#
# Elasticsearch takes care about load balancing, relocating, gathering the
# results from nodes, etc. Experiment with different settings to fine-tune
# your setup.

# Use the Index Status API (<http://localhost:9200/A/_status>) to inspect
# the index status.


################################### Paths ###################################

# Path to directory containing configuration (this file and logging.yml):
#
#path.conf: /path/to/conf

# Path to directory where to store index data allocated for this node.
#
```

```
#path.data: /path/to/data
#
# Can optionally include more than one location, causing data to be striped across
# the locations (a la RAID 0) on a file level, favoring locations with most free
# space on creation. For example:
#
#path.data: /path/to/data1,/path/to/data2

# Path to temporary files:
#
#path.work: /path/to/work

# Path to log files:
#
#path.logs: /path/to/logs

# Path to where plugins are installed:
#
#path.plugins: /path/to/plugins


################################### Plugin ###################################

# If a plugin listed here is not installed for current node, the node will not
  start.
#
#plugin.mandatory: mapper-attachments,lang-groovy


################################### Memory ###################################

# Elasticsearch performs poorly when JVM starts swapping: you should ensure that
# it _never_ swaps.
#
# Set this property to true to lock the memory:
#
#bootstrap.mlockall: true

# Make sure that the ES_MIN_MEM and ES_MAX_MEM environment variables are set
# to the same value, and that the machine has enough memory to allocate
# for Elasticsearch, leaving enough memory for the operating system itself.
#
# You should also make sure that the Elasticsearch process is allowed to lock
# the memory, eg. by using `ulimit -l unlimited`.
```

```
############################# Network And HTTP #############################

# Elasticsearch, by default, binds itself to the 0.0.0.0 address, and listens
# on port [9200-9300] for HTTP traffic and on port [9300-9400] for node-to-node
# communication. (The range means that if the port is busy, it will automatically
# try the next port).

# Set the bind address specifically (IPv4 or IPv6):
#
#network.bind_host: 192.168.0.1

# Set the address other nodes will use to communicate with this node. If not
# set, it is automatically derived. It must point to an actual IP address.
#
#network.publish_host: 192.168.0.1

# Set both 'bind_host' and 'publish_host':
#
network.host: localhost

# Set a custom port for the node to node communication (9300 by default):
#
#transport.tcp.port: 9300

# Enable compression for all communication between nodes (disabled by default):
#
#transport.tcp.compress: true

# Set a custom port to listen for HTTP traffic:
#
#http.port: 9200

# Set a custom allowed content length:
#
#http.max_content_length: 100mb

# Disable HTTP completely:
#
#http.enabled: false



############################### Gateway ###############################

# The gateway allows for persisting the cluster state between full cluster
```

```
# restarts. Every change to the state (such as adding an index) will be stored
# in the gateway, and when the cluster starts up for the first time,
# it will read its state from the gateway.

# There are several types of gateway implementations. For more information, see
# <http://elasticsearch.org/guide/en/elasticsearch/reference/current/modules-gate-
  way.html>.

# The default gateway type is the "local" gateway (recommended):
#
#gateway.type: local

# Settings below control how and when to start the initial recovery process on
# a full cluster restart (to reuse as much local data as possible when using shared
# gateway).

# Allow recovery process after N nodes in a cluster are up:
#
#gateway.recover_after_nodes: 1

# Set the timeout to initiate the recovery process, once the N nodes
# from previous setting are up (accepts time value):
#
#gateway.recover_after_time: 5m

# Set how many nodes are expected in this cluster. Once these N nodes
# are up (and recover_after_nodes is met), begin recovery process immediately
# (without waiting for recover_after_time to expire):
#
#gateway.expected_nodes: 2


############################# Recovery Throttling #############################

# These settings allow to control the process of shards allocation between
# nodes during initial recovery, replica allocation, rebalancing,
# or when adding and removing nodes.

# Set the number of concurrent recoveries happening on a node:
#
# 1. During the initial recovery
#
#cluster.routing.allocation.node_initial_primaries_recoveries: 4
#
# 2. During adding/removing nodes, rebalancing, etc
```

```
#
#cluster.routing.allocation.node_concurrent_recoveries: 2


# Set to throttle throughput when recovering (eg. 100mb, by default 20mb):
#
#indices.recovery.max_bytes_per_sec: 20mb


# Set to limit the number of open concurrent streams when
# recovering a shard from a peer:
#
#indices.recovery.concurrent_streams: 5



################################# Discovery #################################


# Discovery infrastructure ensures nodes can be found within a cluster
# and master node is elected. Multicast discovery is the default.


# Set to ensure a node sees N other master eligible nodes to be considered
# operational within the cluster. This should be set to a quorum/majority of
# the master-eligible nodes in the cluster.
#
#discovery.zen.minimum_master_nodes: 1


# Set the time to wait for ping responses from other nodes when discovering.
# Set this option to a higher value on a slow or congested network
# to minimize discovery failures:
#
#discovery.zen.ping.timeout: 3s


# For more information, see
# <http://elasticsearch.org/guide/en/elasticsearch/reference/current/modules-discov-
  ery-zen.html>


# Unicast discovery allows to explicitly control which nodes will be used
# to discover the cluster. It can be used when multicast is not present,
# or to restrict the cluster communication-wise.
#
# 1. Disable multicast discovery (enabled by default):
#
#discovery.zen.ping.multicast.enabled: false
#
# 2. Configure an initial list of master nodes in the cluster
#    to perform discovery when new nodes (master or data) are started:
#
```

```
#discovery.zen.ping.unicast.hosts: ["host1", "host2:port"]


# EC2 discovery allows to use AWS EC2 API in order to perform discovery.
#
# You have to install the cloud-aws plugin for enabling the EC2 discovery.
#
# For more information, see
# <http://elasticsearch.org/guide/en/elasticsearch/reference/current/modules-discov-
  ery-ec2.html>
#
# See <http://elasticsearch.org/tutorials/elasticsearch-on-ec2/>
# for a step-by-step tutorial.


# GCE discovery allows to use Google Compute Engine API in order to perform discov-
  ery.
#
# You have to install the cloud-gce plugin for enabling the GCE discovery.
#
# For more information, see <https://github.com/elasticsearch/elasticsearch-cloud-
  gce>.


# Azure discovery allows to use Azure API in order to perform discovery.
#
# You have to install the cloud-azure plugin for enabling the Azure discovery.
#
# For more information, see <https://github.com/elasticsearch/elasticsearch-cloud-
  azure>.


################################## Slow Log ##################################


# Shard level query and fetch threshold logging.

#index.search.slowlog.threshold.query.warn: 10s
#index.search.slowlog.threshold.query.info: 5s
#index.search.slowlog.threshold.query.debug: 2s
#index.search.slowlog.threshold.query.trace: 500ms

#index.search.slowlog.threshold.fetch.warn: 1s
#index.search.slowlog.threshold.fetch.info: 800ms
#index.search.slowlog.threshold.fetch.debug: 500ms
#index.search.slowlog.threshold.fetch.trace: 200ms


#index.indexing.slowlog.threshold.index.warn: 10s
#index.indexing.slowlog.threshold.index.info: 5s
#index.indexing.slowlog.threshold.index.debug: 2s
#index.indexing.slowlog.threshold.index.trace: 500ms
```

```
################################ GC Logging ################################


#monitor.jvm.gc.young.warn: 1000ms
#monitor.jvm.gc.young.info: 700ms
#monitor.jvm.gc.young.debug: 400ms


#monitor.jvm.gc.old.warn: 10s
#monitor.jvm.gc.old.info: 5s
#monitor.jvm.gc.old.debug: 2s


################################ Security ################################

# Uncomment if you want to enable JSONP as a valid return transport on the
# http server. With this enabled, it may pose a security risk, so disabling
# it unless you need it is recommended (it is disabled by default).
#
#http.jsonp.enable: true
http.cors.enabled: true
http.cors.allow-origin: "http://elk-srv1.example.com"
```

Step 6. Restart the Elasticsearch service with the **sudo service elasticsearch restart** command. You can also use the **sudo update-rc.d elasticsearch** defaults 95 10 command to start Elasticsearch automatically upon boot.

Install Kibana

The following are the steps necessary to install Kibana in Ubuntu Server:

Step 1 Download Kibana from https://www.elastic.co/downloads/kibana.

Step 2. The Kibana configuration file is config/kibana.yml. Edit the file, as shown in the following example:

```
omar@elk-srv1:~$ vi ~/kibana-4*/config/kibana.yml
```

Step 3. Find the line that specifies **host**. By default, 0.0.0.0 is configured. Replace it with **localhost**. This way Kibana will be accessible only to the local host. In this example, Nginx will be installed, and it will reverse proxy to allow external access.

Step 4. Copy the Kibana files to a more suitable directory. The /opt directory is used in the following example:

```
omar@elk-srv1:~$ sudo mkdir -p /opt/kibana
omar@elk-srv1:~$ sudo cp -R ~/kibana-4*/* /opt/kibana/
```

Step 5. To run Kibana as a service, download a init script with the following command:

```
cd /etc/init.d && sudo wget
https://gist.githubusercontent.com/thisismitch/8b15ac909aed214ad04a/
  raw/bce61d85643c2dc
dfbc2728c55a41dab444dca20/kibana4
```

Step 6. Enable and start the Kibana service with the following commands:

```
omar@elk-srv1:~$ sudo chmod +x /etc/init.d/kibana4
omar@elk-srv1:~$ sudo update-rc.d kibana4 defaults 96 9
omar@elk-srv1:~$ sudo service kibana4 start
```

Installing Nginx

In this example, Nginx is used as a reverse proxy to allow external access to Kibana. Complete the following steps to install Nginx:

Step 1. Use the **sudo apt-get install nginx apache2-utils** command to install Ngnix.

Step 2. You can use **htpasswd** to create an admin user. In this example, secadmin is the admin user:

```
sudo htpasswd -c /etc/nginx/htpasswd.users secadmin
```

Step 3. Edit the Nginx default server block (/etc/nginx/sites-available/default) and update the **server_name** to match your server's name. The following is the /etc/nginx/sites-available/default file contents used in this example:

```
server {
    listen 80;

    server_name elk-srv1.example.com;

    auth_basic "Restricted Access";
    auth_basic_user_file /etc/nginx/htpasswd.users;

    location / {
        proxy_pass http://localhost:5601;
        proxy_http_version 1.1;
        proxy_set_header Upgrade $http_upgrade;
        proxy_set_header Connection 'upgrade';
        proxy_set_header Host $host;
        proxy_cache_bypass $http_upgrade;
    }
}
```

Step 4. Restart Nginx with the **sudo service nginx restart** command.

You should now be able to access Kibana in your browser via the fully qualified domain name (FQDN) or its IP address.

Install Logstash

Complete the following steps to install Logstash in the Ubuntu Server:

Step 1.   Download Logstash from https://www.elastic.co/downloads/logstash. Alternatively, you can add the Logstash repository in Ubuntu and update the package database, as shown here:

```
omar@elk-srv1:~$ echo 'deb http://packages.elasticsearch.org/
  logstash/1.5/debian stable
main' | sudo tee /etc/apt/sources.list.d/logstash.list
omar@elk-srv1:~$ sudo apt-get update
```

Step 2.   Install Logstash with the **sudo apt-get install logstash** command, as shown here:

```
omar@elk-srv1:~$ sudo apt-get install logstash
```

Step 3.   The Logstash configuration files are under /etc/logstash/conf.d. The configuration files are in JSON format. The configuration consists of three sections: inputs, filters, and outputs:

```
input {
    udp {
      port => 9996
      codec => netflow {
        definitions => "/opt/logstash/codecs/netflow/netflow.yaml"
        versions => 9
      }
    }
}

output {
    stdout { codec => rubydebug }
    if ( [host] =~ "172.18.104.1" ) {
      elasticsearch {
        index => "logstash_netflow-%{+YYYY.MM.dd}"
        host => "localhost"
      }
    } else {
      elasticsearch {
        index => "logstash-%{+YYYY.MM.dd}"
        host => "localhost"
      }
    }
}
```

In this example, Logstash is configured to accept NetFlow records from R1 (172.18.104.1). The NetFlow data is exported to Elasticsearch with the logstash_netflow-YYYY.MM.dd index named; where YYYY.MM.dd is the date when the NetFlow data was received. The server is configured to listen on UDP port 9996.

Note   You can find additional examples and resources at https://github.com/santosomar/netflow. You can also contribute with your own examples and code there.

The following template is used for the server to be able to parse the fields from NetFlow:

```
curl -XPUT localhost:9200/_template/logstash_netflow9 -d '{
  "template" : "logstash_netflow9-*",
  "settings": {
    "index.refresh_interval": "5s"
  },
  "mappings" : {
    "_default_" : {
      "_all" : {"enabled" : false},
      "properties" : {
        "@version": { "index": "analyzed", "type": "integer" },
        "@timestamp": { "index": "analyzed", "type": "date" },
        "netflow": {
          "dynamic": true,
          "type": "object",
          "properties": {
            "version": { "index": "analyzed", "type": "integer" },
            "flow_seq_num": { "index": "not_analyzed", "type": "long" },
            "engine_type": { "index": "not_analyzed", "type":
              "integer" },
            "engine_id": { "index": "not_analyzed", "type":
              "integer" },
            "sampling_algorithm": { "index": "not_analyzed", "type":
              "integer" },
            "sampling_interval": { "index": "not_analyzed", "type":
              "integer" },
            "flow_records": { "index": "not_analyzed", "type":
              "integer" },
            "ipv4_src_addr": { "index": "analyzed", "type": "ip" },
            "ipv4_dst_addr": { "index": "analyzed", "type": "ip" },
            "ipv4_next_hop": { "index": "analyzed", "type": "ip" },
            "input_snmp": { "index": "not_analyzed", "type": "long" },
            "output_snmp": { "index": "not_analyzed", "type": "long" },
            "in_pkts": { "index": "analyzed", "type": "long" },
            "in_bytes": { "index": "analyzed", "type": "long" },
            "first_switched": { "index": "not_analyzed", "type": "date" },
```

```
                    "last_switched": { "index": "not_analyzed", "type": "date" },
                    "l4_src_port": { "index": "analyzed", "type": "long" },
                    "l4_dst_port": { "index": "analyzed", "type": "long" },
                    "tcp_flags": { "index": "analyzed", "type": "integer" },
                    "protocol": { "index": "analyzed", "type": "integer" },
                    "src_tos": { "index": "analyzed", "type": "integer" },
                    "src_as": { "index": "analyzed", "type": "integer" },
                    "dst_as": { "index": "analyzed", "type": "integer" },
                    "src_mask": { "index": "analyzed", "type": "integer" },
                    "dst_mask": { "index": "analyzed", "type": "integer" }
                }
              }
            }
          }
        }
      }'
```

The preceding template is used for Elasticsearch to be able to process all indices that start with logstash_netflow9.

Note   Refer to the Elasticsearch documentation for more information at https://www.elastic.co/guide/index.html.

Tip   Do not forget to review examples and provide your own at https://github.com/santosomar/netflow.

Summary

There are numerous commercial and open source NetFlow monitoring and analysis solutions in the market. This chapter provided an overview of these solutions. It provided details on two very popular commercial NetFlow monitoring and analysis solutions: Lancope's StealthWatch and Plixer's Scrutinizer. Many small and medium-sized organizations use open source alternatives for NetFlow monitoring and analysis. This chapter listed several of the most popular open source tools and provided details on several popular toolkits: NFdump, SiLK, Elasticsearch, Logstash, and Kibana. Chapter 6 and Chapter 8 provide several examples of how these commercial and open source tools are used by small, medium, and large organizations.

Chapter 5

Big Data Analytics and NetFlow

This chapter covers the following topics:

- Introduction to big data analytics for cyber security

- NetFlow and other telemetry sources for big data analytics for cyber security

- Open Security Operations Center (OpenSOC)

- Understanding big data scalability: Big data analytics in the Internet of Everything (IoE)

Introduction to Big Data Analytics for Cyber Security

Big data analytics is the practice of studying large amounts of data of a variety of types and a variety of courses to learn interesting patterns, unknown facts, and other useful information. Big data analytics can play a crucial role in cyber security. Many in the industry are changing the tone of their conversation, saying that it is no longer if or when your network will be compromised, but the assumption is that your network has already been hacked or compromised, and suggest focusing on minimizing the damage and increasing visibility to aid in identification of the next hack or compromise.

Advanced analytics can be run against very large diverse data sets to find indicators of compromise (IOCs). These data sets can include different types of structured and unstructured data processed in a "streaming" fashion or in batches. NetFlow plays an important role for big data analytics for cyber security, and you will learn why as you read through in this chapter.

What Is Big Data?

There are a lot of very interesting definitions for the phenomenon called *big data*. It seems that a lot of people have different views of what big data is. Let's cut through the marketing hype and get down to the basics of the subject. A formal definition for big data can be obtained in the Merriam-Webster dictionary: http://www.merriam-webster.com/dictionary/big%20data.

> An accumulation of data that is too large and complex for processing by traditional database management tools.

> Big data usually includes data sets with sizes beyond the ability of commonly used software tools to capture, curate, manage, and process the data within a tolerable elapsed time.

The size of data that can be classified as big data is a moving target. It can range from a few terabytes to yottabytes of data in a single data set. For instance:

■ A petabyte is 1000 terabytes.

■ An exabyte is 1000 petabytes.

■ A zettabyte is 1000 exabytes.

■ A yoyabyte is 1000 zettabytes.

Tip   Cisco has created the Cisco Visual Networking Index (VNI). Cisco VNI is an ongoing initiative to forecast and analyze the growth and use of the Internet, in addition to the data being transferred. You can find details of the Cisco VNI global IP traffic forecast and the methodology behind it at http://www.cisco.com/go/vni.

Unstructured Versus Structured Data

The term *unstructured data* is used when referring to data that does not have a pre-defined data model or is not organized in a predetermined way. Typically, unstructured data is defined as data that is not typically tracked in a "structured" or traditional row-column database. The prime examples of unstructured data are as follows:

■ Multimedia content such as videos, photos, and audio files

■ E-mail messages

■ Social media (Facebook, Twitter, LinkedIn) status updates

■ Presentations

■ Word processing documents

■ Blog posts

■ Executable files

In the world of cyber security, a lot of the network can be also categorized as unstructured:

■ Syslog

■ Simple Network Management Protocol (SNMP) logs

- NetFlow

- Server and host logs

- Packet captures

- Executables

- Malware

- Exploits

Industry experts estimate that the majority of the data in any organization is unstructured, and the amount of unstructured data is growing significantly. There are numerous, disparate data sources. NetFlow is one of the largest single sources, and it can grow to tens of terabytes of data per day in large organizations, and it is expected to grow over the years to petabytes. The differentiation in the usefulness of any big data solution is the merging of numerous data sources and sizes that are all in the same infrastructure and providing the ability to query across all of these different data sets using the same language and tools.

There is an industry concept called *Not-Only SQL* (NoSQL), which is the name given to several databases that do not require SQL to process data. However, some of these databases support both SQL and non-SQL forms of data processing.

Big data analytics can be done in combination of advanced analytics disciplines such as predictive analytics and data mining.

Note   Cisco acquired Cognitive Security in 2013, a company focused on applying artificial intelligence techniques to detect advanced cyber threats. The new Cisco security solutions integrate a range of sophisticated technologies to identify and analyze key threats through advanced behavioral analysis of real-time data.

Extracting Value from Big Data

Any organization can collect data just for the matter of collecting data; however, the usefulness of such data depends on how actionable such data is to make any decisions (in addition to whether the data is regularly monitored and analyzed).

There are three high-level key items for big data analytics:

- **Information management:** An ongoing management and process control for big data analytics.

- **High-performance analytics:** The ability to gain fast actionable information from big data and being able to solve complex problems using more data.

- **Flexible deployment options:** Options for on-premises or cloud-based, software-as-a-service (SaaS) tactics for big data analytics.

There are a few high-level approaches for accelerating the analysis of giant data sets. The following are the most common:

- **Grid computing:** A centralized grid infrastructure for dynamic analysis with high availability and parallel processing.

- **Intra-database processing:** Performing data management, analytics, and reporting tasks using scalable architectures.

- **In-memory analytics:** Quickly solves complex problems using in-memory, multiuse access to data and rapidly runs new scenarios or complex analytical computations.

- **Support for Hadoop:** Stores and processes large volumes of data on commodity hardware. Hadoop will be covered in a few pages in the section "Hadoop."

- **Visualizations:** Quickly visualize correlations and patterns in big data to identify opportunities for further analysis and to improve decision making.

Examples of technologies used in big data analytics are covered in detail later in this chapter.

NetFlow and Other Telemetry Sources for Big Data Analytics for Cyber Security

As discussed in Chapter 1, "Introduction to NetFlow and IPFIX," NetFlow provides detailed network telemetry that allows the administrator to:

- See what is actually happening across your entire network

- Regain control of your network, in case of denial-of-service (DoS) attack

- Quickly identify compromised endpoints and network infrastructure devices

- Monitor network usage of employees, contractors, or partners

- Obtain network telemetry during security incident response and forensics

- Detect firewall misconfigurations and inappropriate access to corporate resources

As previously mentioned, NetFlow data can grow to tens of terabytes of data per day in large organizations, and it is expected to grow over the years to petabytes. However, many other telemetry sources can be used in conjunction with NetFlow to identify, classify, and mitigate potential threats in your network. Figure 5-1 shows examples of these telemetry sources and how they "feed" into a collection engine.

As illustrated in Figure 5-1, NetFlow data, syslog, SNMP logs, server and host logs, packet captures, and files (such as executables, malware, exploits) can be parsed, formatted, and combined with threat intelligence information and other "enrichment data" (network metadata) to perform analytics. This process is not an easy one; this is why Cisco has created an open source framework for big data analytics called *Open Security Operations Center* (OpenSOC). The following section provides an in-depth look at the OpenSOC framework.

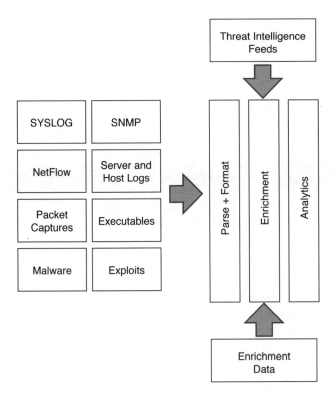

Figure 5-1 *NetFlow and Other Telemetry Sources*

OpenSOC

OpenSOC was created by Cisco to attack the "big data problem" for their Managed Threat Defense offering. Cisco has developed a fully managed service delivered by Cisco Security Solutions to help customers protect against known intrusions, zero-day attacks, and advanced persistent threats. Cisco has a global network of security operations centers (SOCs) ensuring constant awareness and on-demand analysis 24 hours a day, 7 days a week. They needed the ability to capture full packet-level data and extract protocol metadata to create a unique profile of customer's network and monitor them against Cisco threat intelligence. As you can imagine, performing big data analytics for one organization is a challenge, Cisco has to perform big data analytics for numerous customers including very large enterprises. The goal with OpenSOC is to have a robust framework based on proven technologies to combine machine learning algorithms and predictive analytics to detect today's security threats.

The following are some of the benefits of OpenSOC:

■ The ability to capture raw network packets, store those packets, and perform traffic reconstruction

■ Collect any network telemetry, perform enrichment, and generate real-time rules-based alerts

■ Perform real-time search and cross-telemetry matching

■ Automated reports

■ Anomaly detection and alerting

■ Integration with existing analytics tools

Note   OpenSOC is open sourced under the Apache license.

The primary components of OpenSOC include the following:

■ Hadoop

■ Flume

■ Kafka

■ Storm

■ Hive

■ Elasticsearch

■ HBase

■ Third-party analytic tool support (R, Python-based tools, Power Pivot, Tableau, and so on)

The sections that follow cover these components in more detail.

Hadoop

The Apache Hadoop or "Hadoop" is a project supported and maintained by the Apache Software Foundation. Hadoop is a software library designed for distributed processing of large data sets across clusters of computers. One of the advantages of Hadoop is its ability to using simple programming models to perform big data processing. Hadoop can scale from a single server instance to thousands of servers. Each Hadoop server or node performs local computation and storage. Cisco uses Hadoop clusters in OpenSOC to process large amounts of network data for their customers, as part of the Managed Threat Defense solution, and it also uses Hadoop for its internal threat intelligence ecosystem.

Hadoop includes the following modules:

■ **Hadoop Common:** The underlying utilities that support the other Hadoop modules.

■ **Hadoop Distributed File System (HDFS):** A highly scalable and distributed file system.

- **Hadoop YARN:** A framework design for job scheduling and cluster resource management.

- **Hadoop MapReduce (MapR):** A system designed for parallel processing of large data sets based on YARN.

Figure 5-2 illustrates a Hadoop cluster.

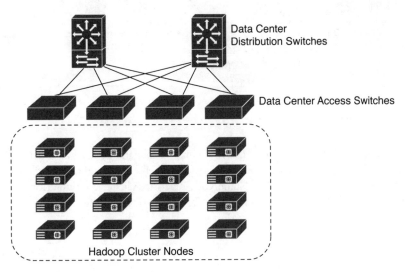

Figure 5-2 *Hadoop Cluster Example*

In Figure 5-2, a total of 16 servers are configured in a Hadoop cluster and connected to the data center access switches for big data processing.

HDFS

HDFS is a highly scalable and distributed file system that can scale to thousands of cluster nodes, millions of files, and petabytes of data. HDFS is optimized for batch processing where data locations are exposed to allow computations to take place where the data resides. HDFS provides a single namespace for the entire cluster to allow for data coherency in a write-once, read-many access model. In other words, clients can only append to existing files in the node. In HDFS, files are separated into blocks, which are typically 64 MB in size and are replicated in multiple data nodes. Clients access data directly from data nodes. Figure 5-3 shows a high-level overview of the HDFS architecture.

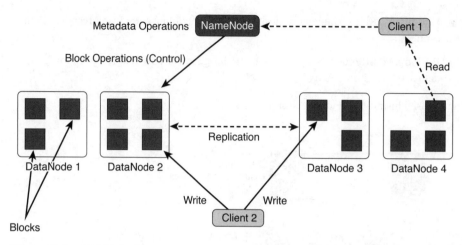

Figure 5-3 *HDFS Architecture*

In Figure 5-3, the NameNode (or Namespace Node) maps a filename to a set of blocks and the blocks to the data nodes where the block resides. There are a total of four data nodes, each with a set of data blocks. The NameNode performs cluster configuration management and controls the replication engine for blocks throughout the cluster. The NameNode metadata includes the following:

- The list of files

- List of blocks for each file

- List of data nodes for each block

- File attributes such as creation time and replication factor

The NameNode also maintains a transaction log that records file creations, deletions, and modifications.

Each DataNode includes a block server that stores data in the local file system, stores metadata of a block, and provisions data and metadata to the clients. DataNodes also periodically send a report of all existing blocks to the NameNode and forward data to other specified DataNodes as needed. DataNodes send a heartbeat message to the NameNode on a periodic basis (every 3 seconds by default), and the NameNode uses these heartbeats to detect any DataNode failures. Clients can read or write data to each data block, as shown in Figure 5-3.

Note   You can obtain more detailed information and download Hadoop at http://hadoop.apache.org.

Flume

OpenSOC uses Flume for collecting, aggregating, and moving large amounts of network telemetry data (like NetFlow, syslog, SNMP, and so on) from many different sources to a centralized data store. Flume is also licensed under the Apache license. Figure 5-4 shows how different network telemetry sources are sent to Flume agents for processing.

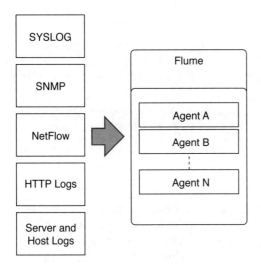

Figure 5-4   *Network Telemetry Sources and Flume*

Flume has the following components and concepts:

- **Event:** A specific unit of data that is transferred by Flume, such as a single NetFlow record.

- **Source:** The source of the data. These sources are either actively queried for new data or they can passively wait for data to be delivered to them. The source of this data can be NetFlow collectors, server logs from Splunk, or similar entities.

- **Sink:** Delivers the data to a specific destination.

- **Channel:** The conduit between the source and the sink.

- **Agent:** A Java virtual machine running Flume that comprises a group of sources, sinks, and channels.

- **Client:** Creates and transmits the event to the source operating within the agent.

Figure 5-5 illustrates Flume's high-level architecture and its components.

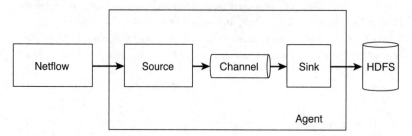

Figure 5-5   *Flume Architecture*

Note   You can obtain more detailed information and download Flume at http://flume.apache.org.

Kafka

OpenSOC uses Kafka as its messaging system. Kafka is a distributed messaging system that is partitioned and replicated. Kafka uses the concept of *topics*. Topics are feeds of messages in specific categories. For example, Kafka can take raw packet captures and telemetry information from Flume (after processing NetFlow, syslog, SNMP, or any other telemetry data), as shown in Figure 5-6.

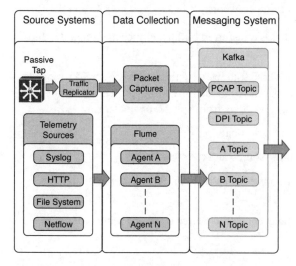

Figure 5-6   *Kafka Example in OpenSOC*

In Figure 5-6, a topic is a category or feed name to which log messages and telemetry information are exchanged (published). Each topic is an ordered, immutable sequence of messages that is continually appended to a commit log.

Kafka provides a single "consumer" abstraction layer, as illustrated in Figure 5-7.

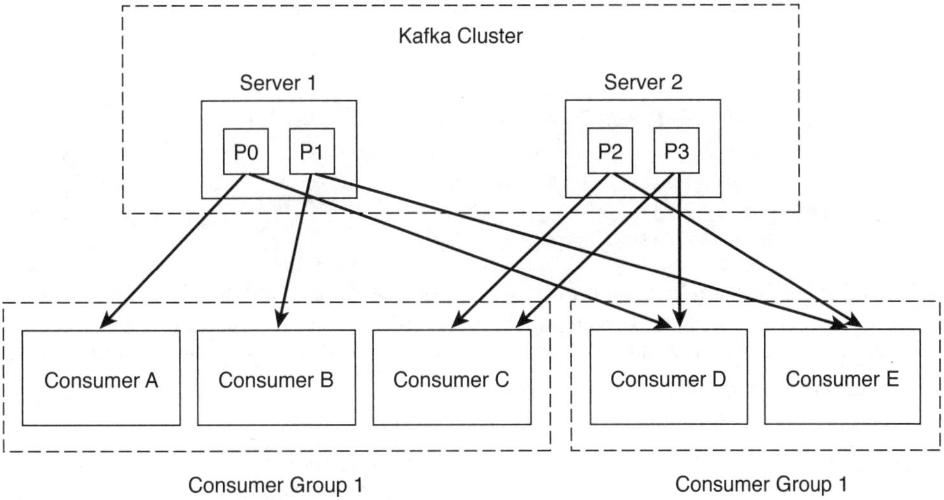

Figure 5-7   *Kafka Cluster and Consumers*

Consumers are organized in consumer groups, and each message published to a topic is sent to one consumer instance within each subscribing consumer group.

Note   Consumers can be in separate processes or on separate machines.

All consumer instances that belong to the same consumer group are processed in a traditional queue load balancing. Consumers in different groups process messages in a publish-subscribe mode, where all the messages are broadcast to all consumers.

In Figure 5-7, the Kafka cluster contains two servers (Server 1 and Server 2), each with two different partitions. Server 1 contains partition 0 (P0) and partition 1 (P1). Server 2 contains partition 2 (P2) and partition 3 (P3). Two consumer groups are illustrated. Consumer Group 1 contains consumers A, B, and C. Consumer Group 2 contains consumers: D and E.

Kafka provides parallelism to provide ordering guarantees and load balancing over a pool of consumer processes. However, there cannot be more consumer instances than partitions.

Note   You can obtain more detailed information and download Kafka at http://kafka.apache.org.

Storm

Storm is an open source, distributed, real-time computation system under the Apache license. It provides real-time processing and can be used with any programming language.

Hadoop consists of two major components: HDFS and MapReduce. The early implementations of Hadoop and MapReduce were designed on batch analytics, which does not provide any real-time processing. In SOCs, you often cannot process data in batches, and so it can take several hours to complete the analysis.

Note   Depending on the amount of data, the number of nodes in the cluster, the technical specifications of each node, and the complexity of the analytics, MapReduce can take anywhere from minutes to hours to perform a job. In security, you need to respond fast!

OpenSOC uses Storm because it provides real-time streaming and because of its amazing ability to process big data, at scale, in real time. Storm can process data at over a million tuples processed per second per node. Figure 5-8 shows how Kafka topics feed information to Storm to provide real-time processing.

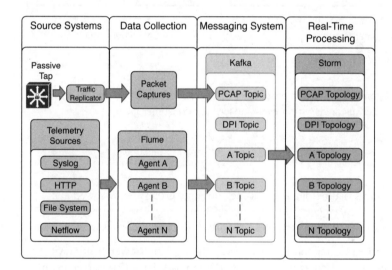

Figure 5-8   *Storm in OpenSOC*

Note   You can obtain more detailed information and download Storm at https://storm.incubator.apache.org.

Hive

Hive is a data warehouse infrastructure that provides data summarization and ad hoc querying. Hive is also a project under the Apache license. OpenSOC uses Hive because of its querying capabilities. Hive provides a mechanism to query data using a SQL-like language that is called HiveQL. In the case of batch processing, Hive allows MapR programmers use their own custom mappers.

Figure 5-9 shows how Storm feeds into Hive to provide data summarization and querying.

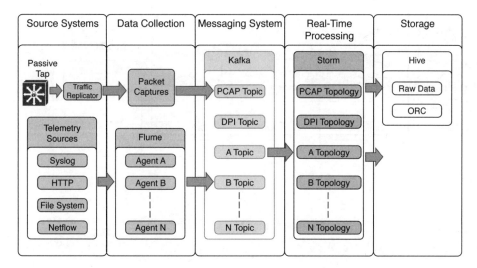

Figure 5-9   *Hive in OpenSOC*

Note   You can obtain more detailed information and download Hive at https://hive.apache.org.

Storm can also feed into HBase and Elasticsearch. These are covered in the following sections.

Elasticsearch

Elasticsearch is a scalable and real-time search and analytics engine that is also used by OpenSOC. Elasticsearch has a very strong set of application programming interfaces (APIs) and query domain-specific languages (DSLs). It provides full query DSL based on JSON to define such queries. Figure 5-10 shows how Storm feeds into Elasticsearch to provide real-time indexing and querying.

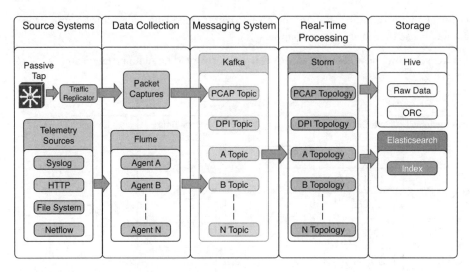

Figure 5-10   *Elasticsearch in OpenSOC*

HBase

HBase is scalable and distributed database that supports structured data storage for large tables. You guessed right: HBase is also under the Apache license! OpenSOC uses HBase because it provides random and real-time read/write access large data sets.

HBase provides linear and modular scalability with consistent database reads and writes.

It also provides automatic and configurable high-availability (failover) support between Region Servers. HBase is a type of "NoSQL" database that can be scaled by adding Region Servers that are hosted on separate servers.

Figure 5-11 shows how Storm feeds into HBase to provide real-time indexing and querying.

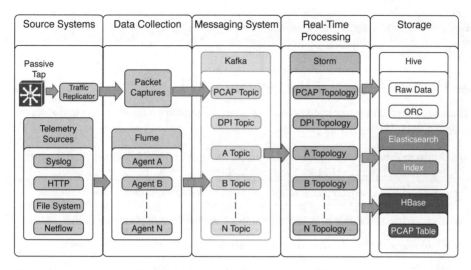

Figure 5-11   *HBase in OpenSOC*

Third-Party Analytic Tools

OpenSOC supports several third-party analytic tools such as:

■ R-based and Python-based tools

■ Power Pivot

■ Tableau

Figure 5-12 shows the complete OpenSOC architecture, including analytics tools and web services for additional search, visualizations, and packet capture (PCAP) reconstruction.

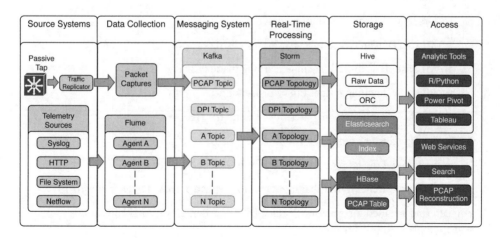

Figure 5-12   *OpenSOC Architecture*

> **Note**   You can download OpenSOC from https://github.com/OpenSOC.

Other Big Data Projects in the Industry

There are other Hadoop-related projects used in the industry for processing and visualizing big data. The following are a few examples:

- **Ambari:** A web-based tool and dashboard for provisioning, managing, and monitoring Apache Hadoop clusters.

- **Avro:** A data serialization system.

- **Cassandra:** A scalable multimaster database with no single points of failure.

- **Chukwa:** A data collection system for managing large distributed systems.

- **Mahout:** A scalable machine learning and data mining library.

- **Pig:** A high-level data-flow language and execution framework for parallel computation.

- **Spark:** A fast and general compute engine for Hadoop data.

- **Tez:** A generalized data-flow programming framework, built on Hadoop YARN.

- **ZooKeeper:** A high-performance coordination service for distributed applications.

- **Berkeley Data Analytics Stack (BDAS):** A framework created by Berkeley's AMPLabs. BDAS has a three-dimensional approach: algorithms, machines, and people. The following are the primary components of BDAS:

  - **Akaros:** An operating system for many-core architectures and large-scale SMP systems

  - **GraphX:** A large-scale graph analytics

  - **Mesos:** Dynamic resource sharing for clusters

  - **MLbase:** Distributed machine learning made easy

  - **PIQL:** Scale independent query processing

  - **Shark:** Scalable rich analytics SQL engine for Hadoop

  - **Spark:** Cluster computing framework

  - **Sparrow:** Low-latency scheduling for interactive cluster services

  - **Tachyon:** Reliable file sharing at memory speed across cluster frameworks

You can find detailed information about BDAS and Berkeley's AMPLabs at https://amplab.cs.berkeley.edu

Understanding Big Data Scalability: Big Data Analytics in the Internet of Everything

Evidently, the challenges of big data analytics include the following:

- Data capture capabilities

- Data management (curation)

- Storage

- Adequate and real-time search

- Sharing and transferring of information

- Deep-dive and automated analysis

- Adequate visualizations

Big data has become a hot topic due to the overabundance of data sources inundating today's data stores as applications proliferate. These challenges will become even bigger as the world moves to the *Internet of Everything* (IoE), a term coined by Cisco. IoE is based on the foundation of the Internet of Things (IoT) by adding network intelligence that allows convergence, orchestration, and visibility across previously disparate systems. IoT is the networked connection of physical objects. IoT is one of many technology transitions that enable the IoE.

The goal is to make networked connections more relevant by turning information into actions that create new capabilities. The IoE consists of many technology transitions, including the IoT. The key concepts are as follows:

- **Machine-to-machine connections:** Including things such as IoT sensors, remote monitoring, industrial control systems, and so on

- **People-to-people connections:** Including collaboration technologies such as TelePresence, WebEx, and so on

- **Machine-to-people connections:** Including traditional and new applications

Big data analytics for cyber security in an IoE world will require substantial engineering to address the huge data sets. Scalability will be a huge challenge. In addition, the endless variety of IoT applications presents a security operational challenge. We are starting to experience these challenges nowadays. For instance, in a factory floor, embedded programmable logic controllers (PLCs) that operate manufacturing systems and robots can be a huge target for bad actors. Do we know all the potential true indicators of compromise so that we can perform deep-dive analysis and perform good incident response?

The need to combine threat intelligence and big data analytics will be paramount in this ever-changing world.

Summary

Today, networks are becoming exponentially bigger and more complex. To maintain visibility and control of the network, many organizations are leveraging or planning to combine big data analytics with real-time, predictive analysis to detect attacks and protect against advanced malware across their networks. This combination can help security professionals address the ever-changing nature of threats that threaten their most important asset, which is data. This chapter provided an overview of the technologies and processes to use big data analytics for cyber security. NetFlow and other telemetry sources play a big role in big data analytics for cyber security. This chapter explained how you can use these telemetry sources to look for indicators of compromise in your network.

Cisco has developed and open source OpenSOC to provide a framework for big data analytics for cyber security. In this chapter, you learned the technologies and architectures used in OpenSOC and how they play a crucial role for security operations. The IoE introduces a lot of security challenges. One of the biggest challenges introduced is the ability to scale to large data sets. It is unavoidable that big data will continue to play a big role in cyber security.

Chapter 6

Cisco Cyber Threat Defense and NetFlow

This chapter covers the following topics:

- Overview of the Cisco Cyber Threat Defense Solution

- The Attack Continuum

- Deploying the Lancope StealthWatch System

- Deploying NetFlow Secure Event Logging in the Cisco ASA

- Configuring NetFlow in the Cisco Nexus 1V

- Configuring NetFlow in the Cisco Nexus 7 Series

- Configuring the Cisco NetFlow Generation Appliance

- Additional Cisco CTD Solution Components

Overview of the Cisco Cyber Threat Defense Solution

In Chapter 1, "Introduction to NetFlow and IPFIX," you learned the benefits of NetFlow and a high-level overview of Cisco's Cyber Threat Defense (CTD) Solution. Cisco has partnered with Lancope to deliver a solution that provides visibility into security threats by identifying suspicious traffic patterns in the corporate network. These suspicious patterns are then augmented with circumstantial information necessary to determine the level of threat associated with a particular incident. This solution allows a network administrator or security professional to analyze this information in a timely, efficient, and cost-effective manner for advanced cyber threats. This chapter provides a detailed coverage of Cisco CTD Solution. Before delving deeper into the details of the Cisco CTD Solution, let's go over the current threat landscape and the attack continuum.

The Attack Continuum

Defending against cyber security attacks is becoming more challenging every day, and it is not going to get any easier. The threat landscape is evolving to a faster, more effective, and more efficient criminal economy profiting from attacks against users, enterprises, services providers, and governments. The organized cyber crime and exchange of exploits is booming and fueling a very lucrative economy. Bad actors nowadays have a clear understanding of the underlying security technologies and their vulnerabilities. Hacker groups now follow software development lifecycles, just like enterprises have their own. These bad actors perform quality-assurance testing against security products before releasing them into the underground economy. They continue to find ways to evade common security defenses. Attackers follow new techniques such as the following:

- Port and protocol hopping

- Encryption

- Droppers

- Social engineering

- Zero-day attacks

Next-generation security defenses must be

- **Visibility driven:** Maintaining complete visibility gathering data from all potential attack vectors across the network fabric, endpoints (including mobile devices), email and web gateways, virtual machines in the data center, and the cloud.

- **Threat focused:** Correlating all collected information with indicators of compromise (IOC) and other contextual information for network security administrators makes better decisions and take action. Keeping up with a constantly evolving threat landscape is almost impossible. Access controls reduce the attack surface, but attackers still get through. Security technologies and solutions must focus on understanding, detecting, and blocking attacks. These solutions require continuous analysis and security intelligence delivered from the cloud and shared across all products for better effectiveness.

- **Platform based:** Security now requires an integrated system of agile and open platforms that cover the network, endpoints, users, and the cloud. These platforms must be scalable and centrally managed for device configuration consistency.

Security technologies and processes should not focus on detection, but also should provide the capability to mitigate the impact after a successful attack. Figure 6-1 illustrates the attack continuum.

Security professionals must maintain visibility and control across the extended network during the full attack continuum:

- Before the attack takes place

- During an active attack

- After an attacker starts to damage systems or steal information

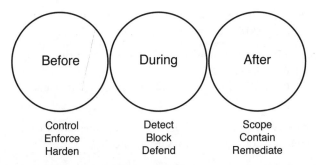

Figure 6-1 *The Attack Continuum*

Cisco next-generation security products provide protection throughout the attack continuum. NetFlow is a vital component of the first version of the Cisco CTD Solution, and continues to play a vital role in its next generation. It provides visibility capabilities that are crucial for all three parts of the attack continuum. Devices such as the Cisco ASA with FirePOWER Services available on the Cisco ASA 5500-X series and ASA 5585-X Adaptive Security Appliances and Cisco's Advanced Malware Protection (AMP) provide a security solution that help discover threats and enforce and harden policies before an attack takes place. In addition, you can detect, block, and defend against attacks that have already taken place with next-generation intrusion prevention systems (NGIPS), and email and web security appliances with AMP. These solutions provide the capabilities to contain and remediate an attack to minimize data loss and additional network degradation.

Cisco CTD Solution Components

In Chapter 1, you learned the different deployment scenarios for NetFlow. These deployment scenarios include the following:

- User access layer

- Wireless LANs

- Internet edge

- Data center

- Firewalls

- NetFlow in site-to-site and remote access virtual private networks (VPNs)

These scenarios still apply for the Cisco CTD Solution.

The Cisco CTD Solution Version 2.0 uses the following next-generation security components:

- **NetFlow and the Lancope StealthWatch System:** For broad network visibility, user and flow context analysis, and incident response and network forensics

- **Cisco FirePOWER and FireSIGHT:** For real-time threat management and deep application inspection

- **Advanced Malware Protection (AMP):** Endpoint control with AMP for endpoints and network malware control with AMP for networks

- **Content Security Appliances and Services such as the Cisco Web Security Appliance (WSA) and Cloud Web Security (CWS):** For dynamic threat control of web traffic, in addition to the Cisco Email Security Appliance (ESA) for dynamic threat control for email traffic

- **Cisco Identity Services Engine (ISE):** For user and device identity integration with Lancope StealthWatch and remediation policy actions using pxGrid

The Cisco CTD Solution supports Flexible NetFlow and NetFlow Version 9. Flexible NetFlow should be used in Cisco IOS Software for the latest technology and features for NetFlow, and should be considered for new deployments because its features allows-user configurable NetFlow record formats. In addition, Flexible NetFlow has several advantages, including tailoring a cache for specific applications not covered by NetFlow predecessor versions. Flexible NetFlow also provides better scalability, because flow record customization for particular application reduces number of flows to monitor.

Figure 6-2 shows a high-level topology of a few components of the Cisco CTD Solution.

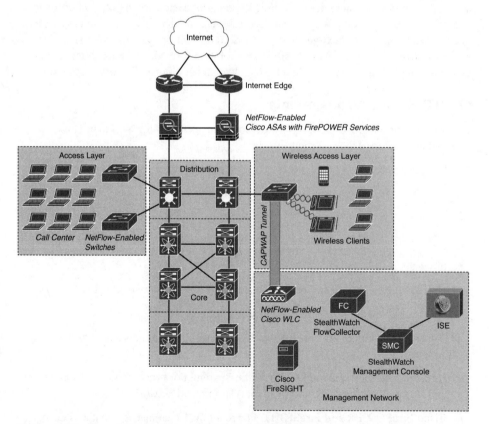

Figure 6-2 *Cisco CTD Solution High-Level Topology*

NetFlow can be enabled at many different network infrastructure devices. In Figure 6-2, access switches, wireless access points managed by the Cisco Wireless LAN Controller (WLC), and Cisco ASA 5500-X Series Next-Generation Firewalls are configured for NetFlow. Lancope's StealthWatch FlowCollector is collecting NetFlow from those devices. StealthWatch FlowCollector is a physical or virtual appliance that collects NetFlow data from infrastructure devices. The StealthWatch Management Console is deployed to provide centralized management for the StealthWatch FlowCollector appliance and provides real-time data correlation, visualization, and consolidated reporting of combined NetFlow and identity analysis.

Cisco FireSIGHT Management Center provides a centralized management and analysis platform for the Cisco NGIPS appliances and the Cisco ASA with FirePOWER Services. It provides support for role-based policy management, including a fully customizable dashboard with advanced reports and analytics.

Tip The FireSIGHT Management Center and the Cisco ASA FirePOWER module require additional licenses. These licenses are installed in the FirePOWER module itself. No additional licenses are required in the Cisco ASA itself.

The Cisco CTD Solution provides identity awareness with a direct correlation between users and specific network events. The identity data can be obtained from the StealthWatch IDentity appliance or through integration with the Cisco Identity Services Engine (ISE). StealthWatch Management Console can also process user information (usernames) within NetFlow records from Cisco ASA appliances. The integration with Cisco ISE provides a rich capability to identify the *who*, *what*, *where*, *when*, and *how* of threats that could penetrate the network.

Note The minimum requirement to perform identity capabilities is to deploy the Cisco ISE and one or more authenticating access devices in a valid Cisco TrustSec Monitoring Mode deployment.

NetFlow Platform Support

The following sections include information about the different platforms that support NetFlow.

Traditional NetFlow Support in Cisco IOS Software

Table 6-1 lists the first Cisco IOS Software release in which traditional NetFlow support was introduced in the following platforms:

- Cisco Catalyst 6500 series switches
- Cisco 7600 series routers
- Cisco 12000 series routers running Cisco IOS Software

- Cisco 10000 series routers

- Cisco Catalyst 4500 series switches

Table 6-1 *Traditional NetFlow Support in Cisco IOS Software*

NetFlow Version/Feature	Software	C6500	C7600	C12000	C10000	C4500
Version 5	12.0(1)	12.1(2)E	12.1(2)E	12.0(14)S	12.0(19)SL	12.1(13)EW
Version 8	12.0(3)T	12.2(14)SX	12.2(14)SX	12.0(6)S	12.0(19)SL	12.1(19)EW
Version 9	12.3	12.2(18)SXF	12.2(18)SXF	12.0(24)S	12.2(31)SB	Not available
Dual Export	12.2(2)T	12.2(17d)SXB	12.2(17d)SXB	Not available	12.2(15)BX	12.1(19)EW
VRF Destination	12.4(4)T	Not available	12.2(33)SRA	12.0(32)S	Not available	Not available
Reliable Export	12.3(4)T	Not available	Not available	Not available	Not available	Not available
IPv4	12.0(1)	12.1(27b)E1	12.2(18)SXF	12.0(22)S	12.2(15)BX	12.1(13)EW
IPv6	12.3(7)T	12.2(33)SXH	12.2(33)SRB	Not available	Not available	Not available
Multicast	12.3	12.2(18)SXF	12.2(18)SXF	Not available	Not available	Not available
BGP Next Hop	12.3	12.2(18)SXF	12.2(33)SRA	12.0(26)S	12.2(31)SB	Not available
Per Interface	Yes	12.2(33)SXH	12.2(33)SRB	No Sub	12.2(15)BX	Not available
Per VRF Interface	Yes	12.2(33)SXH	12.2(33)SRB			Not available
TOS Support	Yes	12.2(17b)SXA	12.2(17b)SXA	Yes	Yes	Not available
Packet Sampling	12.3(24)	Not available	Not available	12.0(11)S	12.2(31)SB	Not available
Min Prefix Aggr.	12.1(2)T	Not available	Not available	Yes	Yes	Not available
MPLS Egress with EXP	Not available	Not available	Not available	Not available	12.2(28)SB	Not available

Table 6-1 *continued*

NetFlow Version/Feature	Software	C6500	C7600	C12000	C10000	C4500
MPLS Egress	12.2(2)T	12.2(33)SXJ	Not available	Not available	Not available	Not available
MPLS Aware	12.3(8)T	Not available	12.2(33)SRA	12.0(24)S	Not available	Not available
MPLS Label Exp.	12.2SB	Not available	12.2(33)SRB	Not available	Not available	Not available
MPLS Aggregate.	Not available	Not available	Not available	Not available	12.2(31)SB	Not available

NetFlow Support in Cisco IOS-XR Software

Table 6-2 lists the first Cisco IOS-XR release in which traditional NetFlow support was introduced in the following platforms:

■ Cisco Carrier Routing System (CRS-X)

■ Cisco 12000 series routers running Cisco IOS Software

■ Cisco ASR 9000 series Aggregation Services Routers

Table 6-2 *NetFlow Support in Cisco IOS-XR Software*

NetFlow Version/Feature	CRS-X	XR-12000	ASR 9000
Version 5	Not supported		
Version 8	Not supported		
Version 9	3.2	3.3.0	4.1
Dual Export	3.4.0	3.4.0	4.1
VRF Destination	3.2	3.3.0	4.1

Flexible NetFlow Support

Table 6-3 lists the first Cisco IOS Software or Cisco IOS-XE Software release in which Flexible NetFlow support was introduced, along with the respective feature, in the following platforms:

■ Cisco Integrated Services Routers

■ Cisco Integrated Services Routers Generation 2 (G2)

■ Cisco 7200 series and Cisco 7300 series routers

■ Cisco ASR 1000 series Aggregation Services Routers

Table 6-3 *Flexible NetFlow Support in ISR, ISR-G2, 7200 Series, 7300 Series, and Cisco ASR 1000 Series Aggregation Services Routers*

Feature	Cisco ISR	Cisco ISR-G2	Cisco 7200 Series Cisco 7300 Series	ASR 1000
New Flexible NetFlow CLI	12.4(9)T	15.0(1)M	12.4(9)T	IOS XE 3.1.1S
Multiple User-Defined Caches	12.4(9)T	15.0(1)M	12.4(9)T	IOS XE 3.1.1S
User-Defined Flow Record	12.4(9)T	15.0(1)M	12.4(9)T	IOS XE 3.1.1S
Normal Cache	12.4(9)T	15.0(1)M	12.4(9)T	IOS XE 3.1.1S
Immediate Cache	12.4(9)T	15.0(1)M	12.4(9)T	IOS XE 3.8.0S
Permanent Cache	12.4(9)T	15.0(1)M	12.4(9)T	IOS XE 3.9.0S
Dynamic TopNTalkers	12.4(22)T	15.0(1)M	12.4(22)T	Not available
FNF EEM Monitor	12.4(22)T	15.0(1)M	12.4(22)T	Not available
Full Flow Support	12.4(9)T	15.0(1)M	12.4(9)T	IOS XE 3.1.1S
Random Sampling 1:M	12.4(9)T	15.0(1)M	12.4(9)T	IOS XE 3.1.1S
NetFlow v5 Export Format	12.4(22)T	15.0(1)M	12.4(22)T	IOS XE 3.1.1S
NetFlow v9 Export Format	12.4(9)T	15.0(1)M	12.4(9)T	IOS XE 3.1.1S
IPFIX Export Format	Not available	15.3(1)T	Not available	IOS XE 3.7.0S
Export over UDP	12.4(9)T	15.0(1)M	12.4(9)T	IOS XE 3.1.1S
Export over IPv6	Not available	15.2(2)T	Not available	IOS XE 3.7.0S
Export in a VRF	12.4(9)T	15.0(1)M	12.4(9)T	IOS XE 3.2.0S
FNF QOS Output Features	12.4(20)T	15.0(1)M	12.4(20)T	IOS XE 3.1.1S
Ingress Support	12.4(9)T	15.0(1)M	12.4(9)T	IOS XE 3.1.1S
Egress Support	12.4(9)T	15.0(1)M	12.4(9)T	IOS XE 3.1.1S
Per Interface	12.4(9)T	15.0(1)M	12.4(9)T	IOS XE 3.1.1S
Per Subinterface	12.4(9)T	15.0(1)M	12.4(9)T	IOS XE 3.1.1S
On VRF Interface	12.4(9)T	15.0(1)M	12.4(9)T	IOS XE 3.1.1S
IPv6 Unicast Flows	12.4(20)T	15.0(1)M	12.4(20)T	IOS XE 3.3.0S
IPv6 Predefined Aggregations	12.4(20)T	15.0(1)M	12.4(20)T	IOS XE 3.3.0S

Table 6-3 *continued*

Feature	Cisco ISR	Cisco ISR-G2	Cisco 7200 Series Cisco 7300 Series	ASR 1000
IPv6 Multicast Flows	12.4(22)T	15.0(1)M	15.0(1)M	Not available
IPv6 Header Section Field	12.4(20)T	15.0(1)M	12.4(20)T	IOS XE 3.3.0S
IPv6 Payload Section Field	12.4(20)T	15.0(1)M	12.4(20)T	IOS XE 3.3.0S
UDP Fields	12.4(20)T	15.0(1)M	12.4(20)T	IOS XE 3.3.0S
TCP Fields	12.4(20)T	15.0(1)M	12.4(20)T	IOS XE 3.3.0S
Application Name (NBAR) Field	Not available	15.2(1)T	Not available	IOS XE 3.1.1S

Table 6-4 lists the first Cisco IOS-XE Software release in which Flexible NetFlow support was introduced, along with the respective feature, in the following platforms:

- Cisco Integrated Services Routers 4400 series
- Cisco Cloud Services Router (CSR) 1000V series

Table 6-4 *Flexible NetFlow Support in the Cisco ISR 4400 Series and the Cisco CSR 1000V Series*

Feature	ISR-4400	CSR-1000V
New Flexible NetFlow CLI	IOS XE 3.8.0S	IOS XE 3.9.0S
Multiple User-Defined Caches	IOS XE 3.8.0S	IOS XE 3.9.0S
User-Defined Flow Record	IOS XE 3.8.0S	IOS XE 3.9.0S
Normal Cache	IOS XE 3.8.0S	IOS XE 3.9.0S
Immediate Cache	IOS XE 3.8.0S	IOS XE 3.9.0S
Permanent Cache	IOS XE 3.9.0S	IOS XE 3.9.0S
Dynamic TopNTalkers	IOS XE 3.12.0S	IOS XE 3.12.0S
FNF EEM Monitor	IOS XE 3.13.0S	IOS XE 3.13.0S
Full Flow Support	IOS XE 3.8.0S	IOS XE 3.9.0S
Random Sampling 1:M Activation	IOS XE 3.8.0S	IOS XE 3.9.0S
Ingress Support	IOS XE 3.8.0S	IOS XE 3.9.0S
Egress Support	IOS XE 3.8.0S	IOS XE 3.9.0S

Table 6-4   *continued*

Feature	ISR-4400	CSR-1000V
Per Interface	IOS XE 3.8.0S	IOS XE 3.9.0S
Per Subinterface	IOS XE 3.8.0S	IOS XE 3.9.0S
On VRF Interface	IOS XE 3.8.0S	IOS XE 3.9.0S
Exporter		
NetFlow v5 Export Format	IOS XE 3.8.0S	IOS XE 3.9.0S
NetFlow v9 Export Format	IOS XE 3.8.0S	IOS XE 3.9.0S
IPFix Export Format	IOS XE 3.8.0S	IOS XE 3.9.0S
Export over UDP	IOS XE 3.8.0S	IOS XE 3.9.0S
Export over IPv4	IOS XE 3.8.0S	IOS XE 3.9.0S
Export over IPv6	IOS XE 3.8.0S	IOS XE 3.9.0S
Exporter MTU Configuration	IOS XE 3.11.0S	IOS XE 3.11.0S
Export in a VRF	IOS XE 3.8.0S	IOS XE 3.9.0S
FNF QOS Output Features	IOS XE 3.8.0S	IOS XE 3.9.0S
IPv6 Flows		
IPv6 Unicast Flows	IOS XE 3.8.0S	IOS XE 3.9.0S
IPv6 Predefined Aggregations	IOS XE 3.8.0S	IOS XE 3.9.0S
IPv6 Header Section Field	IOS XE 3.8.0S	IOS XE 3.9.0S
IPv6 Payload Section Field	IOS XE 3.8.0S	IOS XE 3.9.0S
UDP Fields	IOS XE 3.8.0S	IOS XE 3.9.0S
TCP Fields	IOS XE 3.8.0S	IOS XE 3.9.0S
Application Name (NBAR) Field	IOS XE 3.8.0S	IOS XE 3.9.0S

Table 6-5 lists the first Cisco NX-OS Software release in which Flexible NetFlow support was introduced, along with the respective feature, in the following platforms:

■ Cisco Nexus 7000 series switches

■ Cisco Nexus 1000V

Table 6-5   *Flexible NetFlow Support in the Cisco Nexus 7000 Series Switches and the Cisco Nexus 1000V*

Feature	Nexus 7000	Nexus 1000V
New Flexible NetFlow CLI	4.0	4.0(4)SV1
Multiple User Defined Caches	4.0	4.0(4)SV1

Table 6-5 *continued*

Feature	Nexus 7000	Nexus 1000V
User Defined Flow Record	4.0	Not available
Normal Cache	4.0	4.0(4)SV1
Immediate Cache	Not available	Not available
Permanent Cache	Not available	Not available
Dynamic TopNTalkers	Not available	Not available
FNF EEM Monitor	Not available	Not available
Full Flow Support	4.0	4.0(4)SV1
Random Sampling 1:M	4.0	4.0(4)SV1
Random Sampling N:M	4.0	4.0(4)SV1
Activation		
Ingress Support	4.0	4.0(4)SV1
Egress Support	4.0	4.0(4)SV1
Per Interface	4.0	4.0(4)SV1
Per Subinterface	4.0	Not available
Exporter		
NetFlow v5 Export Format	4.0	4.0(4)SV1
NetFlow v9 Export Format	4.0	4.0(4)SV1
Export over UDP	4.0	4.0(4)SV1
Export over IPv4	4.0	4.0(4)SV1
Export over IPv6	4.2(1)	Not available
FNF QOS Output Features	4.0	Not available
IPv6 Flows		
IPv6 Unicast Flows	4.0	Not available
IPv6 Predefined Aggregations	4.0	Not available
IPv6 Multicast Flows	Not available	Not available
IPv6 Multicast Replication Factor	Not available	Not available
IPv6 Header Section Field	Not available	Not available
IPv6 Payload Section Field	Not available	Not available
UDP Fields	4.0	Not available
TCP Fields	4.0	Not available

NetFlow Support in Cisco ASA

The Cisco ASA supports NetFlow Version 9 services with the NetFlow Secure Event Logging (NSEL) feature. NetFlow support was originally introduced in Cisco ASA Software Version 8.1(1). NetFlow filtering was introduced in 8.1(2) and the Cisco ASA NSEL feature was introduced in 8.2(1).

Deploying the Lancope StealthWatch System

Cisco has partnered with Lancope to deliver this solution. The Lancope StealthWatch System, available from Cisco, aggregates and normalizes considerable amounts of NetFlow data to apply security analytics to detect malicious and suspicious activity. The StealthWatch Management Console provides a rich graphical unit interface (GUI) with many visualizations and telemetry information.

Figure 6-3 shows an example of the many visualizations and reports that can be obtained in the StealthWatch Management Console.

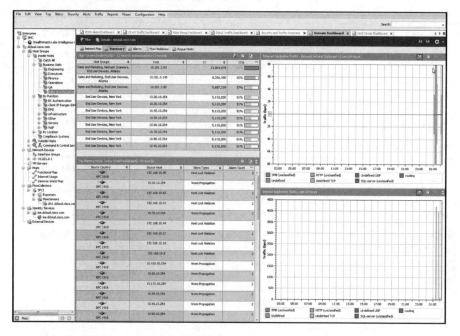

Figure 6-3   *The StealthWatch Management Console Domain Dashboard*

Figure 6-3 shows the Summary tab of the Domain Dashboard. A host (10.201.3.83) has been classified as a high concern host in the inside network. This host belongs to the Sales and Marketing host group in Atlanta. The Concern Index (CI) is a counter that accumulates as a host performs suspicious activity. The higher the number, the more suspicious activity the host has performed. The CI% is an indication of how far this host has deviated from baseline activity for its host group. In Figure 6-3, you can also see that several hosts in the 192.168.10.0 network have generated additional network alarms.

Figure 6-4 shows the StealthWatch Management Console DDoS Traffic Dashboard.

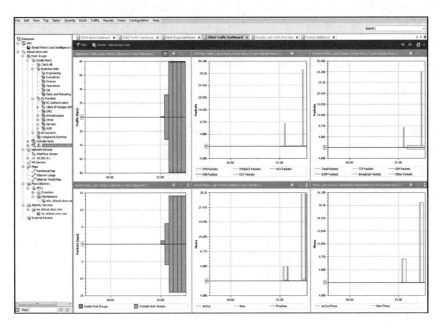

Figure 6-4 *The StealthWatch Management Console DDoS Traffic Dashboard*

The Cisco ISE provides detailed user and device information to Lancope StealthWatch. Figure 6-5 shows the StealthWatch Management Console Identity and Device Table.

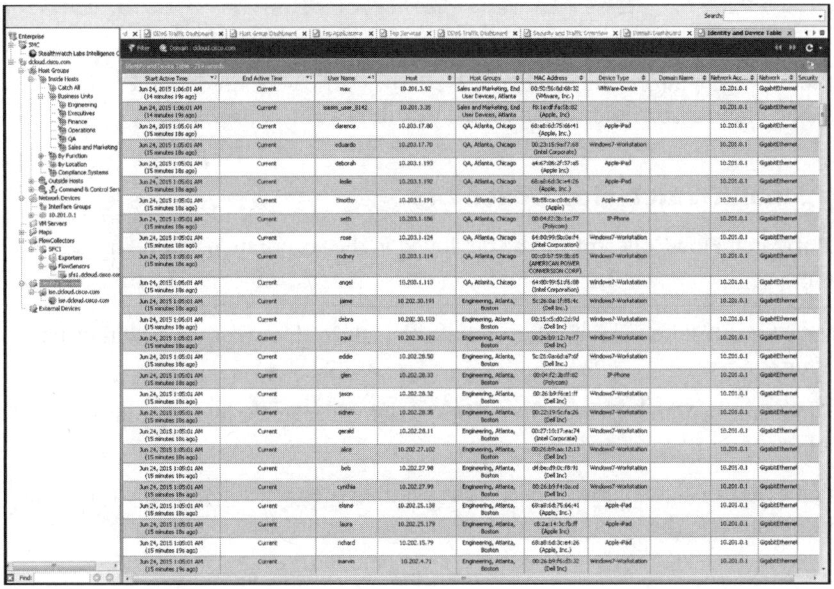

Figure 6-5 *The StealthWatch Management Console Identity and Device Table*

In Figure 6-5, you can see detailed information of active hosts in the inside network, along with the username of the actual user, MAC address identification, the router interface that observed such flow, and the start and end active time, in addition to other connection details.

The following are the primary components of the Lancope StealthWatch System:

- **FlowCollector:** A physical or virtual appliance that collects NetFlow data from infrastructure devices.

- **StealthWatch Management Console:** Used to manage the rest of the Lancope StealthWatch solution.

- **Flow licenses:** Required to aggregate flows at the StealthWatch Management Console. Flow licenses define the volume of flows that may be collected.

The following are optional components of the Lancope StealthWatch System:

- **FlowSensor:** A physical or virtual appliance that can generate NetFlow data when legacy Cisco network infrastructure components are not capable of producing line-rate, unsampled NetFlow data. Alternatively, the Cisco NGA can be used.

- **FlowReplicator:** A physical appliance used to forward NetFlow data as a single data stream to other devices.

Note   For the most up-to-date information about the support in each StealthWatch FlowCollector and FlowSensor appliance models and their specifications, go to Lancope's website at http://lancope.com.

Like all NetFlow generators, the volume of NetFlow traffic generated by the StealthWatch FlowSensor varies based on the monitored traffic profile.

Deploying StealthWatch FlowCollectors

The StealthWatch FlowCollector can be deployed in the corporate network in several ways:

- A single StealthWatch FlowCollector collecting all NetFlow data in a centralized location

- Multiple StealthWatch FlowCollector behind a load balancer in a centralized location

- Multiple StealthWatch FlowCollectors at multiple sites (usually placed close to the source producing the highest number of NetFlow records)

Tip NetFlow collection should be done as close to the NetFlow generator as possible to minimize network bandwidth and overhead impact. In an asymmetric routing situation, all devices in the asymmetric route should send NetFlow records to the same FlowCollector.

Figure 6-6 shows a topology example where a single StealthWatch FlowCollector is deployed collecting all NetFlow data from switches, a router, and a Cisco ASA in a centralized location.

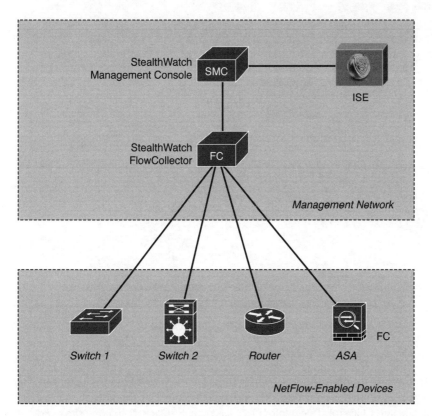

Figure 6-6 *Single StealthWatch FlowCollector Deployment*

Figure 6-7 shows an example topology where three StealthWatch FlowCollectors are deployed behind a load balancer. For example, you can deploy the Citrix NetScaler 1000V on demand, anywhere in the data center, using the Cisco Nexus 1100 Series Cloud Services Platform (CSP) or running as a virtual appliance on VMWare ESXi or KVM. When running on KVM, you can integrate it with OpenStack using the Cisco Prime Network Services Controller. This load-balancing solution will help you scale your StealthWatch FlowCollectors (or any other collectors) more efficiently in your environment.

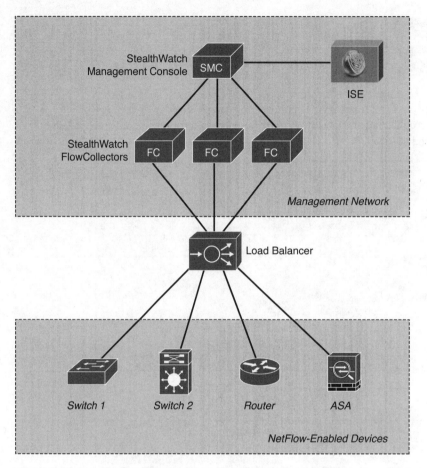

Figure 6-7 *StealthWatch FlowCollectors Behind a Load Balancer*

Figure 6-8 shows an example topology where three StealthWatch FlowCollectors are deployed in a distributed way, with one StealthWatch FlowCollector at each site (New York, Raleigh, and Chicago). This deployment has the advantage of limiting the overhead introduced by NetFlow.

If you have multiple geographically located sites, pay attention to bandwidth limitations between sites. As a best practice, a single FlowCollector should be used for as much related traffic as possible. However, the benefits of centralized collection diminish when the traffic is not similar.

Another best practice is that all NetFlow records belonging to a flow should be sent to the same StealthWatch FlowCollector. Duplicate NetFlow records can be a problem when trying to respond to an incident or analyze traffic patterns. StealthWatch FlowCollectors have a deduplication feature where it guarantees that the flow data is stored properly, while preserving the details about each flow exporter and eliminating the reporting of inflated traffic volumes.

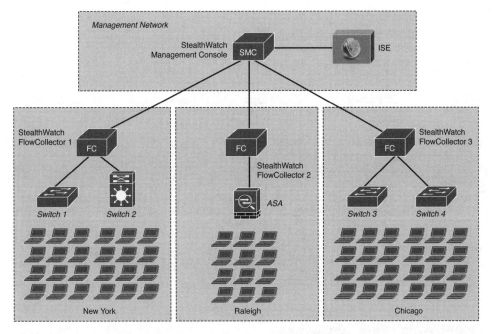

Figure 6-8 *StealthWatch FlowCollectors in Multiple Geographically Dispersed Locations*

When deploying StealthWatch FlowCollectors, you should consider several factors:

- The number of NetFlow generation devices (exporter count).

- The rate of flows per second (fps) that is expected to be received.

- The number of hosts (both inside and outside the network) for which the collector can maintain state. As a best practice, the number of inside hosts should not exceed 60 percent of the host count value.

- The amount of flow data to be stored.

StealthWatch FlowCollectors come in two different form factors: appliances and virtual edition (VE). Table 6-6 lists the different StealthWatch FlowCollector appliances and high-level specifications.

Table 6-6 *StealthWatch FlowCollector Appliances*

Model	Supported Flows per Second	Exporters	Hosts	Storage
StealthWatch FlowCollector 1000	Up to 30,000	Up to 500	Up to 250,000	1.0 TB
StealthWatch FlowCollector 2000	Up to 60,000	Up to 1000	Up to 500,000	2.0 TB
StealthWatch FlowCollector 3000	Up to 120,000	Up to 2000	Up to 1,000,000	4.0 TB

Table 6-7 lists the StealthWatch FlowCollector VE high-level specifications depending on the amount of memory and the number of virtual CPUs.

Table 6-7   *StealthWatch FlowCollector VE*

Number of CPUs	Memory	Exporters	Hosts	Flows per Second
2	4 GB	Up to 250	Up to 125,000	Up to 4500
3	8 GB	Up to 500	Up to 250,000	Up to 15,000
4	16 GB	Up to 1000	Up to 500,000	Up to 22,500
5	32 GB	Up to 1000	Up to 500,000	Up to 30,000

Note   As mentioned earlier in the chapter, for the most up-to-date information about the support in each StealthWatch FlowCollector appliance models and their specifications, go to Lancope's website at http://lancope.com.

StealthWatch FlowReplicators

The StealthWatch FlowReplicator is an optional component of the Cisco CTD Solution. The StealthWatch FlowCollector exists as a physical or virtual appliance. The StealthWatch FlowReplicator supports Cisco NetFlow, IPFIX, and other vendors' flow data. It combines multiple capabilities into a single device to streamline the collection and distribution of network and security data across the corporate network.

Figure 6-9 shows an example topology where the StealthWatch FlowReplicator (FR) is deployed collecting NetFlow, IPFIX, and syslog data from multiple devices in the network.

In Figure 6-9, the StealthWatch FR sends all NetFlow data to the StealthWatch FlowCollector 1 and all IPFIX data to the StealthWatch FlowCollector 2.

The StealthWatch FR can receive data from any connectionless UDP application and syslog messages and then replicate those to network analysis systems. In addition, StealthWatch FR can process Simple Network Management Protocol (SNMP) traps from network infrastructure devices and distribute them to several different SNMP management stations.

StealthWatch Management Console

The StealthWatch Management Console manages, coordinates, and configures all StealthWatch appliances, including the StealthWatch FlowCollector and the StealthWatch FlowReplicator. It is designed to correlate network intelligence across the corporate network primarily using NetFlow. The StealthWatch Management Console can also be configured with the Cisco ISE to receive authenticated session information to correlate flow and identity. The StealthWatch Management Console comes in two different form factors (just like the StealthWatch FlowCollectors): appliances and virtual edition (VE). Table 6-8 lists the different StealthWatch Management Console appliances and high-level specifications.

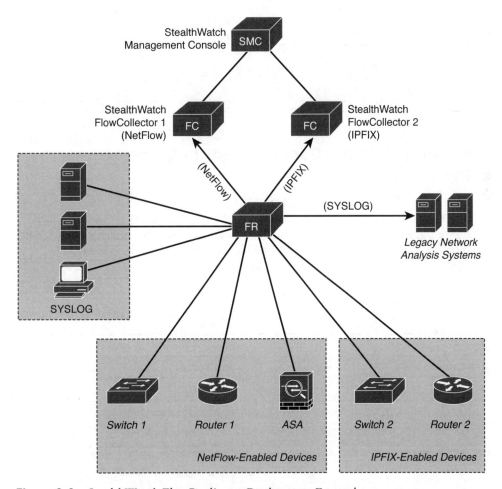

Figure 6-9 *StealthWatch FlowReplicator Deployment Example*

Table 6-8 *StealthWatch Management Console Appliances*

Model	Storage	Memory	Supported FlowCollectors
StealthWatch Management Console 1000	1 TB	8 GB	5
StealthWatch Management Console 2000	2 TB	16 GB	25

Table 6-9 lists the StealthWatch Management Console VE high-level specifications depending on the amount of memory and the number of virtual CPUs.

Table 6-9 *StealthWatch Management Console VE*

Number of CPUs	Memory	Concurrent Users	Supported FlowCollectors
2	4 GB	2	1
3	8 GB	5	3
4	16 GB	10	5

Deploying NetFlow Secure Event Logging in the Cisco ASA

The Cisco ASA family comes in many shapes and sizes, but they all provide a similar set of features. Typically, the smaller the number of the model represents a smaller capacity for throughput. The main standalone appliance model number begins with a 55, but there are also devices in the Cisco ASA family that go into a switch, such as a 6500. Table 6-10 describes the various models of the ASA.

Table 6-10 *Cisco ASA Models*

Cisco ASA 5500 Series Models	Usage
Cisco ASA 5505	Small offices and branch offices
Cisco ASA 5506-X	Small offices and branch offices
Cisco ASA 5510	Small offices and branch offices
Cisco ASA 5512-X	Small offices and branch offices
Cisco ASA 5515-X	Small offices and branch offices
Cisco ASA 5520	Medium-sized offices Internet-edge security appliances
Cisco ASA 5525-X	Medium-sized offices Internet-edge security appliances
Cisco ASA 5540	Medium-sized offices Internet-edge security appliances

Table 6-10 *continued*

Cisco ASA 5500 Series Models	Usage
Cisco ASA 5545-X	Medium-sized offices
	Internet-edge security appliances
Cisco ASA 5550	Large enterprise
	Internet-edge security appliances
Cisco ASA 5555-X	Medium-sized offices
	Internet-edge security appliances
Cisco ASA 5585-X	Data center and large enterprise networks
Cisco ASA Services Module	Data center and large enterprise networks
Cisco ASAv	Virtual ASA used in many different environments

The Cisco ASA NetFlow implementation is also known as NetFlow Secure Event Logging (NSEL). The Cisco ASA supports NetFlow Version 9. NSEL provides a stateful IP flow tracking method that exports only those records that indicate significant events in a flow.

The following are the significant flow events that are tracked:

- Flow create

- Flow teardown

- Flow denied

- Flow update (provide periodic byte counters over the duration of the flow)

Note   The flow-denied events do not support flows that are denied by EtherType access control lists (ACLs). The flow-update events were introduced in Cisco ASA Software Versions 8.4(5) and 9.1(2).

The Cisco ASA NSEL events are typically time driven (similar to traditional NetFlow). However, these events may also be triggered by state changes in the flow.

All NSEL records generated by the Cisco ASA have an Event ID and an Extended Event ID field, which are used to describe the flow event.

Figure 6-10 lists the Cisco ASA NSEL major functions.

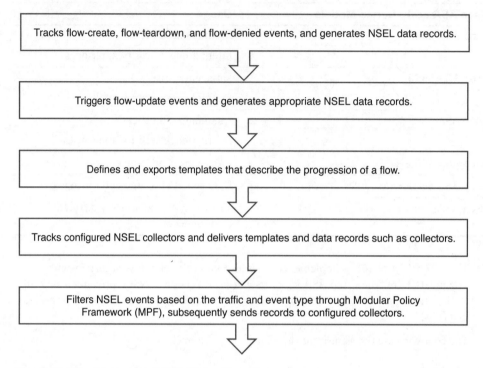

Tracks flow-create, flow-teardown, and flow-denied events, and generates NSEL data records.

Triggers flow-update events and generates appropriate NSEL data records.

Defines and exports templates that describe the progression of a flow.

Tracks configured NSEL collectors and delivers templates and data records such as collectors.

Filters NSEL events based on the traffic and event type through Modular Policy Framework (MPF), subsequently sends records to configured collectors.

Figure 6-10   *Cisco ASA NSEL Major Functions*

NSEL templates describe the format of the data records that are exported by the Cisco ASA. Each NSEL event can have several record formats or templates associated with it.

You can filter NSEL events using the Cisco ASA MPF; the traffic to be filtered or collected is matched based on the order in which classes are configured. It is important to remember that after a match is found, no other classes are checked.

NSEL records can be sent to different collectors, as illustrated in Figure 6-11.

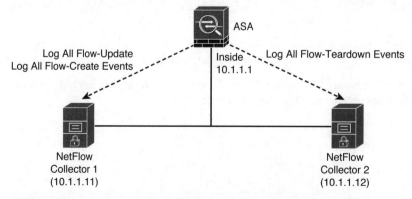

Figure 6-11   *Cisco ASA with Multiple NetFlow Collectors*

In Figure 6-11, a Cisco ASA is configured to send NSEL records to two different NetFlow collectors. In this configuration, the Cisco ASA sends all flow-create and flow-update events to Collector 1 and all flow-teardown events to Collector 2.

Deploying NSEL in Cisco ASA Configured for Clustering

You can configure multiple Cisco ASAs in a cluster. In each cluster, you can combine up to 16 Cisco ASAs into a single traffic processing system. Unlike in failover, each unit of a Cisco ASA cluster actively forwards transit traffic in both the single and multiple context modes; you do not need to artificially separate transit traffic as with active/active failover. Adjacent switches and routers load balance traffic between available cluster members via a cluster-spanned EtherChannel or IP routing.

Figure 6-12 illustrates a cluster with six Cisco ASAs.

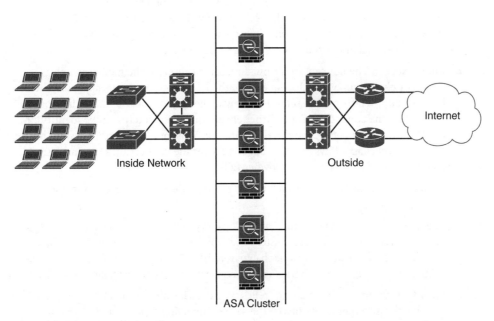

Figure 6-12 *Cisco ASA Cluster*

Any cluster member can fail at any given time without impacting transit traffic or disrupting other cluster units. Each unit always maintains a backup of each stateful connection entry on a different physical ASA. A cluster remains operational when two or more members fail at the same time, but some connections may have to reestablish. You configure and monitor the entire cluster from a single member (including NSEL). The configuration automatically replicates to all other units.

Unit Roles and Functions in Clustering

Unlike with failover, you do not have to make any special role designations when creating a cluster. All operational cluster members forward traffic at all times, but each of them plays one or more dynamic roles:

- **Master and slave units:** Cisco ASA cluster elects one member as the master; all other members become slaves. Similarly to failover, you typically configure clustering on one Cisco ASA and add other units later. That first unit becomes the master and remains in this role until it reloads or fails; you can also manually transition another unit into the master role with the **cluster master unit** command.

- **Flow owner:** A single cluster member must process all packets that belong to a single connection. This ensures symmetry for proper state tracking. For each connection, one unit in the cluster becomes the flow owner. Each cluster member may own some flows. Typically, the unit that receives the first packet for a connection becomes its owner. If the original owner fails while a connection is still active, another unit assumes the ownership of that flow. Typically, any unit receiving a packet for an existing connection with no owner becomes its flow owner. A flow owner always maintains the full stateful connection entry.

- **Flow director:** The concept of a flow director is central to the high-availability aspect of clustering. For each connection, the flow director always maintains the backup stateful information record. A flow owner periodically updates the flow director on the connection state. Other cluster members determine the identity of the flow owner by contacting the flow director. This mechanism of persistent backup flow ownership allows another unit to recover the connection state and assume its ownership if the original flow owner fails.

  Each cluster member knows which unit is the flow director for every possible transit connection.

  The flow director maintains a stub connection entry with a limited set of stateful information. This approach enables a cluster to scale much higher in terms of the maximum connection count. If the flow owner happens to be the flow director for the same connection, another unit creates a backup stub connection entry to maintain high availability.

- **Flow forwarder:** Because a cluster relies on external stateless load balancing, it is possible for different directions of the same connection to land on different units. And because the flow owner must process all packets that belong to a single connection, other units must forward such asymmetrically received packets to the correct owner. A cluster member who receives a non-TCP-SYN packet for an unknown connection queries the respective flow director to determine whether the owner exists.

Clustering NSEL Operations

In a cluster, each Cisco ASA establishes its own connection to the collectors and also manages and advertises its template independently. The fields in the header of the export packet include the following:

- System uptime
- UNIX time that is synchronized across the cluster

These fields are all local to an individual ASA. NetFlow collectors use the combination of the source IP address and source port of the packet to separate different exporters.

> **Note**   The Cisco ASA supports in-cluster upgrades. Cisco ASAs that are participants in a cluster may run different software versions at a certain point in time. Subsequently, the template that each Cisco ASA supports may be different.

Configuring NSEL in the Cisco ASA

The following section includes step-by-step guidance on how to configure NSEL in the Cisco ASA using the Adaptive Security Device Manager (ASDM) and the command-line interface (CLI). The topology in Figure 6-13 is used in the following examples.

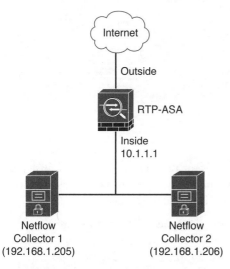

Figure 6-13   *Configuring NSEL in the Cisco ASA*

Figure 6-13 shows the topology of an office in the Research Triangle Park (RTP) in North Carolina. A Cisco ASA is configured with two NetFlow collectors.

Configuring NSEL in the Cisco ASA Using ASDM

In this section, you learn how to configure NSEL in the Cisco ASA. Complete the following steps to configure NSEL in the Cisco ASA using ASDM:

Step 1.   Log in to ASDM and navigate to **Configuration > Device Management > Logging > NetFlow**, as illustrated in Figure 6-14.

Step 2.   Enter the template timeout rate (in minutes). This is the time at which template records are sent to all configured collectors. In this example, the default value is configured (30 minutes).

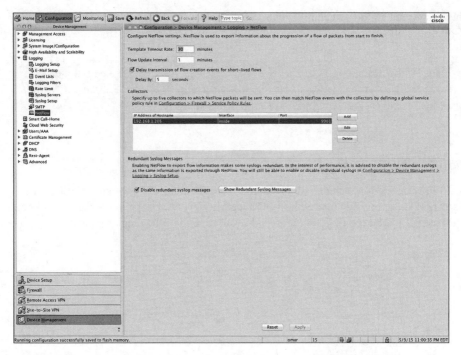

Figure 6-14   *NetFlow Configuration in ASDM*

Step 3.   Enter the flow update interval, which is the time interval between flow-update events. You can configure the flow update interval from 1 to 60 minutes. In this example, the default value is configured (1 minute).

Step 4.   You can configure the Cisco ASA to delay the export of flow-creation events and process a single flow-teardown event instead of a flow-creation event and a flow-teardown event. To do so, check the **Delay Export of Flow Creation Events for Short-Lived Flows** checkbox. In this example, the number of seconds for the delay in the Delay By field is configured to 5 seconds.

Step 5.   You can configure a maximum of five NetFlow collectors. In this example, a NetFlow collector with the IP address 192.168.1.205 is already configured in the inside interface and using UDP port 9901. Let's add a second collector. To configure a collector, click **Add**. The Add NetFlow Collector dialog box will open, as shown in Figure 6-15.

Step 6.   From the drop-down menu, choose the interface to which NetFlow packets will be sent. The inside interface is selected in this example.

Step 7.   Enter the IP address or hostname and the UDP port number in the respective fields. The IP address of the new collector is 192.168.1.206 and the UDP port is 9901.

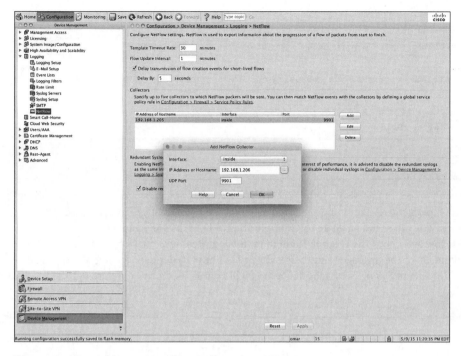

Figure 6-15 *Adding a NetFlow Collector in ASDM*

Step 8.   Click **OK**.

Step 9.   Click **Apply** to apply the changes to the Cisco ASA configuration.

Step 10. Click **Save** to save the configuration.

Configuring NSEL in the Cisco ASA Using the CLI

Example 6-1 demonstrates how to configure NSEL using the CLI.

Example 6-1 *Configuring NSEL Using the CLI*

```
! Log in to the ASA and use the enable command to enter in privilege mode
rtp-asa> enable
Password: ****************
!
! Use the configure terminal command to enter in configuration mode
rtp-asa# configure terminal
!
! Adding a collector (192.168.1.205) and specifying UDP port 9901 for NSEL communi-
  cation.
rtp-asa(config)# flow-export destination inside 192.168.1.205 9901
```

```
!
! Configuring the flow-export delay to 5 seconds.
rtp-asa(config)# flow-export delay flow-create 5
!
! Finishing the configuration and using the write memory command to save the
! configuration in the Cisco ASA.
rtp-asa(config)# end
rtp-asa# write memory
```

NSEL and Syslog

When you configure NSEL in the Cisco ASA, several syslog messages become redundant. It is recommended that you disable all redundant syslog messages. To disable all redundant syslog messages, navigate to **Configuration > Device Management > Logging > NetFlow** and check the **Disable Redundant Syslog Messages** check box. To display the redundant syslog messages and their status, click **Show Redundant Syslog Messages** and the Redundant Syslog Messages dialog box will appear, as shown in Figure 6-16.

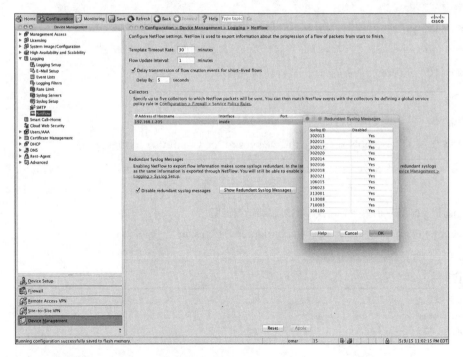

Figure 6-16   *Disabling Redundant Syslog Messages*

Click **OK** to close this dialog box and **Apply** to apply the changes to the Cisco ASA configuration.

Example 6-2 demonstrates how to disable the redundant syslog messages using the CLI.

Example 6-2   *Disabling Redundant Syslog Messages Using the CLI*

```
rtp-asa(config)# no logging message 106015
rtp-asa(config)# no logging message 313001
rtp-asa(config)# no logging message 313008
rtp-asa(config)# no logging message 106023
rtp-asa(config)# no logging message 710003
rtp-asa(config)# no logging message 106100
rtp-asa(config)# no logging message 302015
rtp-asa(config)# no logging message 302014
rtp-asa(config)# no logging message 302013
rtp-asa(config)# no logging message 302018
rtp-asa(config)# no logging message 302017
rtp-asa(config)# no logging message 302016
rtp-asa(config)# no logging message 302021
rtp-asa(config)# no logging message 302020
```

Defining the NSEL Export Policy

The Cisco ASA does not send NetFlow (NSEL) packets to any configured collectors until you classify the traffic type it should be monitoring to generate the NetFlow events. For example, if you want it to monitor all traffic for NetFlow exports, specify a global policy that analyzes all traffic. NetFlow export policy is constructed via the MPF, as previously mentioned in this chapter. Follow these steps to successfully configure an export policy in ASDM:

Step 1.   Navigate to **Configuration > Firewall > Service Policy Rules**, select the **inspection_default policy**, and then choose **Add > Insert After**. ASDM launches an Add Service Policy Rule Wizard.

Step 2.   Click the **Global – Applies to All Interfaces** radio button, as shown in Figure 6-17.

Step 3.   Click **Next**.

Step 4.   Under Create a New Traffic Class, specify a traffic class name of **NetFlow**. Check the **Any Traffic** check box as the traffic match criteria, as shown in Figure 6-18.

Step 5.   Click **Next**.

Step 6.   Under Rule Actions, navigate to the NetFlow tab and click **Add**. A new window opens where you can specify the flow event type, as shown in Figure 6-19.

Step 7.   Select **All** and check the **Send** check box next to the collector's IP address. The collector that was previously configured is displayed.

Step 8.   Click **OK** and then click **Finish** to complete defining a NetFlow export policy.

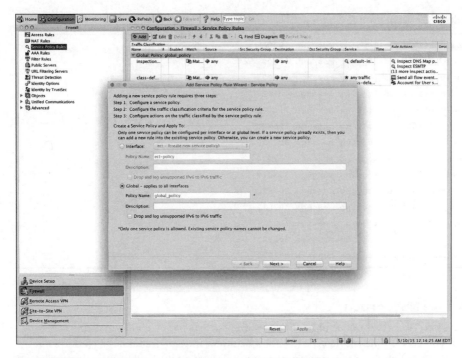

Figure 6-17   *Applying the Global Policy to All Interfaces*

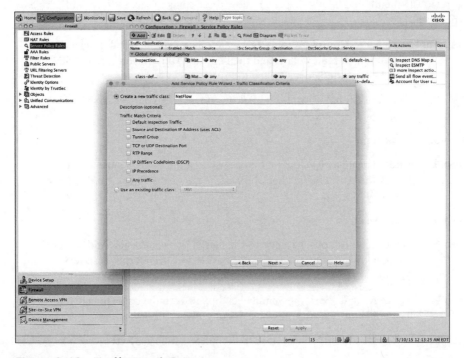

Figure 6-18   *Traffic Match Criteria*

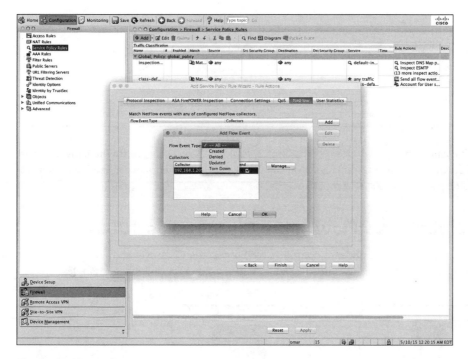

Figure 6-19 *Rule Actions*

Example 6-3 demonstrates how to define the NSEL export policy using the CLI.

Example 6-3 *Defining an NSEL Export Policy*

```
rtp-asa(config)# class-map NetFlow
rtp-asa(config-cmap)# match any
rtp-asa(config-cmap)# policy-map global_policy
rtp-asa(config-pmap)# class NetFlow
rtp-asa(config-pmap-c)# flow-export event-type all destination 192.168.1.205
```

Monitoring NSEL

You can use syslog messages to troubleshoot errors or monitor system usage and performance. You can use the **show flow-export counters** command to display flow export
counters, including statistical data and error data, as demonstrated in Example 6-4.

Example 6-4 show flow-export counters *Command Output*

```
rtp-asa# show flow-export counters
destination: inside 192.168.1.205 9901
  Statistics:
    packets sent                                    348392
```

```
Errors:
  block allocation failure                              0
  invalid interface                                     0
  template send failure                                 0
  no route to collector                                 0
  failed to get lock on block                           0
  source port allocation failure                        0
```

You can list all syslog messages that are captured by NSEL events with the **show logging flow-export-syslogs** command. You can use the **show running-config logging** command to display disabled syslog messages.

Configuring NetFlow in the Cisco Nexus 1000V

This section describes how to configure NetFlow in the Cisco Nexus 1000V virtual switch. The topology illustrated in Figure 6-20 is used in the following examples.

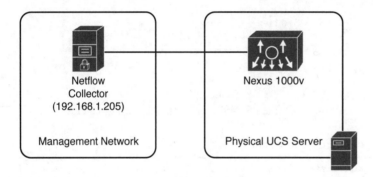

Figure 6-20   *Cisco Nexus 1000V Topology*

You can define new flow records or use the pre-defined Cisco Nexus 1000V flow record. You can use the **show flow record netflow-original** command to display the pre-defined flow records, as shown in Example 6-5.

Example 6-5   *Displaying Predefined Flow Records*

```
nexus1000v# show flow record netflow-original
 Flow record netflow-original:
     Description: Traditional IPv4 input NetFlow with origin ASs
     No. of users: 0
     Template ID: 0
     Fields:
         match ipv4 source address
         match ipv4 destination address
         match ip protocol
         match ip tos
```

```
            match transport source-port
            match transport destination-port
            match interface input
            match interface output
            match flow direction
            collect routing source as
            collect routing destination as
            collect routing next-hop address ipv4
            collect transport tcp flags
            collect counter bytes
            collect counter packets
            collect timestamp sys-uptime first
            collect timestamp sys-uptime last
nexus1000v#
```

Figure 6-21 lists the high-level steps to configure NetFlow in the Cisco Nexus 1000V.

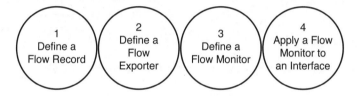

Figure 6-21   *Steps to Configure NetFlow in the Cisco Nexus 1000V*

Defining a Flow Record

Example 6-6 demonstrates how to define a flow record in the Cisco Nexus 1000V.

Example 6-6   *Defining a Flow Record in the Cisco Nexus 1000V*

```
nexus1000v# config terminal
nexus1000v(config)# flow record MyRecord
nexus1000v(config-flow-record)# match ipv4 destination address
nexus1000v(config-flow-record)# collect counter packets
```

In Example 6-6, a flow record called MyRecord is defined. It is configured to match packets based on IPv4 destination addresses. The **collect** subcommand is used to define the information to collect in the flow record. The **counter** keyword can be used collect flow record information in one of the following formats:

■ Bytes

■ Packets

Bytes and packets are collected in 32-bit counters unless the long 64-bit counter is specified. You can also use the **collect timestamp sys-uptime** subcommand to collect the system up time for the first or last packet in the flow. In addition, you can use the **collect transport tcp flags** subcommand to collect the TCP transport layer flags for the packets in the flow.

To show the flow record, you can use the **show flow record** *name* command, as demonstrated in Example 6-7.

Example 6-7   show flow record *Command Output*

```
nexus1000v# show flow record MyRecord
Flow record MyRecord:
    No. of users: 0
    Template ID: 0
    Fields:
        match ipv4 destination address

        collect counter packets
```

Defining the Flow Exporter

Example 6-8 demonstrates how to define a flow exporter in the Cisco Nexus 1000V.

Example 6-8   *Defining a Flow Exporter in the Cisco Nexus 1000V*

```
nexus1000v(config)# flow exporter Exporter1
nexus1000v(config-flow-exporter)# destination 192.168.1.205
nexus1000v(config-flow-exporter)# source mgmt 0
nexus1000v(config-flow-exporter)# transport udp 9901
nexus1000v(config-flow-exporter)# version 9
nexus1000v(config-flow-exporter-version-9)# option exporter-stats timeout 1200
nexus1000v(config-flow-exporter-version-9)# template data timeout 1200
```

In Example 6-8, the **flow exporter Exporter1** command defines the flow exporter. The name of the flow exporter is Exporter1 in this example. The **destination** subcommand specifies the IP address of the destination interface for the flow exporter. The destination in the example is 192.168.1.10.

In Example 6-8, the source interface from which the flow records are sent to the NetFlow collector is management 0 (**mgmt 0**). The destination UDP port is set to 9901. The NetFlow version is set to Version 9. The **option exporter-stats timeout 1100** subcommand specifies the exporter statistics to 1100 seconds. The **template data timeout 1100** subcommand is entered to set the template data resend timer to 1100 seconds.

You can use the **show flow exporter** *name* command to display the flow exporter statistics, as demonstrated in Example 6-9.

Example 6-9   show flow exporter *Command Output*

```
nexus1000v# show flow exporter Exporter1
 Flow exporter Exporter1:
     Destination: 192.168.1.205
     VRF: default (1)
     Destination UDP Port 9901
     Source Interface Mgmt0
     DSCP 2
     Export Version 9
         Exporter-stats timeout 1200 seconds
         Data template timeout 1200 seconds
     Exporter Statistics
         Number of Flow Records Exported 55
         Number of Templates Exported 0
         Number of Export Packets Sent 0
         Number of Export Bytes Sent 0
         Number of Destination Unreachable Events 0
         Number of No Buffer Events 0
         Number of Packets Dropped (No Route to Host) 0
         Number of Packets Dropped (other) 0
         Number of Packets Dropped (LC to RP Error) 0
         Number of Packets Dropped (Output Drops) 1
         Time statistics were last cleared: Never
```

Defining a Flow Monitor

Example 6-10 demonstrates how to define a flow monitor in the Cisco Nexus 1000V.

Example 6-10   *Defining a Flow Monitor in the Cisco Nexus 1000V*

```
nexus1000v(config)# flow monitor MyMonitor
nexus1000v(config-flow-monitor)# exporter Exporter1
nexus1000v(config-flow-monitor)# record MyRecord
nexus1000v(config-flow-monitor)# cache size 10000
```

In Example 6-10, a flow monitor called MyMonitor is configured. The previously configured flow exporter and flow record are applied to the flow monitor. The **cache** size is configured to 10,000 entries. The **cache** is an optional command, but it is useful to limit the impact of the monitor cache on memory and performance.

You can use the **show flow monitor** *name* command to display the flow monitor statistics, as shown in Example 6-11.

Example 6-11   show flow monitor *Command Output*

```
nexus1000v# show flow monitor MyMonitor
 Flow Monitor MyMonitor:
    Use count: 0
    Inactive timeout: 15
    Active timeout: 1800
    Cache Size: 10000
```

Applying the Flow Monitor to an Interface

The final step is to apply the flow monitor to an interface in the Cisco Nexus 1000V. Example 6-12 demonstrates how to assign the previously configured flow monitor to interface veth2.

Example 6-12   *Applying the Flow Monitor to an Interface*

```
nexus1000v(config)# interface veth 2
nexus1000v(config-if)# ip flow monitor MyMonitor output
```

The **output** keyword specifies that the flow monitor will be applied outbound (for output packets).

You can use the **show flow interface** command to display the flow monitor configuration under a given interface, as demonstrated in Example 6-13.

Example 6-13   show flow interface *Command Output*

```
nexus1000v(config-if)# show flow interface veth 2
 Interface veth 2:
    Monitor: MyMonitor
    Direction: Output
```

You can use the **show flow monitor MyMonitor cache** command to display the flow monitor NetFlow cache.

Configuring NetFlow in the Cisco Nexus 7000 Series

The NetFlow configuration in the Cisco Nexus 7000 is practically the same as in the rest of the Nexus switches (including the Cisco Nexus 1000V, which was just covered). The steps are the same:

Step 1.   Define a flow record.

Step 2.   Define a flow exporter.

Step 3.   Define a flow monitor.

Step 4.   Apply the flow monitor to an interface.

NetFlow CLI commands are not available until you enable the NetFlow feature with the **feature netflow** command.

Example 6-14 demonstrates how to define a flow record in the Cisco Nexus 7000.

Example 6-14   *Defining a Flow Record in the Cisco Nexus 7000*

```
n7k(config)# feature netflow
n7k(config)# flow record myRecord
n7k(config-flow-record)# description Custom-Flow-Record
n7k(config-flow-record)# match ipv4 source address
n7k(config-flow-record)# match ipv4 destination address
n7k(config-flow-record)# match transport destination-port
n7k(config-flow-record)# collect counter bytes
n7k(config-flow-record)# collect counter packets
```

Example 6-15 demonstrates how to define a flow exporter in the Cisco Nexus 7000.

Example 6-15   *Defining a Flow Exporter in the Cisco Nexus 7000*

```
n7k(Config)# flow exporter myExporter
n7k(Config-flow-exporter)# destination 192.168.11.2
n7k(Config-flow-exporter)# source Ethernet2/2
n7k(Config-flow-exporter)# version 9
```

Example 6-16 demonstrates how to define a flow monitor with a custom record in the Cisco Nexus 7000.

Example 6-16   *Defining a Flow Monitor with a Custom Record in the Cisco Nexus 7000*

```
n7k(config)# flow monitor myMonitor
n7k(config-flow-monitor)# description Applied Inbound on Ethernet 2/1
n7k(config-flow-monitor)# record myRecord
n7k(config-flow-monitor)# exporter myExporter
```

Example 6-17 demonstrates how to define a flow monitor with an original record in the Cisco Nexus 7000.

Example 6-17   *Defining a Flow Monitor with an Original Record in the Cisco Nexus 7000*

```
n7k(config)# flow monitor myMonitor2
n7k(config-Netflow-Monitor)# description monitor using predefined record
n7k(config-Netflow-Monitor)# record netflow-original
n7k(config-Netflow-Monitor)# exporter myExporter
```

Example 6-18 demonstrates how to adjust the NetFlow timers in the Cisco Nexus 7000.

Example 6-18   *Adjusting the NetFlow Timers in the Cisco Nexus 7000*

```
n7k(config)# flow timeout active 120
n7k(config)# flow timeout inactive 32
n7k(config)# flow timeout fast 32 threshold 100
n7k(config)# flow timeout session
n7k(config)# flow timeout aggressive threshold 75
```

Example 6-19 demonstrates configure sampled NetFlow in the Cisco Nexus 7000.

Example 6-19   *Configuring Sampled NetFlow in the Cisco Nexus 7000*

```
n7k(config)# sampler mySampler
n7k(config-flow-sampler)# mode 1 out-of 1000
```

Example 6-20 demonstrates how to apply a NetFlow monitor and sampler to an interface in the Cisco Nexus 7000.

Example 6-20   *Applying a NetFlow Monitor and Sampler*

```
n7k(config)# interface Ethernet2/1
n7k(config-if)# ip flow monitor myMonitor input sampler mySampler
```

Configuring the Cisco NetFlow Generation Appliance

The Cisco NetFlow Generation Appliance (NGA) can be deployed at strategic sections of a data center or any other places in the corporate network to collect network traffic using Switch Port Analyzer (SPAN) and network taps. Figure 6-22 shows two Cisco NGAs configured to generate NetFlow records for in the data center.

The Cisco NGA supports NetFlow Versions 5 and 9. It also supports IPFIX. The Cisco NGA has four 10G monitoring interfaces and up to four independent flow caches and flow monitors. Subsequently, the Cisco NGA can receive up to 40 gigabits of data and support various combinations of data ports, record templates, and export parameters. This is important to consider when deploying the Cisco NGA in the data center. As a best practice, the Cisco NGA monitoring interfaces should be sourced from network chokepoints to guarantee complete network traffic visibility in the data center.

Initializing the Cisco NGA

To perform the initial system configuration on the Cisco NGA appliance, follow these steps:

Step 1.   Log in to the appliance through the console interface.

Step 2.   The system prompts you to change the password. The default username is root, with a default password of root. It is highly recommended that you change the password to a complex password, using a password that contains at least eight characters and contains numbers, uppercase and lowercase letters, and symbols.

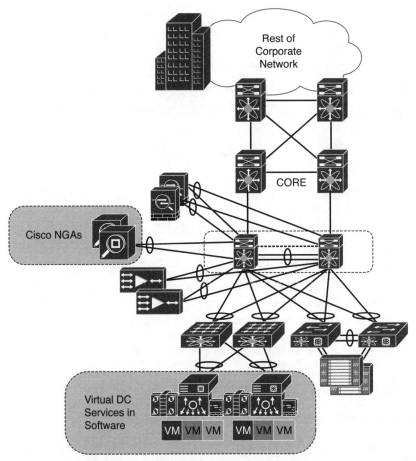

Virtualized Servers with Nexus 1000v and vPath

Figure 6-22   *Cisco NGAs in the Data Center*

Step 3.   Configure the management port IP address and subnet mask information using the following CLI command:

```
ip address 192.168.1.23 255.255.255.0
```

In this example, the Cisco NGA is configured with the IP address 192.168.1.23 and a 24-bit subnet mask (255.255.255.0).

Step 4.   To configure the Cisco NGA's default gateway address, use the **ip gateway** *ip_address* command, as demonstrated here, where the default gateway is 192.168.1.1:

```
ip gateway 192.168.1.1
```

Step 5.   (Optional) Enter the following information for your DNS server IP address using the **ip nameserver** *ip_address* command.

Step 6.   You can use the **show ip** command to verify the configuration.

Step 7.   The next step is to enable the web interface. The Cisco NGA has the ability to autopopulate NetFlow components. Use the **ip http server enable** command to enable the web interface for standard web access or the **ip http secure server enable** for secure web access (recommended).

Step 8.   Press **Enter** to use the default web administrator username (admin).

Step 9.   Enter a password for the web administrator. The Cisco NGA supports only one web user account.

Step 10.   You can direct packets to any of the four data ports on the NGA using either or both of the following methods:

- Enabling SPAN monitoring sessions (otherwise known as port mirroring) from the Cisco Nexus or Cisco Catalyst switches

- Using network taps, which are hardware devices that provide a copy of the packet that flows across a network link

Step 11.   The Cisco NGA can export flow records containing the input and output interface of the device (switch) rather than NGA data port interface index if your traffic source is a Cisco Nexus 5000 or Cisco Nexus 7000 series switch. You must configure the IP address and login credentials of your traffic source as a managed device. As a best practice, configure the IP address of your traffic source in the Cisco NGA as a managed device.

Configuring NetFlow in the Cisco NGA via the GUI

The Cisco NGA supports the following:

- Up to ten NetFlow filters to define which flows are to be sent to certain collectors. This allows you to use your collector's analysis applications and load balance NetFlow data across collectors.

- Up to four managed devices.

- Up to six collectors.

- Up to four independent flow monitors (flow caches) may be active simultaneously. Each monitor supports up to three records (one IPv4 record, one IPv6 record, and one Layer 2 record type).

To configure NetFlow in the Cisco NGA through the web interface, follow these steps:

Step 1.   You can perform the Quick Setup NetFlow configuration (which is the easiest configuration to export NetFlow Version 5 or 9 packets to a collector) by navigating to **Setup > Quick Setup**.

Step 2.   Define a unique name to identify the NetFlow configuration.

Step 3.   Define one or more data ports.

Step 4.   Define the NetFlow collector IP address in the Collector Address (IPv4) field.

Step 5.   Enter the UDP port for communication. The default port is 2055.

Step 6.   Define the NetFlow version (5 or 9).

Step 7.   Click **Submit**.

Step 8.   Select **Cyber_Example_monitor** on the Monitor tab and click **Activate/Inactivate**. This will enable the newly created flow monitor to generate NetFlow information for the input traffic and send it to the NetFlow collector.

Configuring NetFlow in the Cisco NGA via the CLI

This section covers how to configure NetFlow in the Cisco NGA via its CLI. Example 6-21 demonstrates how to create an IPv4 flow record using the key and non-key fields.

Example 6-21   *Creating an IPv4 Flow Record Using the Key and Non-Key Fields*

```
root@omar-nga.cisco.com# flow record IPv4 myRecord
root@omar-nga.cisco.com(sub-record)# match input-interface
root@omar-nga.cisco.com(sub-record)# match ip protocol
root@omar-nga.cisco.com(sub-record)# match destination
root@omar-nga.cisco.com(sub-record)# match source
root@omar-nga.cisco.com(sub-record)# match ip tos
root@omar-nga.cisco.com(sub-record)# match transport destination-port
root@omar-nga.cisco.com(sub-record)# match transport source-port
root@omar-nga.cisco.com(sub-record)# match datalink mac-destination
root@omar-nga.cisco.com(sub-record)# match datalink mac-source
root@omar-nga.cisco.com(sub-record)# collect classification application-id
root@omar-nga.cisco.com(sub-record)# collect counter bytes
root@omar-nga.cisco.com(sub-record)# collect timestamp sys-uptime first
root@omar-nga.cisco.com(sub-record)# collect icmp code
root@omar-nga.cisco.com(sub-record)# collect icmp type
root@omar-nga.cisco.com(sub-record)# collect timestamp sys-uptime last
root@omar-nga.cisco.com(sub-record)# collect ip max-ttl
root@omar-nga.cisco.com(sub-record)# collect ip min-ttl
root@omar-nga.cisco.com(sub-record)# collect counter packets
root@omar-nga.cisco.com(sub-record)# collect transport tcp flags
```

Example 6-22 demonstrates how to define the flow collector.

Example 6-22 *Defining the Flow Collector*

```
root@omar-nga.cisco.com# flow collector myCollector
root@omar-nga.cisco.com(sub-collector)# address 192.168.1.205
root@omar-nga.cisco.com(sub-collector)# transport udp destination-port 2055
```

Example 6-23 demonstrates how to define the flow exporter.

Example 6-23 *Defining the Flow Exporter*

```
root@omar-nga.cisco.com# flow exporter myExporter
root@omar-nga.cisco.com(sub-exporter)# version v9
root@omar-nga.cisco.com(sub-exporter)# template-period 1
root@omar-nga.cisco.com(sub-exporter)# option-period 1
root@omar-nga.cisco.com(sub-exporter)# policy multi-destination
root@omar-nga.cisco.com(sub-exporter)# destination myCollector
```

The name of the flow exporter in Example 6-23 is myExporter. NetFlow Version 9 is used in this example. The Cisco NGA is configured to send NetFlow data templates, option templates, and option data collectors every minute (**1**). The exporting policy is set to **multi-destination** so that the exporter will send the same NetFlow packet to all collectors set in the exporter. You can also configure the exporting policy with the **weighted-round-robin** option. The previously defined collector (**myCollector**) is used in this exporter.

Example 6-24 demonstrates how to define the flow monitor. The flow monitor represents the device's NetFlow database and links together the flow record and the flow exporter with any or all of the four data ports on the NGA.

Example 6-24 *Defining the Flow Monitor*

```
root@omar-nga.cisco.com# flow monitor myMonitor
root@omar-nga.cisco.com(sub-monitor)# record myRecord
root@omar-nga.cisco.com(sub-monitor)# exporter myExporter
root@omar-nga.cisco.com(sub-monitor)# dataport 1
root@omar-nga.cisco.com(sub-monitor)# tunnel inner
root@omar-nga.cisco.com(sub-monitor)# cache size 100
root@omar-nga.cisco.com(sub-monitor)# cache type standard
root@omar-nga.cisco.com(sub-monitor)# cache timeout active 60
root@omar-nga.cisco.com(sub-monitor)# cache timeout inactive 15
```

In Example 6-24, the Cisco NGA's flow monitor is configured to track the innermost IP addresses, by using the **tunnel inner** command. The **tunnel inner** command is used to dictate how the flow monitor will handle network packets that are tunneled and have more than one set of IP addresses. You can also configure the Cisco NGA's flow monitor to track the outermost IP addresses. The total cache memory space to allocate for this monitor instance is set to 100. The cache type is set to standard cache mode. This allows inactive flows to be removed from the cache and memory to be made available for a new flow to use. Alternatively, you can configure permanent cache mode, where flows are never deleted from the cache. The active timeout is set to 60 seconds (recommended) and the inactive timeout is set to 15 seconds.

Tip   You can use the **show cache statistics rates** *monitor_name* command to display the rate of raw traffic being processed and the number of flows being created and forwarded to the exporter engine. Also, you can use the **show collector statistics** *collector_name* command to display the information about NetFlow packets being sent to the collector.

Additional Cisco CTD Solution Components

The following sections describe the additional Cisco CTD Solution components.

Cisco ASA 5500-X Series Next-Generation Firewalls and the Cisco ASA with FirePOWER Services

The Cisco ASA family provides a very comprehensive set of features and next-generation security capabilities. For example, it provides capabilities such as simple packet filtering (normally configured with ACLs) and stateful inspection. The Cisco ASA also provides support for application inspection/awareness. It can listen in on conversations between devices on one side and devices on the other side of the firewall. The benefit of listening in is so that the firewall can pay attention to application layer information.

The Cisco ASA also supports Network Address Translation (NAT) and the ability to act as a Dynamic Host Configuration Protocol (DHCP) server, client, or both. The Cisco ASA supports most of the interior gateway routing protocols, including Routing Information Protocol (RIP), Enhanced Interior Gateway Routing Protocol (EIGRP), and Open Shortest Path First (OSPF). It also supports static routing. It also can be implemented as a traditional Layer 3 firewall, which has IP addresses assigned to each of its routable interfaces. The other option is to implement a firewall as a transparent (Layer 2) firewall, in which the actual physical interfaces receive individual IP addresses, but a pair of interfaces operates like a bridge. Traffic that is going across this two-port bridge is still subject to the rules and inspection that can be implemented by the ASA. In addition, the Cisco ASA is often used a headend or remote-end device for VPN tunnels for both remote-access VPN users and site-to-site VPN tunnels. It supports IPsec and Secure Sockets Layer (SSL)-based remote-access VPNs. The SSL VPN capabilities include support for clientless SSL VPN and the full AnyConnect SSL VPN tunnels.

The Cisco ASA also provides a basic botnet traffic filtering feature. A botnet is a collection of computers that have been compromised and are willing to follow the instructions of someone who is attempting to centrally control them (for example, 200,000 machines all willing [or so commanded] to send a flood of ping requests to the IP address dictated by the person controlling these devices). Often, users of these computers have no idea that their computers are participating in this coordinated attack. The ASA works with an external system at Cisco that provides information about the Botnet Traffic Filter Database and so can protect against this.

Cisco introduced the Cisco ASA FirePOWER module as part of the integration of the SourceFire technology.

Note   SourceFire was a company that Cisco acquired to expand its security portfolio. The Cisco ASA FirePOWER module provides NGIPS, application visibility and control (AVC), URL filtering, and AMP. This module runs as a separate application from the classic Cisco ASA software. The Cisco ASA FirePOWER module can be a hardware module on the ASA 5585-X only or a software module that runs in a solid-state drive (SSD) in all other models.

The Cisco ASA FirePOWER module can be managed by the FireSIGHT Management Center. The FireSIGHT Management Center and the Cisco ASA FirePOWER module require additional licenses. These licenses are installed in the FirePOWER module itself. No additional licenses are required in the Cisco ASA itself.

Note   The Cisco ASA 5500-X Series Next-Generation Firewalls LiveLessons (Workshop): Deploying and Troubleshooting Techniques (ISBN-13: 978-1-58720-570-5) covers step-by-step instructions on how to deploy, configure, and troubleshoot the firewall features of the Cisco ASA 5500-X Series Next-Generation Firewalls, including an introduction of Cisco ASA with FirePOWER Services.

Next-Generation Intrusion Prevention Systems

As a result of the SourceFire acquisition, Cisco expanded its NGIPS portfolio with the following products:

- **Cisco FirePOWER 9300 series appliances:** High-performance appliances designed for service providers and large enterprises. These are modular appliances that can also run Cisco ASA software, Cisco FirePOWER Next-Generation IPS Services, and even Radware's denial of service (DoS) mitigation software.

- **Cisco FirePOWER 8000 series appliances:** High-performance appliances running Cisco FirePOWER Next-Generation IPS Services. These appliances support throughput speeds from 2 Gbps up through 60 Gbps.

- **Cisco FirePOWER 7000 Series Appliances:** These are the base platform for the Cisco FirePOWER Next-Generation IPS software. They support throughput speeds from 50 Mbps up through 1.25 Gbps.

- **Virtual Next-Generation IPS (NGIPSv) for VMware:** Can be deployed in virtualized environments. By deploying the NGIPSv virtual appliances, security administrators can maintain network visibility that is often lost in virtual environments.

FireSIGHT Management Center

Cisco FireSIGHT Management Center provides a centralized management and analysis platform for the Cisco NGIPS appliances and the Cisco ASA with FirePOWER Services. It provides support for role-based policy management, including a fully customizable dashboard with advanced reports and analytics. The following are the models of the Cisco FireSIGHT Management Center appliances:

- **FireSIGHT 750:** Supports a maximum of 10 managed devices (NGIPS or Cisco ASA appliances) and a total of 20 million IPS events.

- **FireSIGHT 1500:** Supports a maximum of 35 managed devices and a total of 30 million IPS events.

- **FireSIGHT 3500:** Supports a maximum of 150 managed devices and a total of 150 million IPS events.

- **FireSIGHT 4000:** Supports a maximum of 300 managed devices and a total of 300 million IPS events.

- **FireSIGHT Virtual Appliance:** Allows you to conveniently provision on your existing virtual infrastructure. It supports a maximum of 25 managed devices.

AMP for Endpoints

Numerous antivirus and antimalware solutions on the market are designed to detect, analyze, and protect against both known and emerging endpoint threats. Before diving into these technologies, you should learn what viruses and malicious software (malware) are and some of the taxonomy around the different types of malicious software.

The following are the most common types of malicious software:

- **Computer viruses:** Malicious software that infects a host file or system area to perform undesirable outcomes such as erasing data, stealing information, or corrupting the integrity of the system. In numerous cases, these viruses multiply again to form new generations of themselves.

- **Worms:** Viruses that replicate themselves over the network, thus infecting numerous vulnerable systems. On most occasions, a worm executes malicious instructions on a remote system without user interaction.

- **Mailers and mass-mailer worms:** A type of worm that sends itself in an email message. Examples of mass-mailer worms are Loveletter.A@mm and W32/SKA.A@m (a.k.a. the Happy99 worm), which sends a copy of itself every time the user sends a new message.

- **Logic bombs:** A type of malicious code that is injected to a legitimate application. An attacker can program a logic bomb to delete itself from the disk after it performs the malicious tasks on the system. Examples of these malicious tasks include deleting or corrupting files or databases and executing a specific instruction after certain system conditions are met.

- **Trojan horses:** Trojan horses are a type of malware that executes instructions determined by the nature of the Trojan to delete files, steal data, and compromise the integrity of the underlying operating system. Trojan horses typically use a form of social engineering to fool victims into installing such software on their computers or mobile devices. Trojans can also act as back doors.

- **Back doors:** A piece of malware or configuration change that allows attackers to control the victim's system remotely. For example, a back door can open a network port on the affected system so that the attacker can connect and control such system.

- **Exploits:** A malicious program designed to "exploit" or take advantage of a single vulnerability or set of vulnerabilities.

- **Downloaders:** A piece of malware that downloads and installs other malicious content from the Internet to perform additional exploitation on an affected system.

- **Spammers:** Spam is referred to as the act of sending unsolicited messages via email, instant messaging, newsgroups, or any other kind of computer or mobile device communications. Spammers are the type of malware whose sole purpose is to send these unsolicited messages with the primary goal of fooling users into clicking on malicious links, replying to emails or such messages with sensitive information, or performing different types of scams. The attacker's main objective is to make money.

- **Key loggers:** A piece of malware that captures the user's keystrokes on a compromised computer or mobile device. It collects sensitive information such as passwords, PINs, personal identifiable information (PII), credit card numbers, and more.

- **Rootkits:** A set of tools that are used by attackers to elevate their privilege to obtain root-level access to be able to completely take control of the affected system.

- **Ransomware:** A type of malware that compromises a system and then demands a ransom from the victim (often to pay the attacker for the malicious activity to cease or for the malware to be removed from the affected system). Two examples of ransomware are Crypto Locker and CryptoWall. These two are malware that encrypts the victim's data and demands the user to pay a ransom for the data to be decrypted and accessible again by the victim.

Numerous types of commercial and free antivirus software are available, including the following:

- avast!

- AVG Internet Security

- Bitdefender Antivirus Free

- ZoneAlarm PRO Antivirus + Firewall and ZoneAlarm Internet Security Suite

- F-Secure Antivirus

- Kaspersky Anti-Virus

- McAfee Antivirus

- Panda Antivirus

- Sophos Antivirus

- Norton AntiVirus

- ClamAV

- Immunet

Note   ClamAV is an open source antivirus engine sponsored and maintained by Cisco and non-Cisco engineers. You can download ClamAV from http://www.clamav.net. Immunet is a free community-based antivirus software maintained by Cisco Sourcefire. You can download Immunet from http://www.immunet.com.

There are numerous other antivirus software companies and products. You can find a comprehensive list and comparison of the different antivirus software available on the market at http://en.wikipedia.org/wiki/Comparison_of_antivirus_software.

Personal firewalls and host intrusion prevention systems (HIPS) are software applications that you can install on end-user machines or servers to protect them from external security threats and intrusions. The term *personal firewall* typically applies to basic software that can control Layer 3 and Layer 4 access to client machines. HIPS provide several features that offer more robust security than a traditional personal firewall, such as host intrusion prevention and protection against spyware, viruses, worms, Trojans, and other types of malware.

Today, more sophisticated software is available on the market that makes basic personal firewalls and HIPS obsolete. For example, Cisco Advanced Malware Protection (AMP) for Endpoints provides more granular visibility and control to stop advanced threats missed by other security layers. Cisco AMP for Endpoints takes advantage of telemetry from big data, continuous analysis, and advanced analytics provided by Cisco's threat intelligence to be able to detect, analyze, and stop advanced malware across endpoints.

Cisco AMP for Endpoints provides advanced malware protection for many operating systems, such as the following:

- Windows

- Mac OS X

- Android

Attacks are getting very sophisticated; they can often evade detection of traditional systems and endpoint protection. Nowadays, attackers have the resources, knowledge, and persistence to beat point-in-time detection. Cisco AMP for Endpoints provides mitigation capabilities that go beyond point-in-time detection. It uses threat intelligence from Cisco to perform retrospective analysis and protection. Cisco AMP for Endpoints also provides device and file trajectory capabilities to allow the security administrator to analyze the full spectrum of the attack. Device trajectory and file trajectory support the following file types in Windows and Mac OS X operating systems:

- MSEXE
- PDF
- MSCAB
- MSOLE2
- ZIP
- ELF
- MACHO
- MACHO_UNIBIN
- SWF
- JAVA

Note The Mac OS X connector does not support SWF files. The Windows connector does not scan Elf, Java, xar(pkg), MACHO, or MACHO_UNIBIN files at the time of this writing. The Android AMP connector scans APK files.

AMP for Networks

Cisco AMP for Networks provides next-generation security services that go beyond point-in-time detection. Cisco AMP for Networks is designed for Cisco FirePOWER network security appliances. It provides continuous analysis and tracking of files and also retrospective security alerts so that the security administrator can take action during and after an attack. Cisco AMP for Networks file trajectory feature tracks file transmissions across the network, and the file capture feature enables security administrators to store and retrieve files for further analysis.

AMP Threat Grid

Cisco acquired a security company called ThreatGRID that provides cloud-based and on-premise malware analysis solutions.

Cisco integrated Cisco AMP and ThreatGRID to provide a solution for advanced malware analysis with deep threat analytics. The Cisco AMP ThreatGRID integrated solution analyzes millions of files and correlates them against hundreds of millions of malware samples. This provides a lot of visibility of attack campaigns and how malware is distributed. This solution provides security administrators with detailed reports of indicators of compromise and threat scores that help them prioritize mitigations and recovery from attacks.

Email Security

Users are no longer accessing email from the corporate network or from a single device. Cisco provides cloud-based, hybrid, and on-premises ESA-based solutions that can help protect any dynamic environment. This section introduces these solutions and technologies, explaining how users can use threat intelligence to detect, analyze, and protect against both known and emerging threats.

There are several types of email-based threats. The following are the most common:

- **Spam:** Unsolicited email messages that can be advertising a service or (typically) a scam or a message with malicious intent. Email spam continuous to be a major threat because it can be used to spread malware.

- **Malware attachments:** Email messages containing malicious software (malware).

- **Phishing:** An attacker's attempt to fool a user that such email communication comes from a legitimate entity or site, such as banks, social media websites, online payment processors, or even corporate IT communications. The goal of the phishing email is to steal user's sensitive information, such as user credentials, bank accounts, and so on.

- **Spear phishing:** Phishing attempts that are more targeted. These phishing emails are directed to specific individual or organizations. For instance, an attacker may perform a passive reconnaissance on the individual or organization by gathering information from social media sites (for example, Twitter, LinkedIn, Facebook) and other online resources. Then the attacker may tailor a more directed and relevant message to the victim, increasing the probability of such user being fooled to follow a malicious link, click an attachment containing malware, or simply reply to the email and provide sensitive information. Another phishing-based attack is called whaling. These attacks specifically target executives and high-profile users within a given organization.

Email Security Appliance

The following are the different ESA models:

- Cisco X-Series Email Security Appliances

  - **Cisco X1070:** High-performance ESA for service providers and large enterprises

- Cisco C-Series Email Security Appliances

  - **Cisco C680:** The high-performance ESA for service providers and large enterprises

- **Cisco C670:** Designed for medium-sized enterprises

- **Cisco C380:** Designed for medium-sized enterprises

- **Cisco C370:** Designed for small to medium-sized enterprises

- **Cisco C170:** Designed for small businesses and branch offices

The Cisco ESA runs Cisco AsyncOS operating system. The Cisco AsyncOS supports numerous features that will help mitigate email-based threats.

The following are examples of the features supported by the Cisco ESA:

- **Access control:** Controlling access for inbound senders according to the sender's IP address, IP address range, or domain name.

- **Antispam:** Multilayer filters based on Cisco SenderBase reputation and Cisco antispam integration. The antispam reputation and zero-day threat intelligence is fueled by Cisco's security intelligence and research group named Talos.

- **Network antivirus:** Network antivirus capabilities at the gateway. Cisco partnered with Sophos and McAfee, supporting their antivirus scanning engines.

- **Advanced Malware Protection (AMP):** Allows security administrators to detect and block malware and perform continuous analysis and retrospective alerting.

- **Data loss prevention (DLP):** The ability to detect any sensitive emails and documents leaving the corporation. The Cisco ESA integrates RSA email DLP for outbound traffic.

- **Email encryption:** The ability to encrypt outgoing mail to address regulatory requirements. The administrator can configure an encryption policy on the Cisco ESA and use a local key server or hosted key service to encrypt the message.

- **Email authentication:** A few email authentication mechanism are supported, including Sender Policy Framework (SPF), Sender ID Framework (SIDF), and DomainKeys Identified Mail (DKIM) verification of incoming mail, and DomainKeys and DKIM signing of outgoing mail.

- **Outbreak filters:** Preventive protection against new security outbreaks and email-based scams using Cisco's Security Intelligence Operations (SIO) threat intelligence information.

Note Cisco SenderBase is the world largest email and web traffic monitoring network. It provides real-time threat intelligence powered by Cisco SIO. The Cisco SenderBase website is located at http://www.senderbase.org.

The Cisco ESA acts as the email gateway the organization, handling all email connections, accepting messages, and relaying them to the appropriate systems. The Cisco ESA can service email connections from the Internet to users inside your network, and from systems inside your network to the Internet. Email connections use Simple Mail Transfer Protocol (SMTP). The ESA services all SMTP connections by default, acting as the SMTP gateway.

Tip Mail gateways are also known as mail exchangers or MX.

The Cisco ESA uses listeners to handle incoming SMTP connection requests. A listener defines an email processing service that is configured on an interface in the Cisco ESA. Listeners apply to email entering the appliance from either the Internet or from internal systems.

The following listeners can be configured:

- Public listeners for email coming in from the Internet.

- Private listeners for email coming from hosts in the corporate (inside) network. These emails are typically from an internal groupware, Exchange, POP, or IMAP email servers.

Cisco ESA listeners are often referred to as SMTP daemons running on a specific Cisco ESA interface. When a listener is configured, the following information must be provided:

- Listener properties such as a specific interface in the Cisco ESA and the TCP port that will be used. The listener properties must also indicate whether it is a public or a private listener.

- The hosts that are allowed to connect to the listener using a combination of access control rules. An administrator can specify which remote hosts can connect to the listener.

- The local domains for which public listeners accept messages.

Cloud Email Security

Cisco Cloud Email Security provides a cloud-based solution that allows companies to outsource the management of their email security management. The service provides email security instances in multiple Cisco data centers to enable high availability.

Cisco Hybrid Email Security

The Cisco Hybrid Email Security solution combines both cloud-based and on-premises ESAs. This hybrid solution helps Cisco customers reduce their onsite email security footprint, outsourcing a portion of their email security to Cisco, while still allowing them to maintain control of confidential information within their physical boundaries. Many organizations need to stay compliant with many regulations that may require them to keep sensitive data physically on their premises. The Cisco Hybrid Email Security solution allows network security administrators to remain compliant and to maintain advanced control with encryption, DLP, and onsite identity-based integration.

Web Security

For any organization to be able to protect their environment against web-based security threats, the security administrators need to deploy tools and mitigation technologies that go far beyond traditional blocking of known bad websites. Nowadays, you can download malware through compromised legitimate websites, including social media sites, advertisements in news and corporate sites, gaming sites, and many more. Cisco has developed several tools and mechanisms to help their customers combat these threats. The core solutions for mitigating web-based threats are the Cisco Cloud Web Security (CWS) offering and the integration of Advanced Malware Protection (AMP) to the Cisco Web Security Appliance (WSA). Both solutions enable malware detection and blocking, continuous monitoring, and retrospective alerting.

Web Security Appliance

The Cisco WSA uses cloud-based intelligence from Cisco to help protect the organization before, during, and after an attack. This "lifecycle" is what is referred to as the attack continuum. The cloud-based intelligence includes web (URL) reputation and zero-day threat intelligence from Cisco's security intelligence and research group named Talos. This threat intelligence help security professionals to stop threats before they enter the corporate network, while also enabling file reputation and file sandboxing to identify threats during an attack. Retrospective attack analysis allows security administrators to investigate and provide protection after an attack when advanced malware might have evaded other layers of defense.

The Cisco WSA can be deployed in explicit proxy mode or as a transparent proxy using the Web Cache Communication Protocol (WCCP). WCCP is a protocol originally developed by Cisco, but several other vendors have integrated it in their products to allow clustering and transparent proxy deployments on networks using Cisco infrastructure devices (routers, switches, firewalls, and so on).

Figure 6-23 illustrates a Cisco WSA deployed as an explicit proxy.

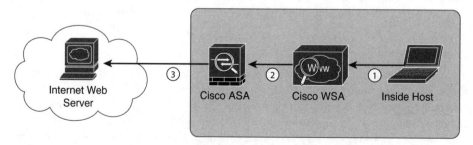

Figure 6-23 *WSA Explicit Proxy Configuration*

The following are the steps illustrated in Figure 6-23:

Step 1. An internal user makes an HTTP request to an external website. The client browser is configured to send the request to the Cisco WSA.

Step 2. The Cisco WSA connects to the website on behalf of the internal user.

Step 3. The firewall (Cisco ASA) is configured to only allow outbound web traffic from the Cisco WSA, and it forwards the traffic to the web server.

Figure 6-24 shows a Cisco WSA deployed as a transparent proxy.

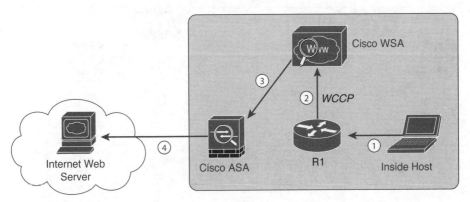

Figure 6-24 *Transparent Proxy Configuration*

The following are the steps illustrated in Figure 6-24:

Step 1. An internal user makes an HTTP request to an external website.

Step 2. The internal router (R1) redirects the web request to the Cisco WSA using WCCP.

Step 3. The Cisco WSA connects to the website on behalf of the internal user.

Step 4. Also in this example, the firewall (Cisco ASA) is configured to only allow outbound web traffic from the WSA. The web traffic is sent to the Internet web server.

Figure 6-25 demonstrates how the WCCS registration works. The Cisco WSA is the WCCP client, and the Cisco router is the WCCP server.

Figure 6-25 *WCCP Registration*

During the WCCP registration process, the WCCP client sends a registration announcement ("Here I am") every 10 seconds. The WCCP server (the Cisco router in this example) accepts the registration request and acknowledges it with an "I See You" WCCP message. The WCCP server waits 30 seconds before it declares the client as "inactive" (engine failed). WCCP can be used in large-scale environments. Figure 6-26 shows a cluster of Cisco WSAs, where internal Layer 3 switches redirect web traffic to the cluster.

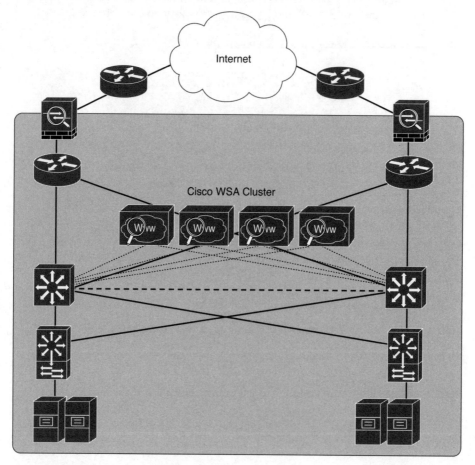

Figure 6-26 *Cisco WSA Cluster Example*

The Cisco WSA comes in different models. The following are the different Cisco WSA models:

- **Cisco WSA S680:** A high-performance WSA designed for large organizations with 6,000 to 12,000 users. A two rack-unit (RU) appliance with 16 (two octa core) CPUs, 32 GB of memory, and 4.8 TB of disk space.

- **Cisco WSA S670:** A high-performance WSA designed for large organizations with 6,000 to 12,000 users. A two RU appliance with 8 (two octa core) CPUs, 8 GB of memory, and 2.7 TB of disk space.

- **Cisco WSA S380:** Designed for medium-sized organizations with 1,500 to 6,000 users. A two RU appliance with six (one hexa core) CPUs, 16 GB of memory, and 2.4 TB of disk space.

- **Cisco WSA S370:** Designed for medium-sized organizations with 1,500 to 6,000 users. A two RU appliance with four (one quad core) CPUs, 4 GB or memory, and 1.8 TB of disk space.

- **Cisco WSA S170:** Designed for small to medium-sized organizations with up to 1,500 users. A one RU appliance with two (one dual core) CPUs, 4 GB of memory, and 500 GB of disk space.

The Cisco WSA runs Cisco AsyncOS operating system. The Cisco AsyncOS supports numerous features that will help mitigate web-based threats. The following are examples of these features:

- **Real-time antimalware adaptive scanning:** The Cisco WSA can be configured to dynamically select an antimalware scanning engine based on URL reputation, content type, and scanner effectiveness. Adaptive scanning is a feature designed to increases the "catch rate" of malware that is embedded in images, JavaScript, text, and Adobe Flash files. Adaptive scanning is an additional layer of security on top of Cisco WSA Web Reputation Filters, which include support for Sophos, Webroot, and McAfee.

- **Layer 4 traffic monitor:** Used to detect and block spyware. It dynamically adds IP addresses of known malware domains to database of sites to block.

- **Third-party DLP integration:** Redirects all outbound traffic to a third-party DLP appliance, allowing deep content inspection for regulatory compliance and data exfiltration protection. It enables an administrator to inspect web content by title, metadata, and size and to even prevent users from storing files to cloud services, such as Dropbox, Google Drive, and others.

- **File reputation:** Using threat information from Cisco Talos. This file reputation threat intelligence is updated every 3 to 5 minutes.

- **File sandboxing:** If malware is detected, the Cisco AMP capabilities can put files in a sandbox to inspect its behavior, combining the inspection with machine-learning analysis to determine the threat level. Cisco Cognitive Threat Analytics (CTA) uses machine-learning algorithms to adapt over time.

- **File retrospection:** After a malicious attempt or malware is detected, the Cisco WSA continues to cross-examine files over an extended period of time.

- **Application visibility and control:** Allows the Cisco ASA to inspect and even block applications that are not allowed by the corporate security polity. For example, an administrator can allow users to use social media sites like Facebook but block micro-applications such as Facebook games.

Cisco Content Security Management Appliance

Cisco Security Management Appliance (SMA) is a Cisco product that centralizes the management and reporting for one or more Cisco ESAs and Cisco WSAs. Cisco SMA consistent enforcement of policy, and enhances threat protection. Figure 6-27 shows a Cisco SMA that is controlling Cisco ESA and Cisco WSAs in different geographic locations (New York, Raleigh, Paris, and London).

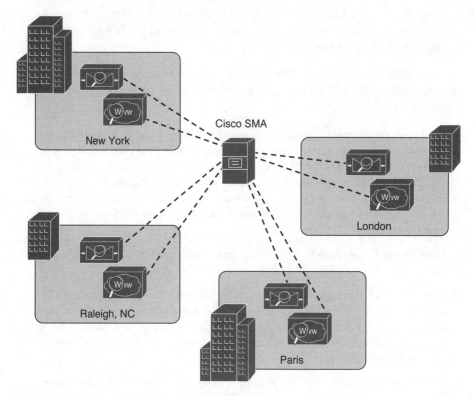

Figure 6-27   *Cisco SMA Centralized Deployment*

The Cisco SMA comes in different models. These models are physical appliances or the Cisco Content Security Management Virtual Appliance (SMAV). The following are the different Cisco SMA models:

- **Cisco SMA M680:** Designed for large organizations with over 10,000 users

- **Cisco SMAV M600v:** Designed for large enterprises or service providers

- **Cisco SMA M380:** Designed for organizations with 1,000 to 10,000 users

- **Cisco SMAV M300v:** Designed for organizations with 1,000 to 5,000 users

- **Cisco SMA M170:** Designed for small businesses or branch offices with up to 1,000 users

- **Cisco SMAV M100v:** Designed for small businesses or branch offices with up to 1,000 users

Note   Cisco also has a Cisco SMAV M000v that is used for evaluations only.

Cisco Cloud Web Security

Cisco Cloud Web Security (CWS_ is a cloud-based security service from Cisco that provides worldwide threat intelligence, advanced threat defense capabilities, and roaming user protection. The Cisco CWS service uses web proxies in Cisco's cloud environment that scan traffic for malware and policy enforcement. Cisco customers can connect to the Cisco CWS service directly by using a proxy autoconfiguration (PAC) file in the user endpoint or through connectors integrated into the following Cisco products:

- Cisco ISR G2 routers

- Cisco ASA

- Cisco WSA

- Cisco AnyConnect Secure Mobility Client

Organizations using the transparent proxy functionality through a connector can get the most out of their existing infrastructure. In addition, the scanning is offloaded from the hardware appliances to the cloud, reducing the impact to hardware utilization and reducing network latency. Figure 6-28 illustrates how the transparent proxy functionality through a connector works.

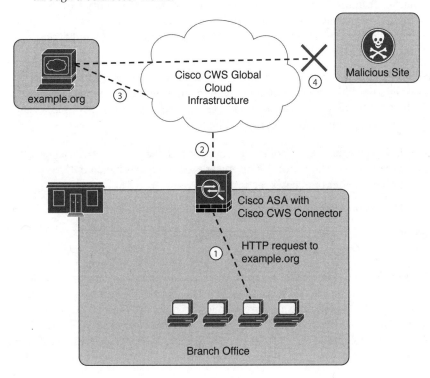

Figure 6-28   *Cisco ASA with Cisco CWS Connector Example*

In Figure 6-28, the Cisco ASA is enabled with the Cisco CWS connector at a branch office. The following steps explain how Cisco CWS protects the corporate users at the branch office:

Step 1.   An internal user makes an HTTP request to an external website (securemeinc.org).

Step 2.   The Cisco ASA forwards the request to Cisco CWS global cloud infrastructure.

Step 3.   It notices that example.org had some web content (ads) that was redirecting the user to a known malicious site.

Step 4.   Cisco CWS blocks the request to the malicious site.

Cisco Identity Services Engine

The Cisco ISE is a comprehensive security identity management solution designed function as a policy decision point for network access. It enables security administrators to collect real-time contextual information from the network, its users, and devices. Cisco ISE is the central policy management platform in the Cisco TrustSec solution. It supports a comprehensive set of authentication, authorization, accounting (AAA), posture, and network profiler features into a single device.

Cisco ISE enables security administrators to provide network guest access management and a wide-ranging client provisioning policies, including 802.1X environments. The support of TrustSec features such as Security Group Tags (SGTs) and Security Group Access Control Lists (SGACLs) makes the Cisco ISE a complete identity services solution. Cisco ISE supports policy sets, which let a security administrator group sets of authentication and authorization policies.

Cisco ISE provides network access control (NAC) features, including posture policies to enforce that end-user devices are configured with the most up-to-date security settings or applications before they enter the network. The following agent types are supported by the Cisco ISE for posture assessment and compliance:

- **Cisco NAC web agent:** A temporary agent that is installed in end-user machines at the time of login. The Cisco NAC Web Agent is no longer visible on the end-user machine after the user terminates the session.

- **Cisco NAC agent:** Installed (permanently) on a Windows or Mac OS X client system.

- **AnyConnect ISE agent:** Installed (permanently) on a Windows or Mac OS X client system.

Cisco ISE provides a comprehensive set of features to allow corporate users to connect their personal devices, such as mobile phones, tablets, laptops, and other network devices to the network. This is what is called bring your own device (BYOD). BYOD introduces many challenges when protecting network services and enterprise data. Cisco ISE provides support for multiple Mobile Device Management (MDM) solutions to enforce policy on endpoints. ISE can be configured redirect users to MDM onboarding portals, prompting them to update their device before they can access the network. Cisco ISE can also be configured to provide Internet-only access to users who are not compliant with MDM policies.

Cisco ISE supports the Cisco Platform Exchange Grid (pxGrid). Cisco pxGrid is a multi-vendor, cross-platform network system that combines different parts of an IT infrastructure, such as the following:

- Security monitoring

- Detection systems

- Network policy platforms

- Asset and configuration management

- Identity and access management platforms

Cisco pxGrid has a unified framework with an open application programming interface (API) designed in a hub-and-spoke architecture. pxGrid is used to enable the sharing of contextual-based information from Cisco ISE session directory to other policy network systems such as Cisco IOS devices and the Cisco ASA.

The Cisco ISE can be configured as a certificate authority (CA) to generate and manage digital certificates for endpoints. Cisco ISE CA supports standalone and subordinate deployments.

Cisco ISE software can be installed on a range of physical appliances or on a VMware server (Cisco ISE VM). The Cisco ISE software image does not support the installation of any other packages or applications on this dedicated platform.

Summary

The Cisco CTD Solution uses Cisco next-generation security products and components, in addition to NetFlow and the Lancope StealthWatch System, for broad network visibility in the attack continuum. This chapter provided an introduction to the attack continuum and the deployment and configuration of NetFlow in key Cisco products such as the Cisco ASA, Cisco NX-OS devices, and the Cisco NGA. Previous chapters covered the NetFlow configuration in Cisco IOS-XE and classic Cisco IOS devices. This chapter also covered the Cisco FirePOWER and FireSIGHT, and Cisco's AMP for endpoint control and network malware control with AMP for networks. It also provided an overview of the content security appliances and services such as the Cisco WSA and Cisco CWS, which provide adaptive threat control of web traffic, in addition to the Cisco ESA, which provides dynamic threat control for email traffic. At the end of the chapter, the Cisco ISE was introduced. The Cisco ISE is used in the Cisco CTD Solution for user and device identity integration with Lancope StealthWatch and remediation policy actions using pxGrid.

## Chapter 7

Troubleshooting NetFlow

This chapter covers the following topics:

- Troubleshooting NetFlow in Cisco IOS Software

- Troubleshooting NetFlow in Cisco IOS-XE Software

- Troubleshooting NetFlow in Cisco NX-OS Software

- Troubleshooting NetFlow in Cisco IOS-XR Software

- Troubleshooting NetFlow in the Cisco ASA

- Troubleshooting NetFlow in the Cisco NetFlow Generation Appliance

Troubleshooting Utilities and Debug Commands

This chapter focuses on the different techniques and best practices available when troubleshooting NetFlow deployments and configurations. It assumes that you already understand the topics covered in previous chapters, such as configuration and deployment of NetFlow in all the supported devices.

Before you start learning in-depth troubleshooting techniques and detailed information about **debug** commands, it is recommended that you understand the impact of debug commands in production environments. Use **debug** commands with caution at all times. The impact of using some of the **debug** commands will depend on your environment and the CPU and memory utilization of your network infrastructure device. In some cases, it is recommended that these commands be used only under the direction of your router technical support representative when troubleshooting specific problems.

Enabling debugging can disrupt operation of an infrastructure device when networks are experiencing high load conditions.

Before debugging, look at your CPU load with the **show processes cpu** command in Cisco IOS, IOS-XE, and IOS-XR devices and with the **show cpu** command in Cisco Adaptive Security Appliance (ASA) devices.

Tip   The whitepaper titled "Troubleshooting High CPU Utilization on Cisco Routers" is a great resource to learn more information about how to analyze CPU utilization in Cisco IOS devices. You can find the whitepaper at http://www.cisco.com/c/en/us/support/docs/routers/10000-series-routers/15095-highcpu.html.

The document in the following link provides information on how to monitor and troubleshoot the performance of a Cisco ASA security appliance: http://www.cisco.com/c/en/us/support/docs/security/asa-5500-x-series-next-generation-firewalls/113185-asaperformance.html.

Cisco routers, switches, and the Cisco ASA can display **debug** outputs to various interfaces, including the console, aux, and vty ports. These devices can also log messages to an internal buffer to an external syslog server.

When you are connected to the console, no extra configuration is needed in order to see the **debug** command output; however, make sure that the logging console level is set to an appropriate level and that logging has not been disabled with the **no logging console** command. Excessive debugs to the console port of a router can cause it to hang or become extremely slow. This is because the router, switch, or Cisco ASA routinely prioritizes console output before other device functions.

If you are connected via Telnet or Secure Shell (SSH), you must use the **terminal monitor** command to see the **debug** output.

Note   SSH is the recommended and most secure connection option of the two.

You can also log messages to an internal buffer. If you enable the logging to an internal buffer, the log messages are copied to an internal buffer instead of to the device displaying them to the console. The buffer is a circular buffer. In other words, newer messages overwrite older messages.

To log messages to an internal buffer, use the **logging buffered** command in Cisco IOS, Cisco IOS-XE, Cisco IOS-XR, and Cisco ASA devices. Example 7-1 shows the different options of the **logging buffered** command in a Cisco IOS router.

Example 7-1   *The logging buffered Command in Cisco IOS Devices*

```
R1(config)# logging buffered ?
  <0-7>               Logging severity level
  <4096-2147483647>  Logging buffer size
  alerts              Immediate action needed        (severity=1)
  critical            Critical conditions            (severity=2)
```

```
debugging          Debugging messages            (severity=7)
discriminator      Establish MD-Buffer association
emergencies        System is unusable            (severity=0)
errors             Error conditions              (severity=3)
filtered           Enable filtered logging
informational      Informational messages        (severity=6)
notifications      Normal but significant conditions (severity=5)
warnings           Warning conditions            (severity=4)
xml                Enable logging in XML to XML logging buffer
```

Example 7-2 shows the different options of the **logging buffered** command in a Cisco ASA.

Example 7-2   *The logging buffered Command in the Cisco ASA*

```
asa(config)# logging buffered ?
configure mode commands/options:
  <0-7>          Enter syslog level (0 - 7)
  WORD           Specify the name of logging list
  alerts         Immediate action needed          (severity=1)
  critical       Critical conditions              (severity=2)
  debugging      Debugging messages               (severity=7)
  emergencies    System is unusable               (severity=0)
  errors         Error conditions                 (severity=3)
  informational  Informational messages           (severity=6)
  notifications  Normal but significant conditions (severity=5)
  warnings       Warning conditions               (severity=4)
```

To display the messages that are logged in the buffer, use the privileged EXEC command **show logging**. Example 7-3 demonstrates how to enable logging buffered at severity 6 (informational), and then an example of the output of the **show logging** command in the Cisco ASA.

Example 7-3   *Example of logging buffered and show logging Commands in the Cisco ASA*

```
asa(config)# logging buffered informational
asa(config)# show logging
Syslog logging: enabled
    Facility: 20
    Timestamp logging: disabled
    Standby logging: disabled
    Debug-trace logging: disabled
    Console logging: disabled
    Monitor logging: disabled
    Buffer logging: level informational, 11 messages logged
    Trap logging: disabled
```

```
    Permit-hostdown logging: disabled
    History logging: disabled
    Device ID: disabled
    Mail logging: disabled
    ASDM logging: level informational, 15635932 messages logged
%ASA-5-111008: User 'enable_15' executed the 'logging buffered informational' command.
%ASA-5-111010: User 'enable_15', running 'CLI' from IP 192.168.1.89, executed
  'logging buffered informational'
%ASA-6-305011: Built dynamic UDP translation from inside:192.168.1.101/19141 to
  outside:172.18.89.12/19141
%ASA-6-305011: Built dynamic UDP translation from inside:192.168.1.101/50613 to
  outside:172.18.89.12/50613
%ASA-6-305011: Built dynamic TCP translation from inside:192.168.1.101/42701 to
  outside:172.99.89.12/42701
%ASA-6-305012: Teardown dynamic TCP translation from inside:192.168.1.101/55345 to
  outside:172.18.89.12/55345 duration 0:00:31
```

Note   For more information about the Cisco ASA logs and syslog messages, go to cisco.com/go/asa or refer to the third edition of the Cisco Press book *Cisco ASA: All-in-One Next-Generation Firewall, IPS, and VPN Services*.

Example 7-4 shows an example of the output of the **show logging** command in a Cisco IOS router. The command is the same in Cisco IOS and Cisco IOS-XE.

Example 7-4   *Example of show logging Command in Cisco IOS and Cisco IOS-XE*

```
R1# show logging
Syslog logging: enabled (0 messages dropped, 3 messages rate-limited, 0 flushes, 0
  overruns, xml disabled, filtering disabled)


No Active Message Discriminator.


No Inactive Message Discriminator.

    Console logging: level debugging, 24 messages logged, xml disabled,
                    filtering disabled
    Monitor logging: level debugging, 0 messages logged, xml disabled,
                    filtering disabled
    Buffer logging:  level debugging, 24 messages logged, xml disabled,
                    filtering disabled
    Exception Logging: size (8192 bytes)
    Count and timestamp logging messages: disabled
    Persistent logging: disabled
```

```
No active filter modules.


    Trap logging: level informational, 28 message lines logged
        Logging Source-Interface:       VRF Name:


Log Buffer (8192 bytes):


*Dec 20 03:16:37.013: %SYS-5-CONFIG_I: Configured from console by console


You can specify the size of the buffer and the severity level of the messages to be
  logged.
```

In the Cisco ASA, you can specify the size of the logging buffer by using the **logging buffer-size** command, as demonstrated in Example 7-5.

Example 7-5   *Example of logging buffer-size Command in the Cisco ASA*

```
asa(config)# logging buffer-size ?
configure mode commands/options:
  <4096-52428800>  Specify logging buffer size in bytes
```

In Cisco IOS and Cisco IOS-XE, you can specify the size of the logging buffer using the **logging buffered** command, as previously shown in Example 7-1.

To clear the log in Cisco IOS and Cisco IOS-XE, you can use the **clear log** command. In the Cisco ASA, you can use the **clear logging buffer** command to clear the internal logging buffer, the **clear logging asdm** command to clear the ASDM logging buffer, and the **clear logging queue** to clear all the logging-related queues. These options are shown in Example 7-6.

Example 7-6   *Cisco ASA clear logging Command Options*

```
asa(config)# clear logging ?
exec mode commands/options:
  asdm    Clear ASDM logging buffer
  buffer  Clear internal logging buffer
  queue   Clear logging related queues
```

Another best practice is to enable millisecond (msec) time stamps in your infrastructure device. In Cisco IOS, you can enable time stamps with the **service timestamps** command, as shown in Example 7-7.

Example 7-7   *The service timestamps Command*

```
R1(config)# service timestamps debug datetime msec
R1(config)# service timestamps log datetime msec
```

In Example 7-7, the **service timestamps debug datetime msec** command is used to enable time stamps for **debug** messages, and the **service timestamps log datetime msec** command is used to enable time stamps for any other log messages.

These commands add time stamps in the format MMM DD HH:MM:SS, indicating the date and time according to the system clock. When the device clock has not been set, the date and time are preceded by an asterisk to indicate that the date and time are probably inaccurate.

With Cisco ASA devices, time stamps are enabled with the **logging timestamp** command.

Tip It is highly recommended that you use a Network Time Protocol (NTP) server to synchronize the clock in all your network infrastructure devices.

Troubleshooting NetFlow in Cisco IOS and Cisco IOS XE Devices

In this section, you will learn several useful commands, tools, and methodologies that are useful when troubleshooting NetFlow configurations in IOS Software. Figure 7-1 shows the network topology of branch office of the fictitious company called SecureMe, Inc. located in Research Triangle Park (RTP), North Carolina. This topology is used as an example for the following scenarios.

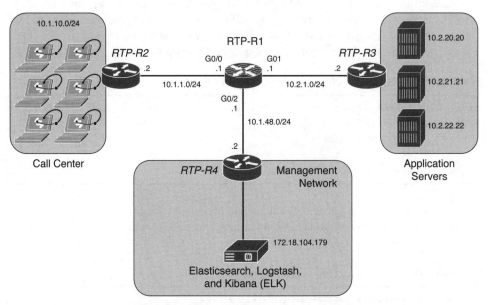

Research Triangle Park, North Carolina Office

Figure 7-1 *Research Triangle Park Branch Office*

The RTP office hosts a call center where more than 200 employees access several internal applications. The security and network administrators want to enable Flexible NetFlow in the router labeled RTP-R1 to monitor the traffic between the hosts in the call center and the application servers. The hosts in the call center are in the 10.1.10.0/24 network, and the application servers are in the 10.2.20.0/24 network, as shown in Figure 7-1. The router RTP-R1 also has a connection to a management network where the security administrator has a server running Elasticsearch, Logstash, and Kibana (otherwise known as ELK). This server is configured with the IP address 172.18.104.179.

Cisco IOS Router Flexible NetFlow Configuration

The goal is for RTP-R1 to monitor all IPv4 traffic coming from the hosts in the call center. Example 7-8 shows the relevant Flexible NetFlow and interface configuration of RTP-R1.

Example 7-8 *RTP-R1 Flexible NetFlow Configuration*

```
flow exporter EXPORTER-1
 description exports to ELK
 destination 172.18.104.179
 transport udp 9995
!
!
flow record RTP-FLOW-RECORD-1
 description basic traffic analysis in RTP
 match ipv4 protocol
 match ipv4 source address
 match ipv4 destination address
 collect counter bytes
 collect counter packets
 collect timestamp sys-uptime first
 collect timestamp sys-uptime last
!
!
flow monitor RTP-FLOW-MONITOR-1
 exporter EXPORTER-1
 record RTP-FLOW-RECORD-1
!
!
interface GigabitEthernet0/0
 ip address 10.1.1.1 255.255.255.0
 ip flow monitor RTP-FLOW-MONITOR-1 input
 duplex auto
 speed auto
 media-type rj45
```

```
!
interface GigabitEthernet0/1
 ip address 10.2.1.1 255.255.255.0
 duplex auto
 speed auto
 media-type rj45
!
interface GigabitEthernet0/2
 ip address 10.1.48.1 255.255.255.0
 duplex auto
 speed auto
 media-type rj45
!
```

In Example 7-8, a flow exporter is configured with the name EXPORTER-1. The destination host is the ELK server with the IP address 172.18.104.179 and configured to send Flexible NetFlow information using UDP port 9995. You can also use the **show running-config flow exporter** command to view all flow exporter configurations, as shown in Example 7-9.

Example 7-9   *show running-config flow exporter Command Output*

```
RTP-R1# show running-config flow exporter
Current configuration:
!
flow exporter EXPORTER-1
 description exports to ELK
 destination 172.18.104.179
 transport udp 9995
!
```

A flow record is configured called RTP-FLOW-RECORD-1. You can also use the **show running-config flow record** to see all flow records that have been configured in the Cisco IOS device, as shown in Example 7-10.

Example 7-10   *show running-config flow record Command Output*

```
RTP-R1# show running-config flow record
Current configuration:
!
flow record RTP-FLOW-RECORD-1
 description basic traffic analysis in RTP
 match ipv4 protocol
 match ipv4 source address
 match ipv4 destination address
```

```
collect counter bytes
collect counter packets
collect timestamp sys-uptime first
collect timestamp sys-uptime last
!
```

This flow record is configured to match IPv4 traffic based on the following:

■ Protocol

■ Source address

■ Destination address

The RTP-FLOW-RECORD-1 flow record is also configured to collect the following information:

■ The total number of bytes transferred in a specific flow

■ The total number of packets in such flow

■ The time when the first packet was seen

■ The time when the most recent packet was seen

You can use the **show flow record** *name* command to see the details of the configured flow record. Example 7-11 includes the output of the **show flow record RTP-FLOW-RECORD-1** command displaying the details of the RTP-FLOW-RECORD-1 flow record.

Example 7-11   *show flow record RTP-FLOW-RECORD-1 Command Output*

```
RTP-R1# show flow record RTP-FLOW-RECORD-1
flow record RTP-FLOW-RECORD-1:
  Description:        basic traffic analysis in RTP
  No. of users:      1
  Total field space: 25 bytes
  Fields:
    match ipv4 protocol
    match ipv4 source address
    match ipv4 destination address
    collect counter bytes
    collect counter packets
    collect timestamp sys-uptime first
    collect timestamp sys-uptime last
```

As you learned in previous chapters, a flow record must have at least one **match** criterion for use as the key field, and usually it has at least one **collect** criterion for use as a non-key field. There are hundreds of possible combinations for the options you can configure in flow records.

You can display several record options by using the **show flow record** command. Example 7-12 shows the output of the **show flow record** command for your reference. The **show flow record** command can show traditional NetFlow collection schemes, IPv4 input NetFlow with origin autonomous systems (AS), and many other fields. The output of this command gives you a good reference of the fields that can be used to customize a Flexible NetFlow record.

Example 7-12   *show flow record Command Output*

```
RTP-R1# show flow record
flow record netflow-original:
  Description:        Traditional IPv4 input NetFlow with origin ASs
! The BGP—Origin AS Validation feature helps prevent network administrators from
  inadvertently
! advertising routes to networks they do not control.
! This feature uses a Resource Public Key Infrastructure (RPKI) server to authenticate
  that
! certain BGP prefixes originated from an expected autonomous system before the
  prefixes
! are allowed to be advertised.
  No. of users:        0
  Total field space:   53 bytes
  Fields:
    match ipv4 tos
    match ipv4 protocol
    match ipv4 source address
    match ipv4 destination address
    match transport source-port
    match transport destination-port
    match interface input
    match flow sampler
    collect routing source as
    collect routing destination as
    collect routing next-hop address ipv4
    collect ipv4 source mask
    collect ipv4 destination mask
    collect transport tcp flags
    collect interface output
    collect counter bytes
    collect counter packets
    collect timestamp sys-uptime first
    collect timestamp sys-uptime last

flow record netflow ipv4 original-input:
  Description:        Traditional IPv4 input NetFlow with ASs
!This includes the router's own AS.
```

```
   No. of users:        0
   Total field space:  53 bytes
   Fields:
     match ipv4 tos
     match ipv4 protocol
     match ipv4 source address
     match ipv4 destination address
     match transport source-port
     match transport destination-port
     match interface input
     match flow sampler
     collect routing source as
     collect routing destination as
     collect routing next-hop address ipv4
     collect ipv4 source mask
     collect ipv4 destination mask
     collect transport tcp flags
     collect interface output
     collect counter bytes
     collect counter packets
     collect timestamp sys-uptime first
     collect timestamp sys-uptime last

flow record netflow ipv4 original-input peer:
   Description:        Traditional IPv4 input NetFlow with peer ASs
 ! This includes the peer AS.
   No. of users:        0
   Total field space:  53 bytes
   Fields:
     match ipv4 tos
     match ipv4 protocol
     match ipv4 source address
     match ipv4 destination address
     match transport source-port
     match transport destination-port
     match interface input
     match flow sampler
     collect routing source as peer
     collect routing destination as peer
     collect routing next-hop address ipv4
     collect ipv4 source mask
     collect ipv4 destination mask
     collect transport tcp flags
     collect interface output
     collect counter bytes
```

```
      collect counter packets
      collect timestamp sys-uptime first
      collect timestamp sys-uptime last
<output omitted for brevity>
```

The following are the highlights of the other NetFlow record options categories that are not displayed in Example 7-12:

- Traditional IPv4 output NetFlow with ASs

- Traditional IPv4 output NetFlow with peer ASs

- AS aggregation schemes

- AS aggregation scheme with peer ASs

- AS and TOS aggregation schemes

- AS and TOS aggregation scheme with peer ASs

- BGP next-hop and TOS aggregation schemes

- BGP next-hop and TOS aggregation scheme with peer ASs

- Destination prefix aggregation schemes

- Destination prefix aggregation scheme with peer AS

- Destination prefix and TOS aggregation schemes

- Destination prefix and TOS aggregation scheme with peer AS

- Source and destination prefixes aggregation schemes

- Source and destination prefixes aggregation scheme with peer ASs

- Prefixes and ports aggregation scheme

- Prefixes and TOS aggregation schemes

- Prefixes and TOS aggregation scheme with peer ASs

- Protocol and ports aggregation scheme

- Protocol, ports, and TOS aggregation scheme

- Source AS and prefix aggregation schemes

- Source AS and prefix aggregation scheme with peer AS

- Source prefix and TOS aggregation schemes

- Source prefix and TOS aggregation scheme with peer AS

- Traditional IPv6 input NetFlow with ASs

- Traditional IPv6 input NetFlow with peer ASs

- Traditional IPv6 output NetFlow with ASs

- Traditional IPv6 output NetFlow with peer ASs

- AS aggregation schemes

- AS aggregation scheme with peer ASs

- BGP next-hop aggregation schemes

- BGP next-hop aggregation scheme with peer ASs

- Destination prefix aggregation schemes

- Destination prefix aggregation scheme with peer AS

- Source and destination prefixes aggregation schemes

- Source and destination prefixes aggregation scheme with peer ASs

- Protocol and ports aggregation scheme

- Source AS and prefix aggregation schemes

- Source AS and prefix aggregation scheme with peer AS

- Basic traffic analysis in RTP

Troubleshooting Communication Problems with the NetFlow Collector

In this scenario, the network security administrator noticed that he was not getting any NetFlow data in his NetFlow collector (the ELK server previously illustrated in Figure 7-1). First, the **show flow exporter** command is used to make sure that the correct destination IP address was configured, as demonstrated in Example 7-13.

Example 7-13 *show flow exporter Command Output*

```
RTP-R1# show flow exporter
Flow Exporter EXPORTER-1:
  Description:             exports to ELK
  Export protocol:        NetFlow Version 9
  Transport Configuration:
    Destination IP address: 172.18.104.179
    Source IP address:      10.1.48.1
    Transport Protocol:     UDP
    Destination Port:       9995
    Source Port:            64715
    DSCP:                   0x0
    TTL:                    255
    Output Features:        Not Used
```

The IP address of the ELK server is correctly configured (172.18.104.179). In addition, the administrator checks that the correct transport protocol (UDP) and destination port (9995 in this example) are configured. The **show flow exporter statistics** is also used. The router displays that 1733 packets have been sent to the exporter, accounting for 145590 bytes of data. Example 7-14 includes the output of the **show flow exporter statistics** command.

Example 7-14 *show flow exporter statistics Command Output*

```
RTP-R1# show flow exporter statistics
Flow Exporter EXPORTER-1:
  Packet send statistics (last cleared 1w4d ago):
    Successfully sent:         1733            (145590 bytes)


  Client send statistics:
    Client: Flow Monitor RTP-FLOW-MONITOR-1
      Records added:           21
        - sent:                21
      Bytes added:             525
        - sent:                525
```

The administrator also uses the **debug flow exporter** command to troubleshoot the communication to the NetFlow collector (ELK server). Example 7-15 demonstrates the **debug flow exporter**.

Example 7-15 *The debug flow exporter Command*

```
RTP-R1# debug flow exporter
*Jan  5 00:21:02.907: FLOW EXP: Export packet sent successfully via fast switch
```

After the **debug flow exporter** command is enabled in Example 7-15, a debug message is shown indicating that a flow exporter packet has been sent to the NetFlow collector. There are several additional options for the **debug flow exporter** command, as shown in Example 7-16.

Example 7-16 *debug flow exporter Command Options*

```
RTP-R1# debug flow exporter ?
  EXPORTER-1   exports to ELK
  error        Flow exporter errors
  event        Flow exporter events
  name         Flow exporter name keyword
  packets      Flow exporter packet information
  <cr>
```

If multiple flow exporters are configured, you can specify the name of the configured exporter you want to troubleshoot. Example 7-17 shows how to enable debug flow exporter just for the EXPORTER-1 exporter.

Example 7-17 *Debugging a Specific Flow Exporter*

```
RTP-R1# debug flow exporter EXPORTER-1
Flow Exporter EXPORTER-1:
  Flow Exporter standard debugging is on
```

The following are the optional keywords of the **debug flow exporter** command:

- **error:** Enables debugging for flow exporter errors

- **event:** Enables debugging for flow exporter events

- **name:** Specifies the name of a configured flow exporter

- **packets:** Packet-level debugging for flow exporters

Remember that NetFlow uses UDP for communication. UDP is connectionless, meaning that the sender transmits data without any confirmation that the destination received the data. Subsequently, the next thing is to make sure that basic IP connectivity between the router and the ELK server is even possible. The administrator uses one of the most fundamental tools available, ping. He notices that he cannot even ping the server, as shown in Example 7-18.

Example 7-18 *ping Command Output*

```
RTP-R1# ping 172.18.104.179
Type escape sequence to abort.
Sending 5, 100-byte ICMP Echos to 172.18.104.179, timeout is 2 seconds:
.....
Success rate is 0 percent (0/5)
```

The administrator then verifies that RTP-R1 has a route for the 172.18.104.179 host by using the **show ip route 172.18.104.179** command, as shown in Example 7-19.

Example 7-19 *show ip route 172.18.104.179 Command Output*

```
RTP-R1# show ip route 172.18.104.179
Routing entry for 172.18.0.0/16
  Known via "static", distance 1, metric 0
  Routing Descriptor Blocks:
  * 10.1.48.3
      Route metric is 0, traffic share count is 1
```

RTP-R1 does have a static route to the 172.18.0.0/16 network, but it was incorrectly configured. The route was pointing to 10.1.48.3 instead of the RTP-R4 router (10.1.48.2) in the management network. After the administrator corrects the route, he was able to ping the ELK server and see all the NetFlow data in the Kibana dashboard.

Additional Useful Troubleshooting Debug and Show Commands

The following are several additional **debug** and **show** commands that are very useful when troubleshooting NetFlow problems in a Cisco IOS device.

Verifying a Flow Monitor Configuration

You can use the **show flow interface** command to verify the configuration of a flow monitor in a specific interface. Example 7-20 shows the output of the **show flow interface GigabitEthernet 0/0** command, detailing the flow monitor configuration of the Gigabit Ethernet 0/0 interface.

Example 7-20   *show flow interface GigabitEthernet 0/0 Command Output*

```
RTP-R1# show flow interface GigabitEthernet 0/0
Interface GigabitEthernet0/0
  FNF:  monitor:          RTP-FLOW-MONITOR-1
        direction:        Input
        traffic(ip):      on
```

As you can see in Example 7-20, the flexible NetFlow flow monitor RTP-FLOW-MONITOR-1 has been associated to interface Gigabit Ethernet0/0. The direction of the traffic that is being monitored by the flow monitor has been configured to **input**. There are two possible values (input and output). When a flow monitor is configured with the **input** keyword, it monitors all traffic is being received by the interface. When a flow monitor is configured with the **output** keyword, it monitors all traffic is being transmitted by such interface.

The **show flow monitor** command can also be used to verify the configuration of an existing flow monitor, as shown in Example 7-21.

Example 7-21   *show flow monitor Command Output*

```
RTP-R1# show flow monitor
Flow Monitor RTP-FLOW-MONITOR-1:
  Description:        User defined
  Flow Record:       RTP-FLOW-RECORD-1
  Flow Exporter:     EXPORTER-1
  Cache:
    Type:              normal
    Status:            allocated
```

```
    Size:                   4096 entries / 229392 bytes
    Inactive Timeout:       15 secs
    Active Timeout:         1800 secs
    Update Timeout:         1800 secs
    Synchronized Timeout:   600 secs
```

You can also specify the name of the flow monitor to display the information for a specific flow monitor. There are two additional optional keywords you can use with this command (cache and statistics), as demonstrated in Example 7-22.

Example 7-22 *show flow monitor Command Options*

```
RTP-R1# show flow monitor RTP-FLOW-MONITOR-1 ?
  cache       Flow monitor cache contents
  statistics  Flow monitor statistics
  |           Output modifiers
  <cr>
```

Example 7-23 displays the status, statistics, and data for the flow monitor named RTP-FLOW-MONITOR-1.

Example 7-23 *show flow monitor RTP-FLOW-MONITOR-1 cache Command Output*

```
RTP-R1# show flow monitor RTP-FLOW-MONITOR-1 cache
  Cache type:                     Normal
  Cache size:                     4096
  Current entries:                   4
  High Watermark:                    5

  Flows added:                      13
  Flows aged:                        9
    - Active timeout   ( 1800 secs)   0
    - Inactive timeout (   15 secs)   9
    - Event aged                      0
    - Watermark aged                  0
    - Emergency aged                  0

IPV4 SOURCE ADDRESS:       10.1.10.10
IPV4 DESTINATION ADDRESS:  10.2.20.21
IP PROTOCOL:               1
counter bytes:             2000
counter packets:           20
timestamp first:           00:52:58.943
timestamp last:            00:53:06.079
```

```
IPV4 SOURCE ADDRESS:         10.1.11.11
IPV4 DESTINATION ADDRESS:    10.2.20.21
IP PROTOCOL:                 1
counter bytes:               1000
counter packets:             10
timestamp first:             00:53:07.743
timestamp last:              00:53:07.884


IPV4 SOURCE ADDRESS:         10.1.12.12
IPV4 DESTINATION ADDRESS:    10.2.20.21
IP PROTOCOL:                 1
counter bytes:               2000
counter packets:             20
timestamp first:             00:53:08.867
timestamp last:              00:53:10.239


IPV4 SOURCE ADDRESS:         10.1.1.2
IPV4 DESTINATION ADDRESS:    10.2.20.21
IP PROTOCOL:                 1
counter bytes:               17700
counter packets:             177
timestamp first:             00:53:18.419
timestamp last:              00:53:20.833
```

Example 7-24 displays the high-level statistics, and data for the flow monitor named RTP-FLOW-MONITOR-1.

Example 7-24   *show flow monitor RTP-FLOW-MONITOR-1 statistics Command Output*

```
RTP-R1# show flow monitor RTP-FLOW-MONITOR-1 statistics
  Cache type:                         Normal
  Cache size:                         4096
  Current entries:                       1
  High Watermark:                        5

  Flows added:                          13
  Flows aged:                           12
    - Active timeout    (  1800 secs)     0
    - Inactive timeout  (    15 secs)    12
    - Event aged                          0
    - Watermark aged                      0
    - Emergency aged                      0
```

Displaying Flow Exporter Templates and Export IDs

An exporter template describes the NetFlow data and the flow set contains the actual data. This allows for flexible export. The **show flow exporter templates** command can be used to display the exporter template information such as the fields in the template, the version of the exporter format, the name of the exporter, the associated flow monitor, and other information. Example 7-25 shows the output of the **show flow exporter templates** command.

Example 7-25 *show flow exporter templates Command Output*

```
RTP-R1# show flow exporter templates
Flow Exporter EXPORTER-1:
  Client: Flow Monitor RTP-FLOW-MONITOR-1
  Exporter Format: NetFlow Version 9
  Template ID   : 256
  Source ID     : 0
  Record Size   : 25
  Template layout
  _____

  |             Field             | Type | Offset | Size |
  --------------------------------------------------------------

  | ipv4 source address           |    8 |      0 |    4 |
  | ipv4 destination address      |   12 |      4 |    4 |
  | ip protocol                   |    4 |      8 |    1 |
  | counter bytes                 |    1 |      9 |    4 |
  | counter packets               |    2 |     13 |    4 |
  | timestamp sys-uptime first    |   22 |     17 |    4 |
  | timestamp sys-uptime last     |   21 |     21 |    4 |
  --------------------------------------------------------------
```

The **show flow exporter export-ids** command is a useful command that can be used as a reference when learning the different NetFlow or IPFIX export fields that can be exported and their IDs. You have three options with this command, as shown in Example 7-26.

Example 7-26 *show flow exporter templates Command Options*

```
RTP-R1# show flow exporter export-ids ?
  ipfix       IPFIX (Version 10)
  netflow-v5  NetFlow Version 5
  netflow-v9  NetFlow Version 9
```

Example 7-27 shows the output of the **show flow exporter export-ids netflow-v9** command. This command output can be used as a reference to learn the NetFlow Version 9 export fields.

Example 7-27   *show flow exporter export-ids netflow-v9 Command Output*

```
RTP-R1# show flow exporter export-ids netflow-v9
Export IDs used by fields in NetFlow-v9 export format:
  misc unsupported                         : 37027
  datalink source-vlan-id                  :     58
  datalink destination-vlan-id             :     59
  datalink encap-size                      :    242
  datalink ethertype                       :    256
  datalink length header                   :    240
  datalink length payload                  :    241
  datalink section header                  :    315
  datalink vlan input                      :     58
  datalink dot1q vlan input                :    243
  datalink dot1q vlan output               :    254
  datalink dot1q ce-vlan                   :    245
  datalink dot1q priority                  :    244
  datalink dot1q ce-priority               :    246
  datalink l2vpn metro vcid                :    247
  datalink l2vpn metro vctype              :    248
  datalink mac source-address              :     56
  datalink mac destination-address         :     80
  datalink mac source address input        :     56
  datalink mac source address output       :     81
  datalink mac destination address input   :     80
  datalink mac destination address output  :     57
  ip version                               :     60
  ip tos                                   :      5
<output omitted for brevity>
```

You can also use the **debug flow exporter** and **debug flow monitor** commands to display flow monitor transactions and flow exporter communications to the NetFlow collector. Example 7-28 shows the output of these commands. In this example, you can see the step-by-step process of how a source interface is selected by the flow exporter and how the flow monitor (mon-1) is created. In addition, you can see that the exporter (exporter-1) is successfully registered to the flow monitor (mon-1). After the flow record (record-1) is created, you can see that the source and destination IP addresses are recorded. At the end of the output of the debugs, you can see that the packet is queued to be sent to the collector.

Example 7-28 *debug flow exporter and debug flow monitor Command Output*

```
*Jan 26 16:43:55.310: FLOW EXP: Source interface Ethernet3/6 has had change of
  IP address
*Jan 26 16:43:55.310: FLOW EXP: Selected Source IP address 0.0.0.0, dst 14.0.0.1
*Jan 26 16:43:55.318: FLOW EXP: Source interface Ethernet3/6 has had change of
  IP address
*Jan 26 16:43:55.318: FLOW EXP: Selected Source IP address 0.0.0.0, dst 14.0.0.1
*Jan 26 16:43:55.462: FLOW EXP: Source interface Ethernet3/6 has had change of
  IP address
*Jan 26 16:43:55.462: FLOW EXP: Selected Source IP address 14.0.0.2, dst 14.0.0.1
*Jan 26 16:43:55.462: FLOW EXP: Source interface Ethernet3/6 has had change of
  IP address
*Jan 26 16:43:55.462: FLOW EXP: Selected Source IP address 14.0.0.2, dst 14.0.0.1
*Jan 26 16:44:02.682: FLOW MON:  'mon-1' created.
*Jan 26 16:44:02.750: FLOW EXP: Exporter exporter-1 successfully registered
  Client mon-1
*Jan 26 16:44:02.834: Flow record: Master(record-1) Created
*Jan 26 16:44:03.694: FLOW EXP: Selected Source IP address 14.0.0.2, dst 14.0.0.1
*Jan 26 16:44:04.694: FLOW MON: Running ip input feature on Ethernet3/7
*Jan 26 16:44:04.694: FLOW MON: Running ip post input feature on Ethernet3/6
*Jan 26 16:44:04.694: FLOW MON: Running ip input feature on Ethernet3/7
*Jan 26 16:44:04.694: FLOW MON: Running ip post input feature on Ethernet3/6
*Jan 26 16:44:04.694: FLOW MON: Running ip input feature on Ethernet3/7
*Jan 26 16:44:04.694: FLOW MON: Running ip post input feature on Ethernet3/6
*Jan 26 16:44:04.694: FLOW MON: Running ip input feature on Ethernet3/7
*Jan 26 16:44:04.694: FLOW MON: Running ip post input feature on Ethernet3/6
*Jan 26 16:44:05.694: FLOW EXP: Time based resending of Template (ID: 256,
  Exporter: em_1)
*Jan 26 16:44:05.694: FLOW EXP: Packet queued for process send
```

There are many application types that can be associated by the exporter. You can use
the **show flow exporter option application table** command to display the detailed
application options that can be used. You can familiarize yourself with all the supported
applications by looking at the output of Example 7-29.

Example 7-29 *show flow exporter option application table Command Output*

```
RTP-R1# show flow exporter option application table

Engine: prot (IANA_L3_STANDARD, ID: 1)
! Different routing protocols are supported, as well as other Layer 3 standard
  tunneling protocols.
```

```
appID   Name            Description
-----   ----            -----------
1:8     egp             Exterior Gateway Protocol
1:88    eigrp           Enhanced Interior Gateway Routing Protocol
1:47    gre             General Routing Encapsulation
1:1     icmp            Internet Control Message Protocol
1:4     ipinip          IP in IP
1:58    ipv6-icmp       ICMP for IPv6
1:115   l2tp            Layer 2 Tunneling Protocol
1:89    ospf            Open Shortest Path First
1:46    rsvp            Resource Reservation Protocol


! The following are the Layer 4 standard protocols supported by the flow exporter
! in Flexible NetFlow.


Engine: port (IANA_L4_STANDARD, ID: 3)


appID   Name            Description
-----   ----            -----------
3:179   bgp             Border Gateway Protocol
3:53    dns             Domain Name Server lookup
3:79    finger          Finger
3:21    ftp             File Transfer Protocol
3:70    gopher          Internet Gopher protocol, online document
                           management.
3:80    http            World Wide Web traffic
3:143   imap            Internet Mail Access Protocol
3:194   irc             Internet Relay Chat
3:88    kerberos        Kerberos Authentication Protocol
3:389   ldap            Lightweight Directory Access Protocol
3:2049  nfs             Network File System
3:119   nntp            Network news transfer protocol
3:123   ntp             Network Time Protocol
3:110   pop3            Post Office Protocol 3
3:1723  pptp            Point-to-Point Tunneling Protocol
3:515   printer         spooler
3:520   rip             Routing Information Protocol
3:554   rtsp            Real Time Streaming Protocol
3:990   secure-ftp      FTP - File Transfer Protocol control over TLS/SSL
3:443   secure-http     Secured HTTP using SSL or TLS
3:993   secure-imap     Internet Message Access Protocol over TLS/SSL
3:994   secure-irc      Secure Internet Relay Chat
3:636   secure-ldap     secure LDAP - Lightweight Directory Access Protocol
3:563   secure-nntp     Secure Network News Transfer Protocol
3:995   secure-pop3     Secure POP3 (Post Office Protocol), standard for
                           e-mail
```

```
3:992   secure-telnet            Telnet protocol over SSL/TLS
3:5060  sip                       Session Initiation Protocol
3:25    smtp                     Simple Mail Transfer Protocol
3:161   snmp                     Simple Network Messaging Protocol
3:1080  socks                    Generic proxy protocol for TCP/IP-based networking
                                   application
3:1700  sqlnet                   DEPRECATED, Please refer to oracle-sqlnet
3:1433  sqlserver                Microsoft SQL Server
3:22    ssh                      Secure Shell
3:3478  stun-nat                  Session Traversal Utilities for NAT (STUN)
3:111   sunrpc                   SUN Remote Procedure Call
3:23    telnet                   Telnet - virtual text-oriented terminal over
                                   network
3:69    tftp                     Trivial File Transfer Protocol
3:5222  xmpp-client              Extensible Messaging and Presence Protocol (XMPP)
                                   Client
3:6000  xwindows                 X-Windows remote access


! In this example, NBAR was not configured and no applications are displayed.
Engine: NBAR (NBAR_CUSTOM, ID: 6)


appID  Name                     Description
-----  ----                     -----------


! The following are the standard Layer 7 supported applications.


Engine: layer7 (CISCO_L7_GLOBAL, ID: 13)


appID  Name                     Description
-----  ----                     -----------
13:0   unclassified             Unclassified traffic
13:1   unknown                  Unknown application
13:69  bittorrent               bittorrent p2p file sharing client
13:80  cifs                     Common Internet File System
13:56  citrix                   Citrix Systems Metaframe 3.0
13:12  cuseeme                  CU-SeeMe desktop video conference
13:13  dhcp                     Dynamic Host Configuration Protocol
13:439 dht                      Distributed sloppy Hash Table protocol
13:70  directconnect            Direct Connect Version 2.0, peer-to-peer file
                                   sharing program
13:67  edonkey                  eDonkey p2p file sharing client
13:49  exchange                 MS-Exchange
13:57  fasttrack                DEPRECATED, traffic will not match
13:58  gnutella                 Gnutella Version2 Traffic, peer-to-peer
                                   file-sharing program
13:64  h323                     H323 Protocol
13:9   ipsec                    IPSec traffic
```

```
13:59    kazaa2                  DEPRECATED, traffic will not match
13:62    mgcp                    Media Gateway Control Protocol
13:1310  ms-rpc                   Microsoft Remote Procedure Call
13:26    netbios                 DEPRECATED, traffic will not match
13:426   netshow                 Microsoft Netshow, media streaming protocol
13:2000  notes                    DEPRECATED, Please refer to lotus-notes
13:47    novadigm                Novadigm EDM
13:32    pcanywhere              Symantec pcAnywhere remote desktop
13:66    rtcp                    Real Time Control Protocol
13:61    rtp                     Real Time Protocol
13:84    sap                     SAP Systems Applications Product in Data
                                   processing
13:63    skinny                  Skinny Call Control Protocol
13:83    skype                   Skype Peer-to-Peer Internet Telephony Protocol
13:453   ssl                     Secure Socket Layer Protocol
13:427   streamwork              Xing Technology StreamWorks player
13:41    syslog                  System Logging Utility
13:114   telepresence-control    Cisco Telepresence-control
13:425   vdolive                 VDOLive streaming video
13:68    winmx                   WinMx file-sharing application
13:113   telepresence-media      telepresence-media stream
13:478   telepresence-data       telepresence-data stream
13:414   webex-meeting           webex-meeting stream
13:81    cisco-phone             Cisco IP Phones and PC-based Unified Communicators
13:472   vmware-view             VMWARE View
13:473   wyze-zero-client        WYZE Zero client
13:5060  sip                      Session Initiation Protocol
13:554   rtsp                    RTSP Protocol
13:496   jabber                  Jabber Protocol
13:5222  xmpp-client              XMPP Client
13:777   ip-camera               IP Video Surveillance Camera
13:778   surveillance-distribution  Surveillance Distribution
RTP-R1#
```

Debugging Flow Records

You can enable debugging for Flexible NetFlow flow records by using the **debug flow record** command in privileged EXEC mode. The **debug flow record** command has several command options, as shown in Example 7-30.

Example 7-30 *debug flow record Command Options*

```
RTP-R1# debug flow record ?
  RTP-FLOW-RECORD-1  User defined
  clone-1            User defined
  default-rtp        User defined
```

```
default-tcp        User defined
detailed           Show detailed information
error              Only show errors
name               Debug a specific Flow Record
netflow            Traditional NetFlow collection schemes
netflow-original   User defined
netflow-v5         User defined
options            Records used to define Flow Exporter options
<cr>
```

When troubleshooting NetFlow communications or record construction problems, you can start by using the **debug flow record error** command. If the output of the **debug flow record error** debugs do not provide you with the information you need to understand the problem, you can then use the **debug flow record detailed** command to display more detailed information

Preventing Export Storms with Flexible NetFlow

A Flexible NetFlow feature called Prevent Export Storms allows a network administrator to avoid "export storms" at a collecting device. These NetFlow export storms can take place especially when multiple Flexible NetFlow-enabled devices are configured to export NetFlow records to the same collector at the same synchronized time. These storms can take place due to the creation of the synchronized cache type. The concept called *export spreading* helps mitigate export storms. Synchronized cache with spreading requires the addition of the interval time stamp field for the synchronized cache.

This feature was introduced in Cisco IOS XE Release 3.11S.

It is recommended to add the interval as a key when no spreading is configured. When export spread is not configured, the default behavior is to immediately export the NetFlow record.

Note The spread time must be smaller than half of the interval. Thus, it will be set to half the interval time or to the configured spread interval, whichever is lower, but not lower than one second.

You should configure spreading when the interval synchronization timeout is lower than 10 seconds. This is so that the asynchronous monitors will be able to aggregate the data within a few seconds.

Note The default spread interval is 30 seconds. The maximum synchronized interval timeout value is 300 seconds. The maximum synchronized interval timeout value could be larger for native Flexible NetFlow monitors.

It is important to understand that the NetFlow/IPFIX header time stamp is set to the time when the record leaves the device, not when the record leaves the NetFlow cache. This is a common misconception. The time stamp fields in the record itself capture the time stamp of the packets and are accounted for in the NetFlow cache.

To configure the Prevent Export Storms feature, use the **flow monitor type performance-monitor** command. Example 7-31 shows an example configuration.

Example 7-31 *Preventing Export Storms*

```
RTP-R1# config terminal
Enter configuration commands, one per line.  End with CNTL/Z.
RTP-R1(config)#flow monitor type performance-monitor RTP-perf-mon
RTP-R1(config-flow-monitor)#cache type synchronized
RTP-R1(config-flow-monitor)#cache timeout synchronized 12 export-spread 5
RTP-R1(config-flow-monitor)#exporter EXPORTER-1
RTP-R1(config-flow-monitor)#end
```

You can use the **show flow monitor type performance-monitor** command to show the details of the performance monitor configuration and statistics, as shown in Example 7-32.

Example 7-32 *show flow monitor type performance-monitor Command Output*

```
RTP-R1# show flow monitor type performance-monitor
Flow Monitor type performance-monitor RTP-perf-mon:
  Description          :User defined
  Flow Record          :default-tcp
  Flow Exporter        :EXPORTER-1
  Cache type           :synchronized
        entries        :2000
        interval       :12 (seconds)
        history size   :0 (intervals)
        timeout        :1 (intervals)
        export spreading:TRUE
        spreading seconds:5 (seconds)
  Interface applied    :0
```

Troubleshooting NetFlow in Cisco NX-OS Software

Several NetFlow troubleshooting commands in NX-OS are very similar to the ones in Cisco IOS and Cisco IOS XE Software. For instance, to view the statistics for the configured flow exporters, you can use the **show flow exporter** command, as shown in Example 7-33.

Example 7-33 *show flow exporter NX-OS Command Output*

```
switch# show flow exporter
Flow Exporter RTP-DC-EXPORTER-1:
Export Version 5
Exporter Statistics
Number of Flow Records Exported 406
Number of Export Packets Sent 1235
Number of Export Bytes Sent 3676523
Number of Destination Unreachable Events 0
Number of No Buffer Events 0
Number of Packets Dropped (No Route to Host) 0
Number of Packets Dropped (other) 0
Number of Packets Dropped (LC to RP Error) 0
Number of Packets Dropped (Output Drops) 0
Time statistics were last cleared: Never
Flow exporter timeout:
Export Version 5
Exporter Statistics
Number of Flow Records Exported 0
Number of Export Packets Sent 0
Number of Export Bytes Sent 0
Number of Destination Unreachable Events 0
Number of No Buffer Events 0
Number of Packets Dropped (No Route to Host) 0
Number of Packets Dropped (other) 0
Number of Packets Dropped (LC to RP Error) 0
Number of Packets Dropped (Output Drops) 0
Time statistics were last cleared: Never
Flow exporter test-exporter:
Description: test server in San Jose CA
Export Version 5
Exporter Statistics
Number of Flow Records Exported 0
Number of Export Packets Sent 0
Number of Export Bytes Sent 0
Number of Destination Unreachable Events 0
Number of No Buffer Events 0
Number of Packets Dropped (No Route to Host) 0
Number of Packets Dropped (other) 0
Number of Packets Dropped (LC to RP Error) 0
Number of Packets Dropped (Output Drops) 0
Time statistics were last cleared: Never
```

To view the configuration of a flow monitor applied to a given interface, you can use the **show flow interface** command, as demonstrated in Example 7-34.

Example 7-34 *show flow interface Command Output in Cisco NX-OS*

```
switch# show flow interface ethernet 0/0
Interface Ethernet0/0
FNF: monitor: RTP-DC-MONITOR-1
direction: Output
traffic(ip): on
```

Example 7-35 demonstrates how to display the status and statistics for the flow monitor named RTP-DC-MONITOR-1.

Example 7-35 *show flow monitor RTP-DC-MONITOR-1 cache Command Output in Cisco NX-OS*

```
switch# show flow monitor RTP-DC-MONITOR-1 cache
SrcAddr   DstAddr   Dir PktCnt ByteCnt
10.1.1.1 10.1.1.2 Egr 246    16412
10.1.1.1 10.1.1.2 Egr 1        70
10.1.1.1 10.1.1.2 Egr 1        74
10.1.1.1 10.1.1.2 Egr 1        74
20.1.1.1 20.1.1.2 Egr 1        74
```

The following are the fields in each column in Example 7-35:

- **SrcAddr:** The source address

- **DstAddr:** The destination address

- **PktCnt:** The number of packets that have been monitored and accounted for

- **ByteCnt:** The number of bytes that have been monitored and accounted for

You can display the status and statistics for a Flexible NetFlow flow monitor by using the **show flow sw-monitor** *name* **statistics** command, as shown in Example 7-36.

Example 7-36 *show flow sw-monitor RTP-DC-MONITOR-1 statistics Command Output in Cisco NX-OS*

```
switch# show flow sw-monitor RTP-DC-MONITOR-1 statistics
Cache type: Normal
Cache size: 4096
Current entries: 4
High Watermark: 6
```

```
Flows added: 124
Flows aged: 115
- Active timeout ( 1800 secs) 0
- Inactive timeout ( 15 secs) 112
- Event aged 0
- Watermark aged 0
- Emergency aged 0
```

Several additional commands can help you display NetFlow configuration statistics and prove useful when troubleshooting NetFlow problems in Cisco NX-OS devices:

- **show flow record netflow layer2-switched input:** Used to display information about Layer 2 NetFlow configuration

- **show flow timeout:** Used to display information about NetFlow timeouts

- **show hardware flow aging:** Used to display information about NetFlow aging flows in hardware

- **show hardware flow entry address table-address type** {ip | ipv6} [**module** *module*]: Used to display information about NetFlow table entries in hardware

- **show hardware flow ip:** Used to display information about NetFlow IPv4 flows in hardware

- **show hardware flow sampler:** Used to display information about the NetFlow sampler in hardware

- **show hardware flow utilization:** Used to display information about NetFlow table utilization in the hardware

- **show sampler** *name*: Used to display information about NetFlow samplers

Troubleshooting NetFlow in Cisco IOS-XR Software

This section covers several tips useful when troubleshooting NetFlow-related problems in Cisco IOS XR devices. Even though most of the commands are very similar to the ones you learned earlier in this chapter for Cisco IOS, Cisco IOS-XE, and Cisco NX-OS platforms, the NetFlow architecture differs significantly in Cisco IOS-XR. In Cisco IOS-XR, NetFlow is not hardware accelerated, but instead it is distributed. Each individual line card runs its own instance of NetFlow, and resources are shared between the interfaces and network processing units (NPUs) on the line card. It is very important that you become familiar with the NetFlow architecture in Cisco IOS-XR to be able to successfully troubleshoot any problems you may encounter.

Figure 7-2 illustrates a high-level architecture of a Cisco ASR 9000 series router line card.

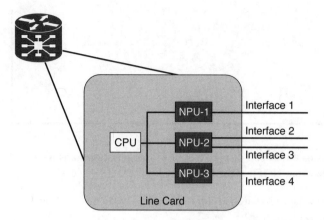

Figure 7-2   *High-Level Architecture of a Cisco ASR 9000 Series Router Line Card*

In Figure 7-2, the first NPU is configured with one interface, the second has two interfaces, and the third NPU has one interface. When you have one interface to one NPU, the full interface rate is available for NetFlow processing. For instance, on a Cisco ASR 9000 series router, it will be 100,000 packets per second (pps) in Trident cards and 200,000 pps in Typhoon-based cards. When two interfaces are enabled on an NPU, the total capacity of such NPUs is shared, depending on the type of the line card.

Figure 7-3 illustrates a diagram that explains the packet and NetFlow configuration flow in a Cisco ASR 9000 running Cisco IOS-XR software. This process is also very similar in Cisco Carrier Routing System (CRS) and Cisco Network Convergence System (NCS) devices.

The following are the steps illustrated in Figure 7-3:

Step 1.   The NetFlow process manager is responsible for sending the configuration parameters to the line card CPU.

Step 2.   The NetFlow execution agent (EA) sends configuration parameters (such as the exporter information, aging timers, and so on) to the NetFlow server.

Step 3.   The NetFlow EA also sends other configuration parameters to the forwarding application-specific integrated circuit (ASIC), such as the NetFlow sampling rate.

Step 4.   Once traffic is collected, the NetFlow sampled packets pass through the sampling policer. The hardware ucode extracts data from the header fields and sends them to the line card CPU (NetFlow producer) to construct a flow record. The line card CPU sends the flow record to the NetFlow cache, and they remain in the line card cache until they are aged due to either timer expiry or cache exhaustion. There are two timers running for flow aging: the active timer and the inactive timer.

Step 5.   The NetFlow server is also responsible for sending the sampled NetFlow records to the NETIO and subsequently to the external NetFlow collector.

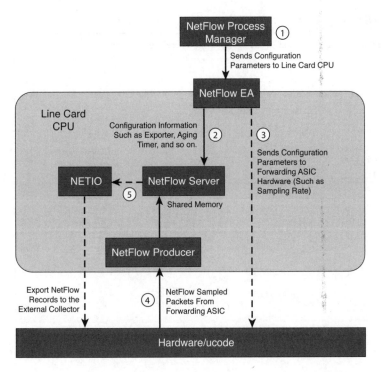

Figure 7-3 *NetFlow Configuration and Packet Flow in Cisco IOS-XR*

Note The recording of flow attributes in supported line cards is done by the line card CPU. All flow packets from the NPs are punted to line card CPU. To prevent flow packets arriving from the network processor (NP) at an overwhelming rate, the punt path is policed by internal programming policers on all the NPs that have NetFlow-enabled interfaces. The policer rate is determined based on the CPU capable rate divided by number of NetFlow enabled interfaces on each NP.

Now that you have learned a few concepts of the NetFlow packet flow and architecture in Cisco IOS XR devices, let's examine some of the **show** commands that are very useful for troubleshooting. Several of these commands are very similar to the commands you learned earlier in this chapter.

Flow Exporter Statistics and Diagnostics

One of the most useful commands to display detailed information about the flow exporter configuration in a Cisco IOS-XR device is the **show flow exporter** command. Example 7-37 shows the output of this command.

Example 7-37   *show flow exporter Command Output in Cisco IOS-XR*

```
RP/0/RP0/CPU0:router# show flow exporter RTP-exp-1 location 0/0/CPU0


Flow Exporter: NFC
Used by flow monitors: RTP-flow-mon-1


Status: Normal
Transport    UDP
Destination 172.18.104.179    (50001)
Source      10.1.1.24         (5956)
Flows exported:                              0 (0 bytes)
Flows dropped:                               0 (0 bytes)


Templates exported:                          1 (88 bytes)
Templates dropped:                           0 (0 bytes)


Option data exported:                        0 (0 bytes)
Option data dropped:                         0 (0 bytes)


Option templates exported:                   2 (56 bytes)
Option templates dropped:                    0 (0 bytes)


Packets exported:                           21 (1008 bytes)
Packets dropped:                             0 (0 bytes)


Total export over last interval of:
  1 hour:                                    0 pkts
                                             0 bytes
                                             0 flows
  1 minute:                                 21 pkts
                                          1008 bytes
                                             0 flows
  1 second:                                  0 pkts
                                             0 bytes
                                             0 flows
```

In Example 7-37, the **location** keyword is used to specify the location where the cache resides. The node-id argument is expressed in the rack/slot/module notation. In this example, the node-id is **0/0/CPU0**.

Tip   You can use the **show platform** command to see the location of all nodes installed in the router.

In the output of the **show flow exporter** command shown in Example 7-37, you can see the following information:

- The flow monitor associated to this exporter (RTP-flow-mon-1 in this example).

- The transport protocol (UDP).

- The exporter destination address.

- The status of the exporter. Normal means that the exporter is active and that the router can export packets. Disabled means that the exporter cannot send packets because the collector is unreachable or the configuration is in complete.

- The flows exported and dropped (in bytes).

- The templates exported and dropped (in bytes).

- The option data exported and dropped (in bytes).

- The option templates exported and dropped (in bytes).

- The average export rate, in bytes per packets. The information there is shown for intervals of the last hour, 1 minute, and 1 second.

Another useful command is the **show flow exporter-map** command demonstrated in Example 7-38.

Example 7-38 *show flow exporter-map Command Output in Cisco IOS-XR*

```
RP/0/RP0/CPU0:router# show flow exporter-map rtp-map1


Flow Exporter Map : rtp-map1
-------------------------------------------------
Id                 : 2
DestinationIpAddr  : 172.18.104.179
SourceIfName       : Loopback0
SourceIpAddr       : 10.1.1.24
DSCP               : 10
TransportProtocol  : UDP
TransportDestPort  : 9995
Export Version: 9
  Common Template Timeout : 1800 seconds
  Options Template Timeout : 1800 seconds
  Data Template Timeout : 600 seconds
  Interface-Table Export Timeout : 1800 seconds
  Sampler-Table Export Timeout : 0 seconds
```

The following are the fields shown in Example 7-38:

- The name of the exporter map (rtp-map1 in this example).

- The ID of the exporter map (2 in this example).

- The destination IP address of the exporter (172.18.104.179).

- The source interface (Loopback 0).

- The source IP address (10.1.1.24).

- The differentiated services code point (DSCP) value for export packets configured with the **flow exporter-map** command.

- The transport protocol. Cisco IOS XR software only supports UDP as the transport protocol.

- The configured destination port for UDP packets.

- The NetFlow version used (version 9 in this example). Only NetFlow Version 9 is supported in Cisco IOS-XR.

- The configured common template timeout.

- The configured options template timeout.

- The configured data template timeout.

- The export timeout value for the interface table.

- The export timeout value for the sampler table.

Flow Monitor Statistics and Diagnostics

You can use the **show flow monitor** command to display flow monitor information for a specific monitor map cache, as shown in Example 7-39. In Example 7-39, the name of the flow monitor is RTP-flow-mon-1, and the location is 0/0/CPU0.

Example 7-39   *show flow monitor Command Output in Cisco IOS-XR*

```
RP/0/RP0/CPU0:router# show flow monitor RTP-flow-mon-1 cache location 0/0/CPU0

Cache summary for Flow Monitor RTP-flow-mon-1:
Cache size:                    65535
Current entries:                   4
High Watermark:                62258
Flows added:                       4
Flows not added:                   0
Ager Polls:                       60
  - Active timeout                 0
  - Inactive timeout               0
```

```
   - TCP FIN flag                      0
   - Watermark aged                    0
   - Emergency aged                    0
   - Counter wrap aged                 0
   - Total                             0
Periodic export:
   - Counter wrap                      0
   - TCP FIN flag                    · 0
Flows exported                        4
Matching entries:                     4


IPV4SrcAddr      IPV4DstAddr       L4SrcPort  L4DestPort BGPDstOrigAS BGPSrcOrigAS
   IPV4DstPrfxLen

IPV4SrcPrfxLen  IPV4Prot IPV4TOS  InputInterface  OutputInterface L4TCPFlags
   ForwardStatus

ForwardReason FirstSwitched   LastSwitched     ByteCount     PacketCount  Dir Sampler ID
10.1.17.2       10.1.18.2       0           0           0           0
   24              24         $
61       normal  HundredGigE /0/0/8       HundredGigE 0/0/0/12     0
   Fwd          0              00
00:02:43:800 00 00:02:49:980 37200       620           In 0
10.1.18.2       .10.1.17.2      0           0           0           0
   24              24         $
61       normal  HundredGigE 0/0/0/12     HundredGigE 0/0/0/8      0
   Fwd          0              00
00:02:43:791 00 00:02:49:980 37200       620           In 0
10.1.17.2       10.1.18.2       0           0           0           0
   24              0          $
61       normal  HundredGigE 0/0/0/8       HundredGigE 0/0/0/12     0
   Fwd          0              00
00:02:43:798 00 00:02:49:980 34720       620           Out 0
10.1.18.2       10.1.17.2       0           0           0           0
   24              0          $
61       normal  HundredGigE 0/0/0/12     HundredGigE 0/0/0/8      0
   Fwd          0              00
00:02:43:797 00 00:02:49:980 34720       620           Out 0
L4SrcPort  L4DestPort BGPDstOrigAS BGPSrcOrigAS IPV4DstPrfxLen
```

In Example 7-39, the cache summary displays general cache information for RTP-flow-mon-1:

■ The cache size for the specified flow monitor map

■ The current number of entries in the cache

■ The high watermark for this cache

- The number of flows added to the cache
- The number of flows not added to the cache

The Ager Polls section displays the following ager statistics:

- The active timeout
- The inactive timeout
- The number of TCP FIN flags
- Watermark aged
- Emergency aged
- Counter wrap aged
- Total count for all the ager polls

The periodic export count section includes statistics for the following:

- Counter wrap
- TCP FIN flag

The last section of the output of Example 7-39 shows the number of flows exported, matching entries, and the actual flow entries.

The **show flow monitor** command is very useful and can be combined in many different combinations depending on the information you want to display and evaluate. The following are several examples of its usage:

- If you want to match on access control lists (ACLs) and one or more fields, use the following options:

  ```
  show flow monitor monitor_name cache match {ipv4 {acl name | source-address
  match_options |destination-address match_options | protocol match_options | tos
  match-options }| ipv6 {acl name | source-address match_options | destination-
  address match_options | protocol match_options | tc match_options}| layer4
  {source-port-overloaded match_options | destination- port-overloaded match_
  options | tcp-flags match_flags_options}| bgp {source-as match_options |
  destination-as match_options}| interface {ingress match_if_options | egress
  match_if_options }| timestamp {first match_options | last match_options}|
  counters {byte match_options | packets match_options}| misc {forwarding-
  status match_options | direction match_dir_options}}
  ```

- You can use the following options to sort flow record information according to a particular field:

  ```
  show flow monitor monitor_name cache sort {ipv4 {source-address | destination-
  address | tos | protocol}| ipv4 {source-address | destination-address | tc |
  protocol}| mpls {label-2 | label-3 | label-4 | label-5 | label-6 | label-type
  | prefix | top-label }| layer4 {source-port-overloaded | destination-
  port-overloaded }| bgp {source-as | destination-as}| timestamp {first |
  last}| counters {bytes | packets}| misc {forwarding-status | direction}{top |
  bottom}
  ```

- You can use the following options to include or exclude one or more fields in the **show flow monitor** command output:

```
show flow monitor monitor_name cache {include | exclude}{ipv4 {source-address
| destination-address | tos | protocol}| ipv6 {source-address | destination-
address | tc | flow-label | option-headers | protocol}| mpls {label-2 |
label-3 | label-4 | label-5 | label-6 | top-label}| layer4 {source-port-overloaded
| destination-port-overloaded}| bgp {source-as | destination-as}| timestamp
{first | last}| counters {bytes | packets}| misc {forwarding-status match_
options | direction match_dir_options}}
```

- The following options can be used to display summarized flow record statistics:

```
show flow monitor monitor_name cache summary location node_id
```

- You can use the following options to display only key field, packet, and byte information for the flow records:

```
show flow monitor monitor_name cache brief location node_id
```

- You can use the following options to display flow record information for a particular node only:

```
show flow monitor monitor_name cache location node_id
```

The **show flow monitor** *monitor_name* **cache summary** command can also be used with any combinations of the following options:

- **format**

- **match**

- **include**

- **exclude**

- **sort**

- **summary**

- **location**

Example 7-40 demonstrates and lists those options.

Example 7-40 *show flow monitor monitor-name **cache summary** Command Options in Cisco IOS-XR*

```
RP/0/RP0/CPU0:router# show flow monitor rtp-map1 cache summary ?

   brief      Show just the key fields
   exclude    Exclude field
   format     Display format
   include    Include field
   location   Specify a location
   match      Match criteria
   sort       Sorting criteria
```

You can use the **show flow monitor-map** command to display information about a configured flow monitor-map, as shown in Example 7-41.

Example 7-41 *show flow monitor-map Command Output*

```
RP/0/RP0/CPU0:router# show flow monitor-map rtp-map1

Flow Monitor Map : rtp-map1
------------------------------------------------
Id:                1
RecordMapName:     ipv4
ExportMapName:     RTP-exp-1
CacheAgingMode:    Permanent
CacheMaxEntries:   10000
CacheActiveTout:   N/A
CacheInactiveTout: N/A
CacheUpdateTout:   60 seconds
```

The following are the fields displayed in the output of the **show flow monitor-map** command shown in Example 7-41:

- The name of the flow monitor map (rtp-map1).

- The flow monitor map ID.

- The name of the export map that is associated with this monitor map (RTP-exp-1).

- The Current aging mode configured on this cache. In this example, Permanent indicates that the removal of entries from the monitor map flow cache is disabled. This is a configurable value that can be configured using the **flow monitor-map** command.

- The number of flow entries currently allowed in the flow cache before the oldest entry is removed. This is a configurable value that can be configured using the **flow monitor-map** command.

- The active flow timeout configured for this cache, in seconds. You can modify the configured active flow timeout using the **flow monitor-map** command.

- The inactive flow timeout configured for this cache, in seconds. This is also configurable using the **flow monitor-map** command.

- The update timeout configured for this cache, in seconds. You guess correctly; this is also configurable using the **flow monitor-map** command.

Displaying NetFlow Producer Statistics in Cisco IOS-XR

Earlier in this chapter, you learned the role of the NetFlow producer. You can display detailed information about the NetFlow producer by using the **show flow platform producer statistics** command and specifying the location of the node of the NetFlow producer you want to examine. Example 7-42 displays the output of the **show flow platform producer statistics** command.

Example 7-42 *show flow platform producer statistics Command Output*

```
RP/0/RP0/CPU0:router# show flow platform producer statistics location 0/0/CPU0
Mon Jan 5 09:25:22.552 UTC
NetFlow Platform Producer Counters:
IPv4 Ingress Packets:             51447246
IPv4 Egress Packets:              51447242
IPv6 Ingress Packets:                    0
IPv6 Egress Packets:                     0
MPLS Ingress Packets:                    0
MPLS Egress Packets:                     0
Drops (no space):                        0
Drops (other):                           0
Unknown Ingress Packets:                 0
Unknown Egress Packets:                  0
Worker waiting:                       8677
SPP Packets:                       4332602
Flow Packets:                     95894488
Flow Packets per SPP Frame:             40
```

Example 7-42 shows the NetFlow Producer statistics for the location 0/0/CPU0. The following counters are displayed:

- The number of IPV4 packets that were received from the remote end

- The number of transmitted IPV4 packets

- The number of Multiprotocol Label Switching (MPLS) packets that were received from the remote end

- The number of transmitted MPLS packets

- The number of packets that the producer could not enqueue to the NetFlow server because the server input ring was full

- The number of packets that the producer could not enqueue to the NetFlow server due to errors other than the server input ring being full

- The number of unrecognized packets received from the remote end that were dropped

- The number of packets transmitted to the remote end that was dropped because they were not recognized by the remote end

- The number of times that the producer needed to use the server

- The number of sequenced packet protocol (SPP) packets transmitted to the remote end

- The number of flow packets transmitted to the remote end

- The number of flow packets per SPP frame transmitted to the remote end

You can clear statistics collected by the NetFlow producer by using the **clear flow platform producer statistics** *location* command in EXEC mode, as follows:

```
RP/0/RP0/CPU0:router# clear flow platform producer statistics location 0/0/CPU0
```

Additional Useful Cisco IOS-XR Show Commands

You can use several additional commands low-level troubleshooting:

- **show flow platform nfea sampler:** Used to display NetFlow sampler map information and statistics.

- **show flow platform nfea interface:** Used to display NetFlow EA information and statistics for a given interface.

- **show flow platform nfea sp location:** Used to display NetFlow EA sampling profile information and statistics for a given location.

- **show flow platform nfea policer np:** Used to display NetFlow EA policer information and statistics for a given node.

- **show flow trace:** Useful to show low level information about the NetFlow manager, NetFlow server, NetFlow EA, and others.

Example 7-43 shows the different options of the **show flow trace** command.

Example 7-43 *show flow trace Command Options*

```
RP/0/RSP0/CPU0:router# show flow trace ?
all       Include traces from all flow subsystems
ea        Include traces from execution agent
ma        Include traces from management agent
mgr       Include traces from manager
platform  Include traces from platform specific component
server    Include traces from server
worker    Include traces from the worker thread
```

Troubleshooting NetFlow in the Cisco ASA

There are a few useful commands when troubleshooting NetFlow in the Cisco ASA. The topology in Figure 7-4 is used in the following examples. A regional office in Austin, Texas, has a Cisco ASA 5525-X configured for NetFlow Secure Event Logging (NSEL).

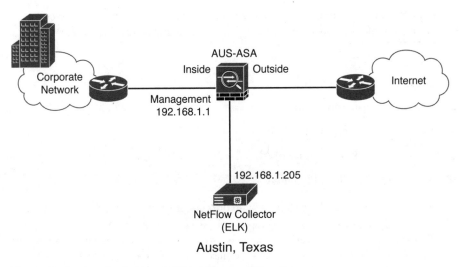

Figure 7-4 *Austin Regional Office Network Topology*

The Cisco ASA in Austin is configured to send NetFlow records to a collector with the IP address of 192.168.1.205, which is reached by the management interface of the Cisco ASA. The network administrator notices that he is not receiving NetFlow information in the collector, even though basic IP connectivity is successful.

First let's see whether NetFlow records (packets) are being sent by the Cisco ASA by using the **show flow-export counters** command, as shown in Example 7-44.

Example 7-44 *show flow-export counters Command Output in the Cisco ASA*

```
aus-asa# show flow-export counters

destination: management 192.168.1.205 9901
  Statistics:
    packets sent                                       369388
  Errors:
    block allocation failure                                0
    invalid interface                                       0
    template send failure                                   0
    no route to collector                                   0
    failed to get lock on block                             0
    source port allocation failure                          0
```

In Example 7-44, the Cisco ASA shows that it has sent 369,388 packets to the NetFlow collector. You can see that the destination is correctly set to 192.168.1.205, which resides in the management interface. You can also see that the ASA is configured to send the NetFlow packets using UDP 9901. The error counters are all zero. The **show**

flow-export counters command can help you determine whether there are any errors in the transmission of NetFlow records/packets because of any of the following reasons:

- Memory block allocation failures

- Invalid interface being configured or sourced

- NetFlow template send failures

- No route to the NetFlow collector

- Failed to get lock on memory block

- UDP source port allocation failures

After analyzing the output of the **show flow-export counters** command, the administrator decides to use the **capture** command to capture all packets sourced from the Cisco ASA to the NetFlow collector. The **capture** command is extremely useful when troubleshooting any communication problems in the Cisco ASA, because it converts the Cisco ASA in a sniffer capturing all packets for a given criteria. The syntax of the **capture** command is as follows:

```
capture capture_name [ type { asp-drop all [ drop-code ] | tls-proxy | raw-data
| lacp | isakmp [ikev1| ikev2] | inline-tag [tag ] | webvpn user webvpn-user }]
[ access-list access_list_name ][ interface asa_dataplane ] [ buffer buf_size ]
[ ethernet-type type ] [ interface interface_name ][ reinject-hide ] [ packet-
length bytes ] [ circular-buffer ] [ trace trace_count ] [ real-time ][ trace ]
[ match prot { host source- ip | source -ip mask | any }{ host destination- ip
| destination -ip mask | any } [ operator port ]
```

Example 7-45 shows the configuration of the **capture** command entered by the administrator in the Cisco ASA in Austin.

Example 7-45 *Collecting NetFlow Packet Captures Using the capture Command*

```
aus-asa(config)# capture netflow-cap interface management match udp host 192.168.1.1
  host 192.168.1.205 eq 9901
```

In Example 7-45, the capture name is **netflow-cap** and the capture is applied to the management interface. The administrator wants to collect all UDP traffic sourced from the management interface of the Cisco ASA (192.168.1.1) to the NetFlow collector (192.168.1.205) over UDP port 9901.

You can use the **show capture** command to review the capture configuration and to make sure that the capture is working and collecting traffic, as shown in Example 7-46.

Example 7-46 *show capture Command Output*

```
aus-asa# show capture
capture netflow-cap type raw-data interface management [Capturing - 15276 bytes]
  match udp host 192.168.1.1 host 192.168.1.205 eq 9901
```

To view the details of the packet capture, use the **show capture** *capture_name* detail command, as demonstrated in Example 7-47.

Example 7-47 *show capture netflow-cap detail Command Output*

```
aus-asa# show capture netflow-cap detail
21 packets captured

  1: 19:09:56.956844 0006.f62a.ee45 000c.294d.1125 0x0800 Length: 946
     192.168.1.1.13955 > 192.168.1.205.9901:  [udp sum ok] udp 904 (ttl 255,
     id 56808)
  2: 19:10:01.984949 0006.f62a.ee45 000c.294d.1125 0x0800 Length: 1242
     192.168.1.1.13955 > 192.168.1.205.9901:  [udp sum ok] udp 1200 (ttl 255,
     id 50882)
  3: 19:10:07.013121 0006.f62a.ee45 000c.294d.1125 0x0800 Length: 714
     192.168.1.1.13955 > 192.168.1.205.9901:  [udp sum ok] udp 672 (ttl 255,
     id 54557)
  4: 19:10:12.041211 0006.f62a.ee45 000c.294d.1125 0x0800 Length: 1414
     192.168.1.1.13955 > 192.168.1.205.9901:  [udp sum ok] udp 1372 (ttl 255,
     id 58539)
  5: 19:10:17.069317 0006.f62a.ee45 000c.294d.1125 0x0800 Length: 1210
     192.168.1.1.13955 > 192.168.1.205.9901:  [udp sum ok] udp 1168 (ttl 255,
     id 44241)
  6: 19:10:22.097407 0006.f62a.ee45 000c.294d.1125 0x0800 Length: 1138
     192.168.1.1.13955 > 192.168.1.205.9901:  [udp sum ok] udp 1096 (ttl 255,
     id 45668)
  7: 19:10:27.125527 0006.f62a.ee45 000c.294d.1125 0x0800 Length: 714
     192.168.1.1.13955 > 192.168.1.205.9901:  [udp sum ok] udp 672 (ttl 255,
     id 47482)
  8: 19:10:32.153632 0006.f62a.ee45 000c.294d.1125 0x0800 Length: 898
     192.168.1.1.13955 > 192.168.1.205.9901:  [udp sum ok] udp 856 (ttl 255,
     id 47263)
  9: 19:10:37.181722 0006.f62a.ee45 000c.294d.1125 0x0800 Length: 686
     192.168.1.1.13955 > 192.168.1.205.9901:  [udp sum ok] udp 644 (ttl 255,
     id 41339)
 10: 19:10:42.209828 0006.f62a.ee45 000c.294d.1125 0x0800 Length: 874
     192.168.1.1.13955 > 192.168.1.205.9901:  [udp sum ok] udp 832 (ttl 255,
     id 42217)
 11: 19:10:47.237948 0006.f62a.ee45 000c.294d.1125 0x0800 Length: 1382
     192.168.1.1.13955 > 192.168.1.205.9901:  [udp sum ok] udp 1340 (ttl 255,
     id 37157)
 12: 19:10:52.266023 0006.f62a.ee45 000c.294d.1125 0x0800 Length: 922
     192.168.1.1.13955 > 192.168.1.205.9901:  [udp sum ok] udp 880 (ttl 255,
     id 46611)
 13: 19:10:57.294143 0006.f62a.ee45 000c.294d.1125 0x0800 Length: 1398
     192.168.1.1.13955 > 192.168.1.205.9901:  [udp sum ok] udp 1356 (ttl 255,
     id 36149)
 14: 19:11:01.869629 0006.f62a.ee45 000c.294d.1125 0x0800 Length: 1514
     192.168.1.1.13955 > 192.168.1.205.9901:  [udp sum ok] udp 1472 (ttl 255,
     id 55718)
 15: 19:11:06.897795 0006.f62a.ee45 000c.294d.1125 0x0800 Length: 1118
     192.168.1.1.13955 > 192.168.1.205.9901:  [udp sum ok] udp 1076 (ttl 255,
     id 42311)
```

```
   16: 19:11:11.925885 0006.f62a.ee45 000c.294d.1125 0x0800 Length: 854
        192.168.1.1.13955 > 192.168.1.205.9901:  [udp sum ok] udp 812 (ttl 255,
           id 61926)
   17: 19:11:16.953991 0006.f62a.ee45 000c.294d.1125 0x0800 Length: 758
        192.168.1.1.13955 > 192.168.1.205.9901:  [udp sum ok] udp 716 (ttl 255,
           id 56845)
   18: 19:11:21.982111 0006.f62a.ee45 000c.294d.1125 0x0800 Length: 418
        192.168.1.1.13955 > 192.168.1.205.9901:  [udp sum ok] udp 376 (ttl 255,
           id 56342)
   19: 19:11:27.010253 0006.f62a.ee45 000c.294d.1125 0x0800 Length: 1006
        192.168.1.1.13955 > 192.168.1.205.9901:  [udp sum ok] udp 964 (ttl 255,
           id 54177)
   20: 19:11:30.156318 0006.f62a.ee45 000c.294d.1125 0x0800 Length: 1474
        192.168.1.1.13955 > 192.168.1.205.9901:  [udp sum ok] udp 1432 (ttl 255,
           id 52633)
   21: 19:11:35.172537 0006.f62a.ee45 000c.294d.1125 0x0800 Length: 1502
        192.168.1.1.13955 > 192.168.1.205.9901:  [udp sum ok] udp 1460 (ttl 255,
           id 45542)
21 packets shown
```

In Example 7-47, a total of 21 packets were captured, and you can see the details of each packet. To view the actual dump of each of the packets collected, you can use the **show capture** *capture_name* **dump** command, as shown in Example 7-48.

Example 7-48   *show capture netflow-cap dump Command Output*

```
aus-asa# show capture netflow-cap dump
21 packets captured

   1: 19:09:56.956844       192.168.1.1.13955 > 192.168.1.205.9901:  udp 904
0x0000        000c 294d 1125 0006 f62a ee45 0800 4500    ..)M.%...*.E..E.
0x0010        03a4 dde8 0000 ff11 5641 c0a8 0101 c0a8    ........VA......
0x0020        01cd 3683 26ad 0390 7bb1 0009 000c 47de    ..6.&...{.....G.
0x0030        3675 54ab 27d4 0005 a318 0000 0000 0100    6uT.'...........
0x0040        0068 0017 0850 c0a8 01cd 0000 0004 c0a8    .h...P..........
0x0050        0101 0000 ffff 0103 03c0 a801 cdc0 a801    ................
0x0060        0100 0000 0001 0000 0000 014a bc93 8432    ...........J...2
0x0070        0000 014a bc93 8432 0000 0000 0000 0000    ...J...2........
0x0080        0000 0000 0000 0000 0000 0000 0000 0000    ................
0x0090        0000 0000 0000 0000 0000 0000 0000 0000    ................
0x00a0        0000 0000 0000 0107 0080 0017 0850 c0a8    .............P..
0x00b0        01cd 0000 0004 c0a8 0101 0000 ffff 0103    ................
0x00c0        03c0 a801 cdc0 a801 0100 0000 0005 07e2    ................
0x00d0        0000 014a bc93 8432 0000 0224 0000 0000    ...J...2...$....
0x00e0        0000 014a bc93 8432 0017 0850 c0a8 01cd    ...J...2...P....
0x00f0        0000 0004 c0a8 0101 0000 ffff 0103 03c0    ................
```

```
0x0100        a801 cdc0 a801 0100 0000 0002 07e2 0000        ...............
0x0110        014a bc93 8432 0000 0224 0000 0000 0000        .J...2...$......
0x0120        014a bc93 8432 0100 0068 0017 0851 c0a8        .J...2...h...Q..
0x0130        0159 eede 0004 ac12 6c2b 0035 0008 1100        .Y......l+.5....
0x0140        000a 756e 24ac 126c 2bee de00 3501 0000        ..un$..l+...5...
0x0150        0000 014a bc93 8568 0000 014a bc93 8568        ...J..h...J...h
0x0160        433a 1af1 2bc0 c8ca 0000 0000 0000 0000        C:...+..........
0x0170        0000 0000 0000 0000 0000 0000 0000 0000        ................
0x0180        0000 0000 0000 0000 0000 0000 0000 0107        ................
0x0190        00c0 0017 0851 c0a8 0159 eede 0004 ac12        .....Q...Y......
0x01a0        6c2b 0035 0008 1100 000a 756e 24ac 126c        l+.5......un$..l
0x01b0        2bee de00 3505 07e2 0000 014a bc93 8586        +...5......J....
0x01c0        0000 0020 0000 0127 0000 014a bc93 8568        ... ...'...J...h
0x01d0        0017 0851 c0a8 0159 eede 0004 ac12 6c2b        ...Q...Y......l+
0x01e0        0035 0008 1100 000a 756e 24ac 126c 2bee        .5......un$..l+.
0x01f0        de00 3502 07e2 0000 014a bc93 8586 0000        ..5......J......
0x0200        0020 0000 0127 0000 014a bc93 8568 0017        . ...'...J...h..
0x0210        081d c0a8 0182 d751 0004 4a7d 8965 01bb        .......Q..J}.e..
0x0220        0003 0600 00ae 6359 0c4a 7d89 65d7 5101        ......cY.J}.e.Q.
0x0230        bb05 0000 0000 014a bc93 86c6 0000 0a3b        .......J.......;
0x0240        0000 0352 0000 014a bc92 94d6 0000 0100        ...R...J........
0x0250        0068 0017 0852 c0a8 0185 cc0f 0004 0c95        .h...R..........
0x0260        da49 01bb 0003 0600 00ae 6359 0c0c 95da        .I........cY....
0x0270        49cc 0f01 bb01 0000 0000 014a bc93 92b0        I..........J....
0x0280        0000 014a bc93 92b0 433a 1af1 2bc0 c8ca        ...J....C:...+...
0x0290        0000 0000 0000 0000 0000 0000 0000 0000        ................
0x02a0        0000 0000 0000 0000 0000 0000 0000 0000        ................
0x02b0        0000 0000 0000 0107 00fc 0017 0852 c0a8        .............R..
0x02c0        0185 cc0f 0004 0c95 da49 01bb 0003 0600        .........I......
0x02d0        00ae 6359 0c0c 95da 49cc 0f01 bb05 07ed        ..cY....I.......
0x02e0        0000 014a bc93 9364 0000 0034 0000 0034        ...J...d...4...4
0x02f0        0000 014a bc93 92b0 0017 0852 c0a8 0185        ...J.......R....
0x0300        cc0f 0004 0c95 da49 01bb 0003 0600 00ae        ......I.........
0x0310        6359 0c0c 95da 49cc 0f01 bb02 07ed 0000        cY....I.........
0x0320        014a bc93 9364 0000 0034 0000 0034 0000        .J...d...4...4..
0x0330        014a bc93 92b0 0017 07f0 c0a8 01cc 007b        .J.............{
0x0340        0004 c63c 16f0 007b 0003 1100 00ae 6359        ...<...{......cY
0x0350        0cc6 3c16 f000 7b00 7b05 07eb 0000 014a        ..<...{.{......J
0x0360        bc93 9788 0000 0000 0000 0000 0000 014a        ..............J
0x0370        bc92 acdc 0017 07f0 c0a8 01cc 007b 0004        .............{..
0x0380        c63c 16f0 007b 0003 1100 00ae 6359 0cc6        .<...{......cY..
0x0390        3c16 f000 7b00 7b02 07eb 0000 014a bc93        <...{.{......J..
0x03a0        9788 0000 0030 0000 0030 0000 014a bc91        .....0...0...J..
0x03b0        bbf0
<output omitted>
```

> **Note**   For more information about the Cisco ASA **capture** command, see http://
> www.cisco.com/c/en/us/td/docs/security/asa/asa-command-reference/A-H/cmdref1/
> c1.html#pgfId-2147322.

Clearly, the Cisco ASA is sending the NetFlow packets to the NetFlow collector correctly. After reviewing the output of all the aforementioned commands, the network
administrator logs in to the NetFlow collector (ELK server) and notices that its logstash
NetFlow configuration file (logstash-netflow.conf in this example) was configured
incorrectly. It had 10.1.1.1 for the NetFlow source instead of the Cisco ASA management interface IP address. The highlighted line in Example 7-49 shows the entry in the
logstash-netflow.conf file that was configured incorrectly.

Example 7-49   *Incorrectly Configured Logstash-netflow.conf file*

```
input {
  udp {
    port => 9901
    codec => netflow {
      definitions => "/home/administrator/logstash-1.4.2/lib/logstash/codecs/
        netflow/netflow.yaml"
      versions => [9]
    }
  }
}


output {
 stdout { codec => rubydebug }
 if ( [host] =~ "10.1.1.1" ) {
    elasticsearch {
      index => "logstash_netflow5-%{+YYYY.MM.dd}"
      host => "localhost"
    }
  } else {
    elasticsearch {
      index => "logstash-%{+YYYY.MM.dd}"
      host => "localhost"
    }
  }
}
```

When troubleshooting NetFlow communication problems in the Cisco ASA, basic troubleshooting tools such as the **capture** command and other simple **show** commands can save you
hours of troubleshooting. These are considered the "Swiss army knives" that can help during
the troubleshooting of many communication and IP connectivity issues in the Cisco ASA.

Troubleshooting NetFlow in the Cisco NetFlow Generation Appliance

This section provides information about several commands that can prove useful when troubleshooting problems in the Cisco NetFlow Generation Appliance (NGA).

Gathering Information About Configured NGA Managed Devices

A managed device is a device that replicates network packets to the Cisco NGA data ports for monitoring and producing NetFlow packets to collector devices. For example, a Cisco NGA data port can be connected to a different managed device, such as a Cisco Nexus series switch. The NGA downloads internal information about the switch (managed device), so it can populate the input and output interface for flow records that are sent to collectors.

Note If no managed device is configured for a particular data port, the NGA populates the input and output interface fields in flow records with a value corresponding to its own local data port on which the flow was received.

To view the details about the configured managed devices, use the **show managed-device** command, as shown in Example 7-50.

Example 7-50 *show managed-Device Command Output*

```
root@rtp-nga.cisco.com# show managed-device

        Managed Device:          10.1.1.10
        ID:                      1
        Username:                md-user
        Dataport:                2,4
```

In Example 7-50, the IP address of the configured managed device is 10.1.1.10. The ID is the identifier of the managed device; in this case, the managed device ID is 1. The username used to communicate to the managed device is md-user and the data ports are 2 and 4.

Note The data ports are configured with the **dataport ports** command. These are the data ports where NGA is receiving network traffic from the managed device. Each ports is a comma-separated string (for example, 2,4 for data port 2 and data port 4).

Gathering Information About the Flow Collector

You can obtain information about the configured flow collector using the **show flow collector** command. Before we review that command, let us look at all the options of the **show flow** command, as shown in Example 7-51.

Example 7-51   *show flow Command Options*

```
root@rtp-nga.cisco.com# show flow ?
     collector    - Show flow collector
     exporter     - Show flow exporter
     filter       - Show flow filter
     monitor      - Show flow monitor
     record       - Show flow record
     sampling     - Show flow sampling information received at data ports
```

You can use the **show flow** command to display information about the following:

■ All the configured collectors in the NGA

■ The configured exporter

■ Any flow filters configured in the device

■ Information about the configured flow monitor

■ Information about configured flow records

■ NetFlow sampling information received at any of the data ports

To display and analyze information about the flow collectors configured in the system, you can use the **show flow collector** command, as demonstrated in Example 7-52.

Example 7-52   *show flow collector Command Output*

```
root@NGA.cisco.com# show flow collector
        Collector name:                 rtp-collector-1
        Description:
        IP address:                     172.18.104.179
        DSCP value:                     0
        Transport:                      UDP
        Port number:                    9995

        Collector name:                 rtp-collector-2
        Description:
        IP address:                     172.18.104.180
        DSCP value:                     0
        Transport:                      UDP
        Port number:                    9995

root@rtp-nga.cisco.com#
```

In Example 7-52, two flow collectors are configured (rtp-collector-1 and rtp-collector-2). The IP address of rtp-collector-1 is 172.18.104.179, and the IP address of rtp-collector-2 is 172.18.104.180. Both are configured to communicate using UDP port 9995.

Gathering Information About the Flow Exporter

The **flow exporter** *name* command is used to specify various parameters for an export session between the Cisco NGA and one or more collectors that the exporter will use to send NetFlow packets. The Cisco NGA flow exporter includes parameters such as the following:

- The version **format** of NetFlow packets to be sent

- How frequent the exporter sends template and option data

- Destination name and a description of the exporter

You can use the **show flow exporter** command to view and analyze the flow exporter configuration in the Cisco NGA, as shown in Example 7-53.

Example 7-53   *show flow exporter Command Output*

```
root@rtp-nga.cisco.com# show flow exporter rtp-exporter
        Exporter name:          rtp-exporter
        Description:             Exporter in RTP NGA
        Export version:         v9
        Template timeout:       20 minutes
        Options timeout:        30 minutes
        Policy:                 Multi-destination
        Destination name:       rtp-collector-1
```

In Example 7-53, the exporter name is rtp-exporter. The exporter is configured to export NetFlow Version 9 packets. The template timeout is set to 20 minutes, and the options timeout is set to 30 minutes. The policy is set to multi-destination.

Note   When the exporter policy is configured to multi-destination, the exporter sends the same NetFlow packet to all collectors set in the exporter. When the exporter policy is configured as a policy weighted-round-robin, the Cisco NGA load balances the NetFlow packets among collectors set in the exporter.

In this example, the destination name is rtp-collector-1.

Gathering Information About Flow Records

To gather information about specific flow records, you can use the **show flow record** command, as shown in Example 7-54.

Example 7-54   *show flow record Command Output*

```
root@rtp-nga.cisco.com# show flow record rtp-record-1


        Record name:                    rtp-record-1
        Record type:                    IPv4
        Record description:             RTP record example 1
        Number of match fields:         10
        Match field:                    MAC source address
        Match field:                    MAC destination address
        Match field:                    Ethertype field
        Match field:                    Input Interface
        Match field:                    Output Interface
        Match field:                    IPv4 destination address
        Match field:                    IPv4 source address
        Match field:                    IP protocol
        Match field:                    Destination port
        Match field:                    Source port
        Number of collect fields:       7
        Collect field:                  Packet count
        Collect field:                  Byte count
        Collect field:                  Maximum TTL/hop limit
        Collect field:                  Minimum TTL/hop limit
        Collect field:                  First timestamp
        Collect field:                  Last timestamp
        Collect field:                  TCP header flags
root@rtp-nga.cisco.com#
```

As you can see in Example 7-54, the **show flow record** command displays the following information:

- The flow record name (rtp-record-1 in this example)

- The flow record type (IPv4 in this example)

- The flow record description entered by the administrator

- The number of match fields configured for such flow record (10 in this example)

- The actual match fields

- The number of collect fields configured for the flow record (7 in this example)

- The actual collect fields

Gathering Information About the Flow Monitor

In the Cisco NGA, the flow monitor is a conceptual device that takes network traffic from data ports and generates flow records based on parameters configured at the flow exporter and flow monitor. It subsequently sends the flow information to the exporter, which can apply filter rules, packs the flow records into NetFlow packets, and sends the NetFlow packets to collectors.

The Cisco NGA supports up to four active flow monitors and up to six flow collectors. You can use the **show flow exporter** command to display and analyze information about the configured flow monitor, as shown in Example 7-55.

Example 7-55 *show flow monitor Command Output*

```
root@rtp-nga.cisco.com# show flow monitor rtp-monitor

        Monitor name:            rtp-monitor
        Description:
        Exporter name:           example-exporter
        Record name:             example-record
        Dataport:                2,3
        Tunnel:                  Inner
        Cache size:              40 %
        Cache type:              Standard
        Cache active timeout:    1800 seconds
        Cache inactive timeout:  15 seconds
        Cache session timeout:   Disabled
        Monitor Status:          Inactive

root@rtp-nga.cisco.com#
```

Show Tech-Support

As in other Cisco devices such as Cisco IOS, Cisco IOS-XE, Cisco IOS-XR, Cisco NX-OS, and Cisco ASA, the Cisco NGA has its own version of the **show tech-support** command (**show tech** for short). This is the most comprehensive **show** command that is used for low-level troubleshooting in the Cisco NGA. The **show tech** command includes numerous device statistics, logs, and low-level information that can be useful for advanced users and for Cisco's Technical Assistance Center (TAC).

Example 7-56 includes a short snippet of the **show tech** command.

Example 7-56 *show tech Command Output*

```
root@rtp-nga.cisco.com# show tech-support
! NTP Server Configuration
! In this example two NTP servers are configured
NGA synchronize time to:        NTP
NTP server1:                    10.1.2.161
NTP server2:                    10.1.2.162
NGA time zone:
```

```
Current system time:                Sun Jul 26 16:58:46 UTC 2015

! The version of the NGA appliance. In this example, no patches have been
! installed on the system.
NGA application image version: 1.0(2) RELEASE SOFTWARE [fc2]
Product Id: NGA3240-K9
Disk 0 size: 999 GB
Disk 1 size: 3 GB
Installed patches:

No patches are installed on this system.

! IP address, DNS server, HTTP server, TACACS+, Telnet and SSH configuration
  information

IP address:              10.1.1.215
Subnet mask:             255.255.255.0
IP Broadcast:            10.1.1.55
DNS Name:                rtp-nga.cisco.com
Default Gateway:         10.1.1.1
Nameserver(s):           144.254.254.254
HTTP server:             Disabled
HTTP secure server:      Enabled
HTTP port:               80
HTTP secure port:        443
TACACS+ configured:      No
Telnet:                  Disabled
SSH:                     Enabled

! IP address, DNS server, HTTP
SNMP Agent:    rtp-snmp-02.cisco.com    10.1.5.14

SNMPv1:  Enabled
SNMPv2C: Enabled

! Detailed file system and low level process information

sysDescr        Cisco NetFlow Generation Appliance (NGA3240-K9), Version 1.0(2)
  RELEASE SOFTWARE [fc2]
Compiled Oct 29 2012 19:50:40
Copyright (c) 2012 by Cisco Systems, Inc.
sysObjectID     enterprises.9.1.1539
sysContact
sysName
sysLocation
```

```
NAM_TARGET=NFA_X520
NAM_TARGET_ID=13
MP=no
NAM_PROD_NO=NFA_X520
NAM_PROD_DESCR="Cisco NetFlow Generation Appliance (NFA_X520)"
NAM_VERSION="1.0(2) RELEASE SOFTWARE [fc2]"
NFA_MODEL=NGA3240-K9
NAM_PID=NGA3240-K9
NAM_SN=FCH1825V223
NAM_VID=V01
MEGARAID=1
NAM_LOCAL_DISK=/dev/sda
NAM_ROOT_PARTITION=/dev/sda1
NAM_NVRAM_PARTITION=/dev/sda2
NAM_STORAGE1_PARTITION=/dev/sda3
NAM_STORAGE_PARTITION=/dev/sda3
NAM_DISK=1002GB
NAM_DISK0=999GB
NAM_DISK1=3GB


  PID TTY       STAT   TIME COMMAND
    1 ?         Ss     0:25 init [3]
    2 ?         S      1:29 [kthreadd]
 2619 ?         S<s    0:00 udevd --daemon
 4694 ?         Ss     0:00 /sbin/syslogd
 4702 ?         Ss     0:00 /sbin/klogd -x -c 4
 4716 ?         Ss     0:00 /usr/sbin/inetd
 4723 ?         Ss     0:00 /usr/sbin/sshd
 4757 ?         Ss     0:00 /usr/sbin/ntpd -u 102:102 -c /etc/ntp.conf
 4768 ?         Ssl    0:01 /usr/sbin/nscd
 4832 ?         Ss     0:00 /usr/sbin/atd
 4852 ?         Ss     0:00 /usr/sbin/cron
 4862 ?         Ssl 1105:26 /usr/local/nam/bin/mond -d
 4864 ?         Ss     0:00 /usr/local/nam/bin/devconfd
 4866 ?         S      0:00 /bin/bash /usr/local/nam/bin/rd_wd
 4877 ?         Ss     0:00 /usr/local/nam/bin/configd
 4879 pts/0     Ss+    0:00 /usr/local/nam/bin/cli -n
 4882 ?         Ssl    0:00 /usr/local/nam/bin/dmand/dmand
 4888 tty1      Ss+    0:00 /sbin/getty 38400 tty1
 4889 tty2      Ss+    0:00 /sbin/getty 38400 tty2
 4891 ttyS1     Ss+    0:00 /sbin/getty -L ttyS1 9600 vt100
 5062 ttyS0     Ss+    0:00 /sbin/getty -L ttyS0 9600 vt100
 5106 ?         Ss     0:11 /usr/local/apache/bin/httpd -DSSL -k start
 5107 ?         S      0:00 /usr/local/apache/bin/httpd -DSSL -k start
 5108 ?         S      0:00 /usr/local/apache/bin/httpd -DSSL -k start
```

```
 5109 ?         S        0:00 /usr/local/apache/bin/httpd -DSSL -k start
 5110 ?         S        0:00 /usr/local/apache/bin/httpd -DSSL -k start
 5111 ?         S        0:00 /usr/local/apache/bin/httpd -DSSL -k start
 5121 ?         S        0:00 /usr/local/apache/bin/httpd -DSSL -k start
 5125 ?         S        0:00 /usr/local/apache/bin/httpd -DSSL -k start
 5126 ?         S        0:00 /usr/local/apache/bin/httpd -DSSL -k start
 5127 ?         S        0:00 /usr/local/apache/bin/httpd -DSSL -k start
 5170 ?         S        0:00 /usr/local/apache/bin/httpd -DSSL -k start
10683 ?         S        0:00 sleep 2m
10684 ?         Ss       0:00 sshd: root@pts/1
10688 pts/1     Ss+      0:00 -cli
10713 pts/1     R+       0:00 /bin/ps ax


! Underlying Linux IP configuration information


Address              HWtype  HWaddress          Flags Mask          Iface
10.203.5.193         ether   00:00:0c:9f:f3:88  C                   eth0


eth0      Link encap:Ethernet  HWaddr 1C:6A:7A:18:11:00
          inet addr:10.203.5.215  Bcast:10.203.5.223  Mask:255.255.255.224
          UP BROADCAST RUNNING MULTICAST  MTU:1500  Metric:1
          RX packets:146408 errors:0 dropped:0 overruns:0 frame:0
          TX packets:481794 errors:0 dropped:0 overruns:0 carrier:0
          collisions:0 txqueuelen:1000
          RX bytes:42372760 (40.4 MiB)  TX bytes:654152312 (623.8 MiB)


eth1      Link encap:Ethernet  HWaddr 1C:6A:7A:18:11:01
          BROADCAST MULTICAST  MTU:1500  Metric:1
          RX packets:0 errors:0 dropped:0 overruns:0 frame:0
          TX packets:0 errors:0 dropped:0 overruns:0 carrier:0
          collisions:0 txqueuelen:1000
          RX bytes:0 (0.0 b)  TX bytes:0 (0.0 b)


eth2      Link encap:Ethernet  HWaddr 90:E2:BA:70:FF:28
          UP BROADCAST RUNNING PROMISC MULTICAST  MTU:1500  Metric:1
          RX packets:0 errors:0 dropped:0 overruns:0 frame:0
          TX packets:0 errors:0 dropped:0 overruns:0 carrier:0
          collisions:0 txqueuelen:1000
          RX bytes:0 (0.0 b)  TX bytes:0 (0.0 b)


eth3      Link encap:Ethernet  HWaddr 90:E2:BA:70:FF:29
          UP BROADCAST RUNNING PROMISC MULTICAST  MTU:1500  Metric:1
          RX packets:0 errors:0 dropped:0 overruns:0 frame:0
          TX packets:0 errors:0 dropped:0 overruns:0 carrier:0
          collisions:0 txqueuelen:1000
          RX bytes:0 (0.0 b)  TX bytes:0 (0.0 b)
```

```
eth4      Link encap:Ethernet  HWaddr 90:E2:BA:70:FE:D8
          UP BROADCAST RUNNING PROMISC MULTICAST  MTU:1500  Metric:1
          RX packets:0 errors:0 dropped:0 overruns:0 frame:0
          TX packets:0 errors:0 dropped:0 overruns:0 carrier:0
          collisions:0 txqueuelen:1000
          RX bytes:0 (0.0 b)  TX bytes:0 (0.0 b)

eth5      Link encap:Ethernet  HWaddr 90:E2:BA:70:FE:D9
          UP BROADCAST RUNNING PROMISC MULTICAST  MTU:1500  Metric:1
          RX packets:0 errors:0 dropped:0 overruns:0 frame:0
          TX packets:0 errors:0 dropped:0 overruns:0 carrier:0
          collisions:0 txqueuelen:1000
          RX bytes:0 (0.0 b)  TX bytes:0 (0.0 b)

lo        Link encap:Local Loopback
          inet addr:127.0.0.1  Mask:255.255.255.255
          UP LOOPBACK RUNNING  MTU:16436  Metric:1
          RX packets:7122 errors:0 dropped:0 overruns:0 frame:0
          TX packets:7122 errors:0 dropped:0 overruns:0 carrier:0
          collisions:0 txqueuelen:0
          RX bytes:732348 (715.1 KiB)  TX bytes:732348 (715.1 KiB)


! Active connection information (similar to the output of the netstat Linux command.


Active Internet connections (servers and established)
Proto Recv-Q Send-Q Local Address            Foreign Address              State
tcp        0      0 *:ssh                    *:*                         LISTEN
tcp        0      0 localhost:9911           *:*                         LISTEN
tcp        0      0 *:telnet                 *:*                         LISTEN
tcp        0      0 localhost:9914           *:*                         LISTEN
tcp        0      0 *:https                  *:*                         LISTEN
tcp        0      0 localhost:46147          localhost:9911              ESTABLISHED
tcp        0      0 localhost:38998          localhost:9911              ESTABLISHED
tcp        0      0 localhost:9911           localhost:46150             ESTABLISHED
tcp        0      0 localhost:46145          localhost:9911              ESTABLISHED
tcp        0      0 localhost:46150          localhost:9911              ESTABLISHED
tcp        0      0 localhost:676            localhost:9911              TIME_WAIT
tcp        0      0 localhost:46148          localhost:9911              ESTABLISHED
tcp        0      0 localhost:9911           localhost:46145             ESTABLISHED
tcp        0      0 localhost:9911           localhost:38998             ESTABLISHED
tcp        0      0 localhost:46149          localhost:9911              ESTABLISHED
tcp        0      0 localhost:9911           localhost:46147             ESTABLISHED
tcp        0    236 localhost:9911           localhost:688               ESTABLISHED
tcp        0      0 localhost:9911           localhost:46148             ESTABLISHED
tcp        0      0 localhost:9911           localhost:60524             ESTABLISHED
tcp        0      0 localhost:60525          localhost:9911              ESTABLISHED
```

```
tcp        0        0 localhost:9911              localhost:46149          ESTABLISHED
tcp        0        0 localhost:688              localhost:9911           ESTABLISHED
tcp        0        0 localhost:9911              localhost:60525          ESTABLISHED
tcp        0        0 localhost:60524            localhost:9911           ESTABLISHED
tcp        0        0 localhost:9911              localhost:46146          ESTABLISHED
tcp        0        0 localhost:46146            localhost:9911           ESTABLISHED
udp        0        0 mel-csxpod1-nga-02.cisc:ntp *:*
udp        0        0 localhost:ntp              *:*
udp        0        0 *:ntp                      *:*
udp        0        0 *:snmp                     *:*
udp        0        0 *:41812                    *:*
udp        0        0 *:53497                    *:*
udp        0        0 *:57775                    *:*
Active UNIX domain sockets (servers and established)
Proto RefCnt Flags       Type      State       I-Node Path
unix  14      [ ]         DGRAM                 6027   /dev/log
unix  2       [ ACC ]     STREAM    LISTENING   6218   /var/run/nscd/socket
unix  2       [ ]         DGRAM                 16414  /usr/local/nam/bin/
                                                         devconfd_ipc_path
unix  2       [ ]         DGRAM                 357    @/org/kernel/udev/udevd
unix  2       [ ]         DGRAM                 25326
unix  2       [ ]         DGRAM                 24940
unix  2       [ ]         DGRAM                 15781
unix  2       [ ]         DGRAM                 1551
unix  2       [ ]         DGRAM                 15758
unix  2       [ ]         DGRAM                 2835
unix  2       [ ]         DGRAM                 2766
unix  2       [ ]         DGRAM                 6231
unix  2       [ ]         DGRAM                 15686
unix  2       [ ]         DGRAM                 6088
unix  2       [ ]         DGRAM                 6058
unix  2       [ ]         DGRAM                 6028
Active IPX sockets
Proto Recv-Q Send-Q Local Address              Foreign Address
   State


Linux mel-csxpod1-nga-02.cisco.com 3.0.0-nam #1 SMP PREEMPT Fri Jul 13 14:04:48 PDT
   2012 x86_64 GNU/Linux


queue 0: rc=32768, rs=524288, bs=134217728 (order 9)
niantic_data_rx_resources: adapter 3, queue 0 (48): allocated 32768 pkts.
niantic_data_rx_resources: adapter 3, queue 1: rc=32768, rs=524288, bs=134217728
   (order 9)
niantic_data_rx_resources: adapter 3, queue 1 (49): allocated 32768 pkts.
...
<and many many more logs>
```

As you can see in Example 7-56, the **show tech** command is very comprehensive, including tons of information that can be useful to troubleshoot installation, configuration, and communication issues in the Cisco NGA.

Additional Useful NGA show Commands

The following are several additional **show** commands that can prove useful when troubleshooting problems in the Cisco NGA:

- **show audit-trail:** Used to show the status of audit trail.

- **show cache statistics cumulative** *monitor_name*: Used to show statistic information at the internal cache level from processing network traffic received at NGA data ports.

- **show cache statistics rates** *monitor_name*: Displays flow stats information at the internal cache level with rate derived from the last minute.

- **show cdp settings:** Displays Cisco Discovery Protocol (CDP) settings.

- **show collector statistics** *collector_name*: Displays flow statistics at the flow collector level, both cumulative and last-minute rates. This displays how many packets and flows have been sent to each collector.

- **show dataport statistics cumulative:** Displays statistics at the data port level where network traffic arrives at NGA for processing.

- **show dataport statistics rates:** Displays statistics at the data port level with rates computed for the last minute.

- **show dataport statistics rates queues:** Displays how balanced packets are at each data port queues. Generally, queues at the data ports should be fairly balanced for the best performance.

- **show exporter statistics** *exporter_name*: Displays flow statistics at the flow exporter level.

- **show flow filter** *filter_name*: Displays all flow filters configured in the system.

- **show inventory:** Displays the product ID and serial number of NGA device.

- **show ip:** Displays IP network settings.

- **show log config:** Displays logging of configuration done via **config network ftp-url** command.

- **show log patch:** Displays logging results from patch commands.

- **show log upgrade:** Displays logging results from upgrade commands.

- **show patches:** Displays all patches that have been installed in the system.

- **show snmp:** Displays SNMP settings in the system.

Summary

In this chapter, you learned many different commands, debugs, and tools that are useful when troubleshooting NetFlow problems in Cisco IOS, Cisco IOS-XE, Cisco NX-OS, and Cisco IOS-XR devices, as well as in the Cisco ASA 5500-X series Next-Generation Firewalls and the Cisco NetFlow Generation Appliances. The first step in understanding what **show** commands to use is to become familiar with them even during normal operations. Also, determine what **debug** commands to use by using them with caution. In the beginning of this chapter, several tips and information about **debug** commands were provided as a general guidance when using these types of commands.

## Chapter 8

Case Studies

This chapter covers several case studies and real-life scenarios on how NetFlow is deployed in large enterprises and in small and medium-sized businesses. The following case studies are covered:

- Using NetFlow for anomaly detection and identifying denial-of-service attacks

- Using NetFlow for incident response and forensics

- Using NetFlow for monitoring guest users and contractors

- Using NetFlow for capacity planning

- Using NetFlow to monitor cloud usage

Using NetFlow for Anomaly Detection and Identifying DoS Attacks

Denial-of-service (DoS) attacks and distributed denial-of-service (DDoS) attacks are very disruptive for organizations of all types and sizes. An example of a DDoS is using a botnet to attack a target system. If an attack is launched from a single device with the intent to cause damage to an asset, the attack could be considered a DoS attempt, as opposed to a DDoS.

DDoS attacks can generally be divided into the following three categories:

- Direct DDoS attacks

- Reflected DDoS attacks

- Amplification attacks

Direct DDoS Attacks

Direct DDoS attacks occur when the source of the attack generates the packets, regardless of protocol, application, and so on, that are sent directly to the victim of the attack. Figure 8-1 illustrates a direct DDoS attack where numerous infected systems that are part of a botnet send spoofed TCP SYN packets to web servers in the corporate network.

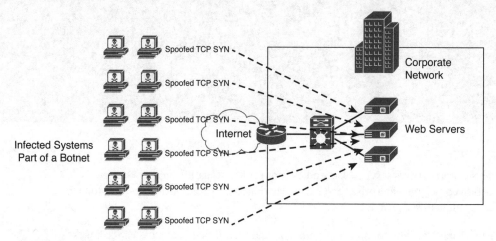

Figure 8-1   *Direct DDoS Example*

Reflected DDoS Attacks

Reflected DDoS attacks occur when the sources of the attack are sent spoofed packets that appear to be from the victim, and then the sources become unwitting participants in the DDoS attacks by sending the response traffic back to the intended victim. UDP is often used as the transport mechanism because it is more easily spoofed due to the lack of a three-way handshake. This type of reflected DDoS attack is illustrated in Figure 8-2.

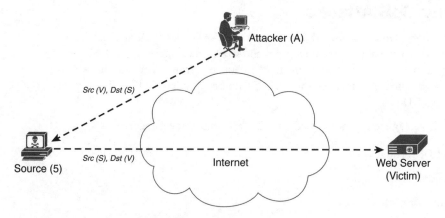

Figure 8-2   *Reflected DDoS Example*

In the example shown in Figure 8-2, the attacker (A) manipulates a host (source) to attack a victim (V) web server. An example of this is when the attacker sends Network Time Protocol (NTP) request packets to the source (S), who thinks these packets are legitimate. The source (S) then responds to the NTP requests by sending the responses to the victim (V), who was never expecting these NTP packets from source (S).

Tip   NTP is just an example of a protocol that can be used for these types of DDoS attacks. Other protocols such as Domain Name System (DNS) can also be very effective.

Amplification Attacks

Amplification attacks are a form of reflected attacks in which the response traffic (sent by the unwitting participants) is made up of packets that are much larger than those that were initially sent by the attacker (spoofing the victim). An example of this is when DNS queries are sent for which the DNS responses are much larger in packet size than the initial query packets. As a result, the victim is flooded by large DNS responses for which it never actually issued queries. Figure 8-3 illustrates an example of a DNS amplification attack.

In Figure 8-3, an attacker sends spoofed DNS requests to DNS open resolvers on the Internet. These spoofed DNS requests are small 64-byte packets. The DNS responses are then sent to the victim by these open DNS resolvers.

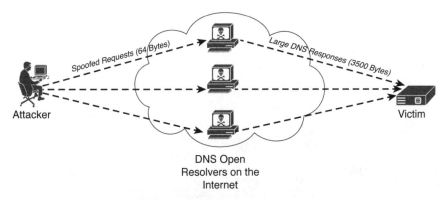

Figure 8-3   *DNS Amplification Attack Example*

Tip   The Open Resolver Project is a nonprofit initiative to report information about DNS open resolvers on the Internet. It provides reports and statistics of millions of open resolvers. Their site allows you to search for open resolvers based on your IP address space. You can learn more about the Open Resolver Project at http://openresolverproject.org.

Another example of amplification attacks are misused of web-based applications such as Wordpress. For instance, the Wordpress Pingback feature has been exploited in the past by miscreants to attack other websites. The legitimate intent of a pingback is to create a blog or website comment that is created when you link to another blog post (if "pingbacks" are enabled). Some systems automate this and maintain automated lists linking back to sites that covered their blog post. In order to implement pingback, Wordpress implements an XML-RPC API function. This function will then send a request to the site to which you would like to send a "pingback".

An attacker can include the "victim" URL with a random parameter such as "victim.com? 123456=123456" to prevent caching. Subsequently, the Wordpress install will send a request to the victim's site.

Identifying DDoS Attacks Using NetFlow

NetFlow is extremely useful for anomaly detection and identifying DoS and DDoS attacks. The following sections cover how enterprises and services providers use NetFlow to identify DDoS attacks.

Using NetFlow in Enterprise Networks to Detect DDoS Attacks

The following examples demonstrate how an enterprise uses NetFlow to detect DDoS. Figure 8-4 shows a topology of an enterprise network.

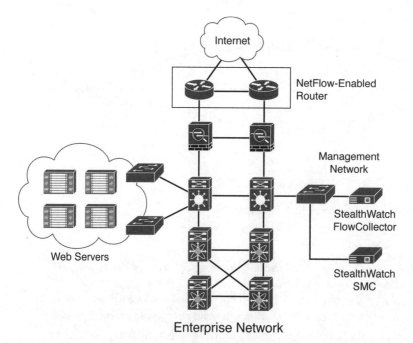

Figure 8-4   *Enterprise Network with NetFlow-Enabled Internet-Edge Routers*

The following are some of the key devices in the topology illustrated in Figure 8-4:

- Two Internet-edge routers configured with NetFlow
- Two Cisco Adaptive Security Appliance (ASA) firewalls
- Four web servers providing customer (public-facing) sites and applications
- Lancope StealthWatch FlowCollector (FC) in the management network
- Lancope StealthWatch System Management Console (SMC) to administer the StealthWatch FlowCollector (FC) in the management network

In this example, the FC collects and analyzes NetFlow data produced by the two NetFlow-enabled routers. The SMC manages the FC creating normal traffic baselines providing visibility, reporting, and management functions.

Example 8-1 shows the Flexible NetFlow configuration of one of the Internet-edge routers.

Example 8-1   *Internet-Edge Router Flexible NetFlow Configuration*

```
flow record INTERNET-ASR-FLOW-RECORD-1
 description Used for basic traffic analysis
 match ipv4 destination address
 collect interface input
!
!
flow exporter INTERNET-EXPORTER-1
 description exports to Flow Collector
 destination 10.10.10.100
!
!
flow monitor INTERNET-ASR-FLOW-MON-1
 description monitor for IPv4 Internet traffic
 record INTERNET-ASR-FLOW-RECORD-1
 exporter INTERNET-EXPORTER-1
 cache entries 200000
!
interface GigabitEthernet0/1
 ip address 209.165.200.233 255.255.255.248
 ip flow monitor INTERNET-ASR-FLOW-MON-1 input
```

In Example 8-1, a flow record called INTERNET-ASR-FLOW-RECORD-1 is configured to match all IPv4 packets in the input interface. A flow exporter (INTERNET-EXPORTER-1) is configured to send NetFlow packets to the StealthWatch FC (10.10.10.100). The flow record and flow exporter are associated to the flow monitor (INTERNET-ASR-FLOW-MON-1), and then the flow monitor is applied on interface Gigabit Ethernet 0/1 (external interface) of the Internet-edge router.

One day, thousands of compromised hosts are controlled by a command-and-control (C&C) system managed by an attacker. These compromised hosts (botnet) start sending millions of spoofed packets toward the enterprise network web servers, as illustrated in Figure 8-5.

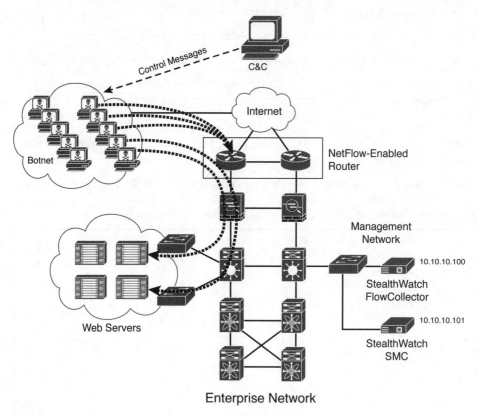

Figure 8-5   *DDoS Against Enterprise Web Servers*

Once the DDoS event is detected, the StealthWatch SMC alerts the administrator.

Systems such as Lancope's StealthWatch System can integrate with packet scrubbing solutions. An example of one is Radware's DefensePro. Radware's DefensePro can be configured to provide DDoS attack mitigation and scrubbing (including Secure Sockets Layer [SSL]-based attacks). DefensePro is installed in dedicated hardware to be able to scale while mitigating DDoS attacks. The SMC can interact with DefensePro to divert the suspicious flows to the scrubbing device using Border Gateway Protocol (BGP). DefensePro blocks the attack traffic and forwards only the clean traffic to the destination. This is illustrated in Figure 8-6.

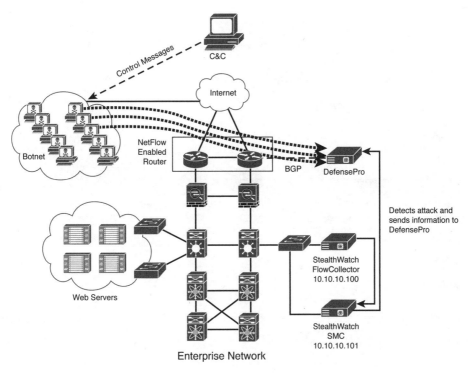

Figure 8-6   *Enterprise DDoS Scrubbing*

Note   The carrier-grade Cisco Firepower 9300 provides DDoS protection capabilities with Radware DefensePro, and it also can be used in these type of scenarios. The Cisco Firepower 9300 also provides Cisco ASA firewalling and virtual private networking (VPN) capabilities. The Cisco Firepower 9300 platform supports up to three security modules. One of the modules can be configured with Cisco ASA software. A second module can be deployed with Firepower Threat Defense including Advanced Malware Protection (AMP), Next-Generation IPS (NGIPS), and URL filtering. A third module can be configured with Radware DefensePro.

Using NetFlow in Service Provider Networks to Detect DDoS Attacks

The following examples demonstrate how a service provider (SP) uses NetFlow to detect DDoS. Figure 8-7 shows a topology of a service provider network.

In Figure 8-7, a service provider has a series of Lancope StealthWatch FCs configured in a distributed manner. Each FC is managed by the SMC. The SMC interacts with a series of scrubbing servers redirecting attack traffic to the scrubbing center. These scrubbing servers provide protection to the SP customers (Enterprise A and B) and even other peering service providers.

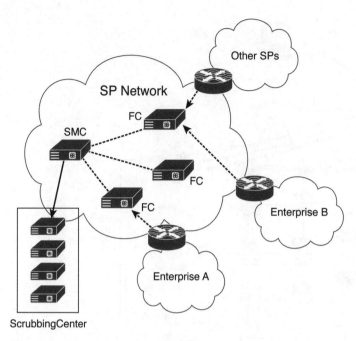

ScrubbingCenter

Figure 8-7   *SP Network DDoS Scrubbing*

Using NetFlow for Incident Response and Forensics

NetFlow and IPFIX can be used for incident response and forensics. The following sections cover two case studies on how two organizations use NetFlow to help during the investigation and forensics analysis of two network security incidents.

Credit Card Theft

In this case study, a large retail organization is the victim of a large breach where attackers stole over 100,000 credit card numbers. The retailer headquarters is in San Francisco, California, and has two large secondary offices in Toronto, Canada, and Austin, Texas. This retailer also has more than 1,000 stores in the United States and Canada. Figure 8-8 illustrates these offices and stores.

The breach was not detected for several months after the attackers had already penetrated the network. The retailer had firewalls and intrusion prevention devices, but those were not enough to detect or mitigate the attack. The attack was thought to be an insider job, because the malware that was extracting the credit card numbers was very sophisticated and tailored to such an organization. The breach was detected only because law enforcement contacted the victimized organization, telling them that thousands of fraudulent credit card transactions had been detected on credit cards that were last legitimately used at the retailer.

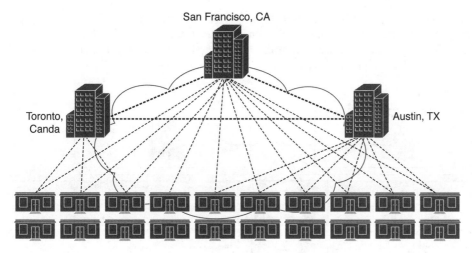

San Francisco, CA

Toronto,
Canda

Austin, TX

Figure 8-8   *Retailer High-Level Network Topology*

After the organization started their incident response and forensics investigation, they decided to deploy NetFlow in routers at the edge of the data center. The topology in Figure 8-9 illustrates the network at the San Francisco headquarters and the two routers that were configured with NetFlow.

The data center has numerous servers that are dedicated for credit card processing applications (software), as illustrated in Figure 8-10.

After deploying NetFlow in their data center edge routers, the retailer observed that numerous DNS requests were being sent from the credit card processing servers to DNS servers outside of their country (United States). The most interesting fact was that such DNS servers were in embargoed countries where the retailer previously had never transacted any business. In addition, most of these DNS requests were being sent during off-hours (mostly around 2:00 to 4:00 a.m. local time).

The retailer was able to inspect NetFlow traffic and detect the country where the credit card information was sent by using the MaxMind Geo location database. MaxMind provides IP intelligence to thousands of companies to locate their Internet visitors and perform analytics. MaxMind has a product called minFraud service, which helps businesses prevent fraudulent online transactions and reduce manual review.

Note   You can obtain more information about MaxMind at https://www.maxmind.com. You can also get access to their database files and open source utilities at https://github. com/maxmind.

The attackers were sending stolen credit card data over DNS using tunneling. DNS is a protocol that enables systems to resolve domain names (for example, example.com) into IP addresses (for example, 93.184.216.34). DNS is not intended for a command channel or even tunneling. However, attackers have developed software that enabled tunneling over DNS. Because traditionally DNS it is not designed for data transfer, it is less inspected in terms of security monitoring. Undetected DNS tunneling (otherwise known as *DNS exfiltration*) represents a significant risk to any organization.

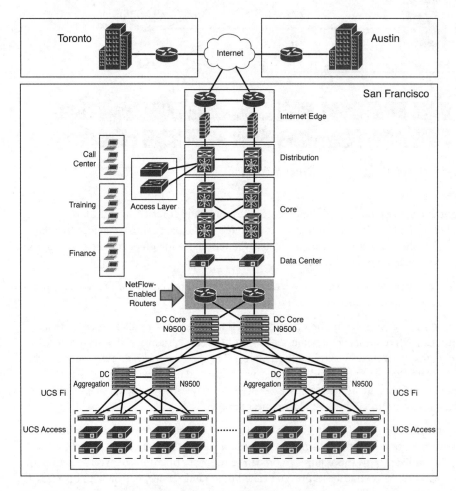

Figure 8-9 *San Francisco Headquarters NetFlow Routers*

In this case, the credit cards were base64 encoded and sent over DNS requests (tunneling) to cyber criminals abroad. Attackers nowadays use different DNS record types and encoding methods to exfiltrate data from victims' systems and networks. The following are some examples of encoding methods:

■ Base64 encoding

■ Binary (8-bit) encoding

- NetBIOS encoding

- Hex encoding

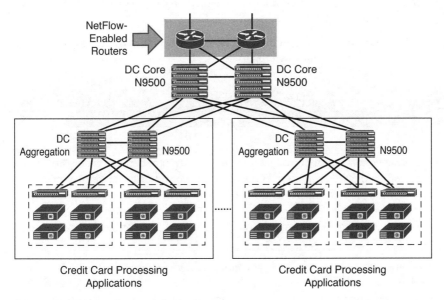

Figure 8-10 *Credit Card Processing Servers*

Several utilities have been created to perform DNS tunneling (for the good and also for the bad). The following are a few examples:

- **DeNiSe:** A Python tool for tunneling TCP over DNS.

- **dns2tcp:** Written by Olivier Dembour and Nicolas Collignon in C, it supports KEY and TXT request types.

- **DNScapy:** Created by Pierre Bienaime, this Python-based Scapy tool for packet generation even supports SSH tunneling over DNS, including a SOCKS proxy.

- **DNScat or DNScat-P:** This Java-based tool created by Tadeusz Pietraszek supports bidirectional communication through DNS.

- **DNScat (DNScat-B):** Written by Ron Bowes, this tool runs on Linux, Mac OS X, and Windows. DNScat encodes DNS requests in NetBIOS encoding or hex encoding.

- **Heyoka:** This tool written in C supports bidirectional tunneling for data exfiltration.

- **Iodine:** Written by Bjorn Andersson and Erik Ekman in C, Iodine runs on Linux, Mac OS X, and Windows, and can even be ported to Android.

- **Nameserver Transfer Protocol (NSTX):** Creates IP tunnels using DNS.

- **OzymanDNS:** Written in Perl by Dan Kaminsky, this tool is used to set up an SSH tunnel over DNS or for file transfer. The requests are base32 encoded, and responses are base64-encoded TXT records.

- **psudp:** Developed by Kenton Born, this tool injects data into existing DNS requests by modifying the IP/UDP lengths.

- **Feederbot and Moto:** This malware using DNS has been used by attackers to steal sensitive information from many organizations.

> **Note**   Some of these tools were not created with the intent to steal data, but cyber criminals have used them for their own purposes.

The retailer's network security personnel were able to perform detailed analysis of the techniques used by the attackers to steal this information and discovered the types of malware and vulnerabilities being exploited in systems in the data center. Network telemetry tools such as NetFlow are invaluable when trying to understand what is happening (good and bad) in the network, and it is a crucial tool for incident response and network forensics.

Retailers or any organizations that process credit cards or electronic payments are often under regulation from the Payment Card Industry Data Security Standard (PCI DSS). PCI DSS was created to encourage and maintain cardholder data security and expedite the consistent use of data security methodologies. This standard enforces a baseline of technical and operational requirements. PCI DSS applies to the following:

- Banks

- "Brick-and-mortar" and online retailers

- Merchants

- Processors

- Acquirers

- Issuers

- Service providers or any other organization that store, process, or transmit cardholder data (CHD) and/or sensitive authentication data (SAD)

The PCI DSS defines general requirements for the following:

- Building and maintaining secure networks

- Protecting cardholder data

- Enforcing vulnerability management and patching programs

- Implementing adequate access control measures

- Consistently monitoring networks and its systems

- Guaranteeing the maintenance of information security policies

As you can see from this list, adequate monitoring of systems is an underlying and fundamental requirement. NetFlow, intrusion prevention systems, and others are often used to maintain this required visibility into what is happening in the network.

Theft of Intellectual Property

According to Merriam-Webster's dictionary, intellectual property is "something (such as an idea, invention, or process) that derives from the work of the mind or intellect; an application, right, or registration relating to this." Intellectual property (and other forms of expression) is often protected by patent, trademark, and copyright (in addition to state and federal laws). In today's world, cyber and corporate espionage is a huge business. Many types of attackers (for example, corporations, cyber criminals, and nation states) are after information with independent economic value, such as the following:

- Blueprints

- Chemical formulas

- Research and development documents

- Marketing strategies

- Manufacturing processes

- Source code

- A song

- A book

- Documentation guides

In 1996, to maintain the health and competitiveness of the U.S. economy, the United States Congress passed the Economic Espionage Act to protect trade secrets from bad actors.

In the following case study, a mobile phone manufacturer in the United States was a victim of intellectual property theft (also known as *trade secret theft*). The company has their headquarters in San Jose, California, and a development campus in Bangalore, India. The two sites connect over an IPsec site-to-site tunnel, as illustrated in Figure 8-11.

San Jose, CA   Bangalore, India

Figure 8-11 *Mobile Phone Company Site-to-Site IPsec tunnel*

An attacker was able to steal many design documents and source code from this company. He compromised internal systems in the San Jose site, and then used those systems as stepping-stones to gain access to development resources at the campus in Bangalore over the very same IPsec tunnel that was designed to keep all communication between San Jose and Bangalore encrypted. Figure 8-12 illustrates the steps that the attacker followed to compromise the user's system in San Jose.

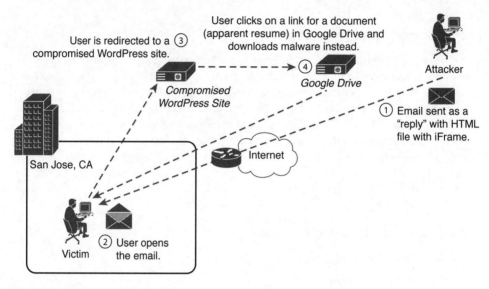

Figure 8-12   *Fake Resume Compromise to User in San Jose*

The following are the steps illustrated in Figure 8-12.

Step 1.   The attacker sends an e-mail to the victim. The attacker sends the e-mail "as a reply" to make it look like a reply to an existing e-mail and not something that was sent unsolicited. In addition, the e-mail had an HTML file attached. The file size was only 250 bytes. This HTML file had an iFrame that will redirect the user to a compromised WordPress site. The HTML file is as follows:

```
<html>
<head></head>
<body>
<iframe src="http://compromised-wordpress-site/resume.php"
  width="1024" height="768" style="position:absolute;left:-10118px;">
  </iframe>
</body>
</html>
```

This HTML iFrame is used to trick the user into visiting http://compromised-wordpress-site/resume.php.

Step 2.   The user opens the e-mail and the attached HTML file.

Step 3.   The user is redirected to the compromised WordPress site that was in the iFrame of the HTML file.

Step 4.   The WordPress site had a link to a Google Drive document that "appeared to be a resume." The user clicks the Google Drive document link and downloads malware that is installed on his machine and used by the attacker to elevate privileges and take control of his machine.

Once the attacker takes control of the victim's system, it uses it to gain access to design documents and source code from the engineering campus in Bangalore. Figure 8-13 illustrates the steps that the attacker followed.

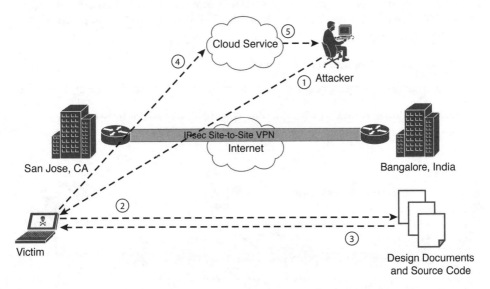

Figure 8-13   *Attacker Stealing Design Documents and Source Code*

The following are the steps illustrated in Figure 8-13:

Step 1.   The attacker takes full control of the victim's computer.

Step 2.   The victim is a development director who has access to design documents and source code in the Bangalore site.

Step 3.   The attacker leverages those permissions to gain access to such design documents and source code.

Step 4.   The design documents and source code are uploaded to a trusted cloud service site.

Step 5.   The attacker downloads the design documents and source code from the cloud service site.

The mobile phone company has NetFlow enabled in the router in the San Jose head-quarters. The network security administrator notices a spike in traffic being downloaded from the Bangalore site by the victim and also notices a lot of traffic being sent to the cloud service site. After further investigation, the network security administrator determines that this is not normal and blocks the victim user from sending any data to the Internet and contacts the user.

Using NetFlow for Monitoring Guest Users and Contractors

NetFlow is a great tool to monitor guest users and contractors. In the following case study, an enterprise allows guest wireless users to connect to their office network and also provides wireless access to contractors. The following are the policies for each of the types of users:

■ **Guest users:** Only Internet access is allowed.

■ **Contractors:** Internet access and access to three internal application servers is allowed.

Figure 8-14 illustrates how wireless guest users and contractors are authenticated and allowed to the network.

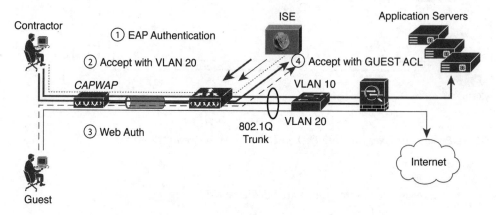

Figure 8-14   *Wireless Guest Users and Contractors*

In Figure 8-14, contractors and guest users connect to the wireless network and are authenticated by the Cisco Identity Services Engine (ISE). Contractors are assigned to the contractor VLAN (VLAN 10), which allows them to connect to the three application servers and to the Internet. The following are the steps illustrated in Figure 8-14 to authenticate and allow guest users to connect to the Internet:

Step 1.   Guest user authenticates to the wireless network (EAP authentication).

Step 2.   Guest user is assigned to VLAN 20.

Step 3.   Guest user is authenticated via WebAuth.

Step 4.   An access control list (ACL) called GUEST ACL is also applied to prevent them from connecting to the corporate network and to allow them to connect only to the Internet.

NetFlow is configured in the Cisco Wireless LAN Controller (WLC) to monitor guest users and contractors. The following are the high-level steps to configure NetFlow to monitor wireless guest users and contractors in the WLC. Only the single static flow record type can be exported from the Cisco WLC, as opposed to Flexible NetFlow in Cisco IOS devices:

Step 1.   Configure the NetFlow exporter.

Step 2.   Configure the NetFlow monitor.

Step 3.   Associate the record and export with the monitor.

Step 4.   Associate the monitor with a WLAN.

The topology in Figure 8-15 is used for the example that follows. The Cisco WLC is configured to export NetFlow records to a server running Elasticsearch, Logstash, and Kibana (ELK).

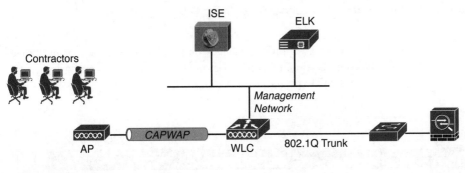

Figure 8-15   *WLC Exporting NetFlow Records to ELK*

The following are the steps taken to configure NetFlow in the Cisco WLC web admin interface:

Step 1.   Configure the NetFlow exporter:

    a.   Log in to the WLC and navigate to **Wireless > NetFlow > Exporter**, as shown in Figure 8-16.

    b.   Click **New** to add a new exporter. Enter the exporter name, IP address, and the port number. In this example, the exporter name is ELK-server, the IP address is 10.10.10.88, and the port number is 9995, as shown in Figure 8-16.

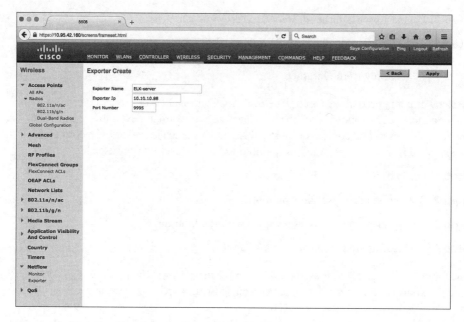

Figure 8-16   *Configuring the Exporter in the Cisco WLC*

    c. Click **Apply** to apply the changes, and click **Save Configuration** to save
        the configuration. Figure 8-17 shows the configured exporter in the
        Cisco WLC Exporter List screen.

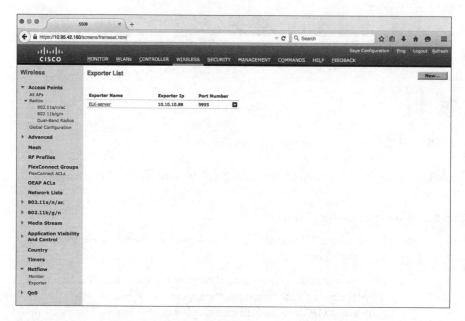

Figure 8-17   *Cisco WLC NetFlow Exporter List*

Step 2.   Configure the NetFlow monitor:

a.   In the web admin interface, navigate to **Wireless > NetFlow > Monitor**.

b.   Click **New** and enter the monitor name, as shown in Figure 8-18.

c.   On the Monitor List page, click the monitor name to open the **NetFlow Monitor > Edit** page, as shown in Figure 8-19.

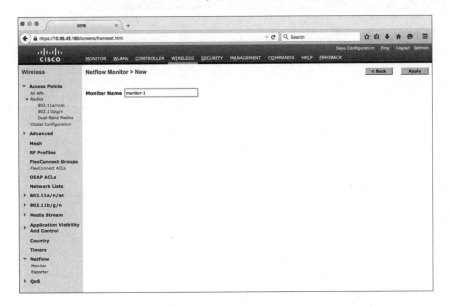

Figure 8-18   *Entering the Monitor Name*

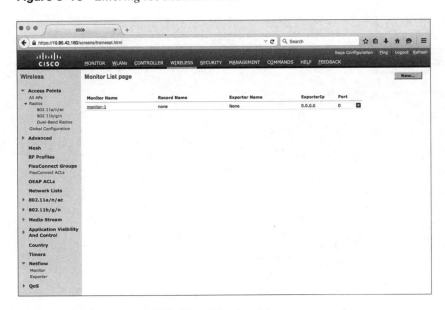

Figure 8-19   *Cisco WLC NetFlow Monitor List*

Step 3. Select the exporter name and the record name from the respective drop-down lists, as shown in Figure 8-20. Only single static flow record type can be exported from the Cisco WLC, as opposed to Flexible NetFlow in Cisco IOS devices.

Figure 8-20 *Selecting the Exporter and Record*

Click **Apply** to apply the changes, and click **Save Configuration** to save the configuration. Figure 8-21 shows the updated Monitor List page.

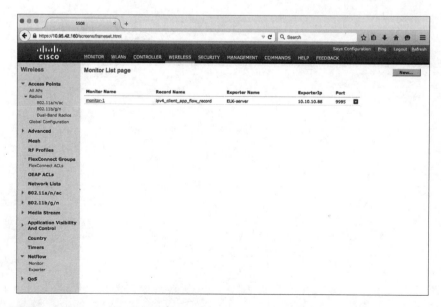

Figure 8-21 *Updated Monitor List page*

Step 4.   Associate a NetFlow monitor with a WLAN:

   a.   Navigate to **WLANs** and click the WLAN ID to open the **WLANs > Edit page**.

   b.   On the QoS tab, choose the NetFlow monitor from the NetFlow Monitor drop-down list, as shown in Figure 8-22.

   c.   Click **Apply** to apply the changes, and click **Save Configuration** to save the configuration.

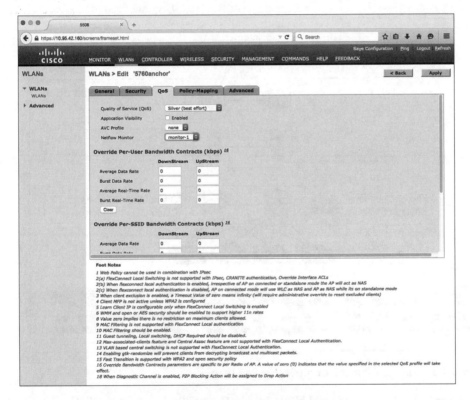

Figure 8-22   *Associating the NetFlow Monitor with a WLAN*

Note   In this example, the WLAN IDs will be the WLANs for guest users and contractors. If you configure multiple WLAN IDs, you need to repeat step 4 for each of the WLANs.

Using NetFlow for Capacity Planning

Capacity planning allows network administrators to assess future network requirements based on business forecasts. As more and more organizations are adopting cloud services, their infrastructure capacity needs are also quickly changing. Network administrators can use NetFlow as a capacity-planning tool to help foresee future needs and adapt quickly.

In the following case study, a network administrator uses NetFlow analysis to determine his organization's bandwidth needs to accommodate the growth over a period of time and to decide on the changes to be implemented. In addition, he would like to identify bandwidth bottlenecks and wasted bandwidth.

Figure 8-23 illustrates the network topology used in this case study. This is a medium-sized enterprise with offices in San Juan, Puerto Rico. This enterprise is a video production company. Their corporate users utilize numerous cloud-based services, in addition to many different online tools, to produce and review their client videos.

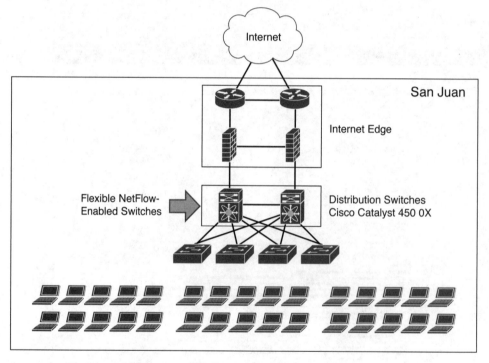

Figure 8-23   *Video Producing Company in San Juan*

The network administrator enables Flexible NetFlow in the distribution switches shown in Figure 8-17 (Cisco Catalyst 4500X switches).

Example 8-2 shows the Flexible NetFlow configuration in the Cisco Catalyst 4500X distribution switches.

Example 8-2   *Distribution Switch Flexible NetFlow Configuration*

```
flow exporter Exporter1
 destination 10.1.20.3
 !
 !
flow record Record1
```

```
 match ipv4 source address
 match ipv4 destination address
 collect counter bytes long
 collect counter packets long
!
!
flow monitor mon1
 record Record1
 exporter Exporter1
 cache timeout active 60
 cache timeout inactive 30
!
!
interface GigabitEthernet 2/1
 ip flow monitor mon1 layer2-switched input
!
interface GigabitEthernet 2/2
 ip flow monitor mon1 input
```

The Cisco Catalyst 4500X distribution switches are configured to send NetFlow records to a collector with the IP address 10.1.20.3.

Note The Cisco Catalyst 4500 series switches support ingress flow statistics collection for switched and routed packets. However, they do not support Flexible NetFlow on egress traffic.

The **ip flow monitor mon1 layer2-switched input** interface subcommand is used in interface Gigabit Ethernet 2/1 to allow the collection of flow records even when the packet is bridged. In the Cisco Catalyst 4500X, NetFlow is supported on multiple targets. These targets include port, VLAN, per-port per-VLAN (Flexible NetFlow can be enabled on a specific VLAN on a given port), and on a port-channel interface (instead of on individual member ports).

Using NetFlow to Monitor Cloud Usage

The growing demand for cloud-based applications and their increased rate of adoption has resulted in massive pressure on network administrators. They must continuously monitor network traffic behavior to guarantee network uptime for necessary operational processes. NetFlow data can be collected from infrastructure devices to identify the following:

■ Cloud services that are being accessed by network users

■ The number of unique IP addresses being used

■ The volume of traffic to such cloud service providers and the impact on bandwidth by cloud applications

■ Unauthorized protocol and application usage

In addition, rogue cloud applications, often referred to as *shadow IT*, can be identified by deploying NetFlow. The ease of use of public cloud services has also led to an increase in rogue cloud applications. Many network administrators and other company officials are often unaware of the number of cloud applications (often unauthorized applications) that are used by their employees.

Note   Cisco also provides a cloud consumption assessment service for their customers. You can find more information about the Cisco Cloud Consumption Professional Services at http://www.ipv6.cisco.com/web/partners/services/programs/collaborative/downloads/datasheet_c78_729142_080513.pdf.

This new paradigm of shadow IT introduces a new set of challenges for business leaders. These challenges include determining how to manage the costs and risks associated with cloud adoption and how to establish effective cloud management processes.

In the following case study, a network administrator is tasked to monitor how often users use cloud providers, specifically Amazon Web Services (AWS). The network administrator immediately thought about using NetFlow on routers close to the Internet edge of their network.

The topology illustrated in Figure 8-24 is used in this case study.

In this case, the company does not use Cisco Adaptive Security Appliances (ASAs), but instead uses a third-party firewall solution. NetFlow is enabled in the routers behind the corporate firewalls.

After the network administrator enables NetFlow in the routers, he struggles to figure out how to monitor what traffic is destined for the AWS. Luckily, Amazon documents all the IP address ranges that they use in all their availability zones and cloud services at http://docs.aws.amazon.com/general/latest/gr/aws-ip-ranges.html.

Tip   The IP address ranges can also be downloaded in JSON format from https://ip-ranges.amazonaws.com/ip-ranges.json.

After further analysis, the network administrator notices that users are using cloud services hosted in AWS 10 to 15 times more than anticipated, in terms of connections and the amount of data being transferred. In addition, he noticed that some of these services are even competitive services to those offered by their own company. He uses this data to work with his InfoSec team to develop company-wide policies for cloud usage and uses the existing NetFlow capabilities in his network to continue to monitor such usage.

Rogue cloud-based applications and services can consume a lot of bandwidth, which in turn could result in an interruption of important business applications. The network administrator also used NetFlow data to define quality of service (QoS) policies and set priorities for several critical applications. The administrator used NetFlow data reports with Type of Service (ToS) and DSCP fields to monitor the bandwidth usage by application and to measure the effectiveness of the deployed QoS policies.

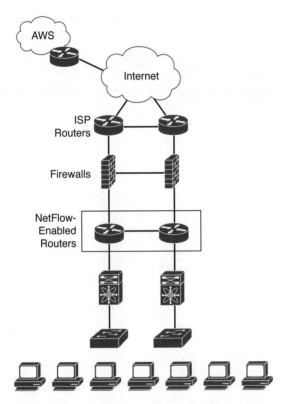

Figure 8-24 *NetFlow to Monitor Cloud Usage*

Summary

This chapter covered several case studies describing how NetFlow can be used for many different security and nonsecurity applications. You learned how you can use NetFlow for anomaly detection and to identify DoS attacks. Both enterprises and services providers can use NetFlow to mitigate DDoS attacks, including direct, reflected, and amplification DDoS attacks. NetFlow is also a very useful tool for incident response and forensics. In this chapter, several case studies showed how an enterprise used NetFlow to detect threat actors when attempting to steal credit card and other personally identifiable information (PII) data from its network. You also learned how another enterprise used NetFlow to detect a sophisticated attacker who compromised internal system to steal intellectual property and company trade secrets. Additional case studies covered how to use NetFlow to monitor guest users and contractors, capacity planning, and cloud usage.

Index

N

![CISCO]

ciscopress.com: Your Cisco Certification and Networking Learning Resource

Subscribe to the monthly Cisco Press newsletter to be the first to learn about new releases and special promotions.

Visit **ciscopress.com/newsletters.**

While you are visiting, check out the offerings available at your finger tips.

–Free Podcasts from experts:
  • OnNetworking
  • OnCertification
  • OnSecurity

Podcasts

View them at **ciscopress.com/podcasts.**

–Read the latest author **articles** and **sample chapters** at **ciscopress.com/articles**.

–Bookmark the Certification Reference Guide available through our partner site at **informit.com/certguide**.

Connect with Cisco Press authors and editors via Facebook and Twitter, visit informit.com/socialconnect.

CISCO

Connect, Engage, Collaborate

The Award Winning Cisco Support Community

Attend and Participate in Events

Ask the Experts
Live Webcasts

Knowledge Sharing

Documents
Blogs
Videos

Top Contributor Programs

Cisco Designated VIP
Hall of Fame
Spotlight Awards

Multi-Language Support

https://supportforums.cisco.com